# fully
# engaged

"When Jesus stated that 'as the Father sent me, so I send you,' he committed all subsequent followers to go in the manner of his own sending: through the twin impulses of mission and incarnation. The so-called quiet in the land need to recover this original and originating way of Jesus in order to be faithful in this generation. This book is a great reminder of the latent potentials embedded into the Anabaptist tradition."

**—Alan Hirsch, award-winning author of books on missional Christianity**

"Digging deep into the rich wells of Anabaptist tradition and reflecting on its contributions through the being, doing, and saying of the church in mission, *Fully Engaged* offers valuable insight and marks a way forward for followers of Jesus inside and far beyond this radical tradition."

**—Ruth Padilla DeBorst, theologian and board member, Latin American Theological Fellowship**

"*Fully Engaged* is a timely book exploring the critical question of what it means to be a missional church with Anabaptist roots. The honest reflections and testimonies in the book offer tools and snapshots threaded with a deep yearning to recover the true identity and the work of the church."
—**Hyun Hur and Sue Park-Hur, codirectors of ReconciliAsian**

"This collection of essays, impressive in both depth and scope, is a distinctive contribution to the ongoing 'missional church' adventure—an opportunity for the Anabaptist voice to be heard alongside many other conversation partners. There are rich resources here, from experienced missiologists and pioneering practitioners, that are vital for the future of the Mennonite church and the whole of the Christian community."
—**Stuart Murray, author of *The Naked Anabaptist***

# fully
# engaged

## MISSIONAL CHURCH IN AN ANABAPTIST VOICE

EDITED BY Stanley W. Green AND James R. Krabill

**Herald Press**

Harrisonburg, Virginia
Kitchener, Ontario

**Library of Congress Cataloging-in-Publication Data**

Fully engaged : missional church in an anabaptist voice / Stanley W. Green and James R. Krabill, editors.

    pages cm

Includes bibliographical references.

    ISBN 978-0-8361-9944-4 (pbk. : alk. paper) 1. Church. 2. Mission of the church. 3. Christianity--21st century. 4. Church renewal. 5. Anabaptists--Doctrines. 6. Mennonite Church USA--Doctrines. 7. Emerging church movement. I. Green, Stanley Walter, 1954- editor.

    BV600.3.F85 2015

    266'.97--dc23

                       2015009656

Unless otherwise noted, Scripture text is quoted, with permission, from the *New Revised Standard Version*, © 1989, Division of Christian Education of the National Council of Churches of Christ in the United States of America.

Five of the essays in this collection are adaptations of earlier publications and are used here by permission. They include chapter 2, first appearing as "From Preservation to Engagement: Together Sharing All of Christ with All of Creation" in the *Mennonite* (November 2007); chapter 5, adapted from the *Mission Insight* series, no. 1 (1999), ed. James R. Krabill; and chapters 3, 13, and 16, from the *Missio Dei* series, ed. James R. Krabill, no. 16 (2008), no. 18 (2010), and no. 2 (2003), respectively.

*To faithful witnesses in the Anabaptist stream whose lives were fully engaged in sharing the whole gospel of Jesus, wherever they were*

This book was made possible as a gift
to you through the generosity of

# G & S Titanium, Inc.
# Wooster, Ohio

**Mennonite Mission** Network

The mission agency of
Mennonite Church USA

# Contents

## PART 5 Missional Journeys: Congregations and Conferences

## PART 6 Missional Journeys: Multicultural Initiatives

# Acknowledgments

We want to thank each of the authors who submitted chapters. We appreciate the important sharing each contributor has made to the ongoing conversation on our journey toward fuller engagement with God's purposes in the world. We are also grateful to have been partners with the Mennonite Church USA Executive Board on our common quest to resource the church. We appreciate the leadership that conceived the "Purposeful Plan" and the invitation to Mennonite Mission Network to contribute to the shape of that plan.

We are thankful to our publisher, Herald Press, and are especially grateful to Valerie Weaver-Zercher and Amy Gingerich for providing helpful counsel that contributed in no small measure to the shape of this volume. Furthermore, we are grateful to Lyz Weaver, who provided valuable assistance in helping us gather the necessary details to complete this project, and to David Miller, who prepared the bibliographical materials at the end of the book.

Finally, we are also grateful to our spouses, Ursula and Jeanette, who blessed us in our busyness during the journey of our other love, the church, in its trek toward fuller alignment with God's purposes.

# Introduction

*Stanley W. Green and James R. Krabill*

## That word . . . *missional*

It is not incidental that we have chosen *fully engaged* rather than *missional* as the primary identifier in the title of this book. There are plenty of Anabaptists who could make the claim that they had been working at missional themes long before *missional church* language came onto the scene. They would observe that they now continue to do the same work of engaging the world with a new vocabulary to assist them.

Most Mennonites have embraced the language of the missional church, believing that it aptly describes the mission passion and commitment that they aspire to. Others, however, contend that *missional church* terminology feels contrived. As such, it invites suspicion. Some in this camp also worry that *missional* is a new buzzword that will soon fade as other fads have done before now. We have thus deliberately put the emphasis on being *fully engaged*, believing that this framing suggests the depth and significance of the changes demanded if congregations are to become truly missional in their ethos and praxis.

The formal encounter of twentieth-century Mennonites with the missional church movement came, in the main, in the context of a denominational merger. In the course of discernment during the integration process, we were strongly urged by one of our consultants, Patrick Keifert, to "find a usable future in your past." In the quest for a usable future that would reach beyond adjusted polities and revised structures, the goal became transformation at every level of the church. The promise wrapped up in our embrace of a vision to become a missional people was infused with the hope of being fully aligned with God's purposes in the world and a recovery of the essence for which the church exists: God's mission.

## Recapturing as Anabaptists the "subversive remembrance" of missional engagement

Particularly in the last century, Mennonites were not immune to the enticements of Christendom, despite the fact that the memory of our missionally engaged roots persisted even when we were beguiled by and susceptible to accommodations to mainstream churchly culture. Even if most Anabaptists had experienced a drift away toward a certain kind of Christendom marked by a cultural captivity, the decision to move back toward fuller missional engagement resonated with the deeply held convictions about mission being inherent in the true nature of the church.

The predilection in Christendom to separate mission from the church and to believe that the church can exist separately from its mission was in serious tension with an early Anabaptist understanding that the church is not simply a *sending* body, but a *sent* body—a fresh rediscovery that came to be broadly affirmed within the missional church movement. Quite apart from the actual practice of later Anabaptists, this deeply ingrained understanding—even subversive remembrance—lived on from an early Anabaptist conviction that the church and mission *are not* and *cannot be* separate realities. Indeed, the earliest Anabaptists demonstrated in both their words and acts of witness that to be the church is to be about God's holistic mission of salvation, healing, reconciliation, justice, and freedom in the world.

A real hazard for Mennonites on the journey toward becoming more fully engaged was the danger of being hijacked. The temptation to a smug arrogance, and even a spirit of condescension, born out of an assumption that Anabaptists had always inveighed against the pernicious effects of Christendom, is real and needs yet to be resisted. It would be too easy to allow ourselves to become puffed up by an appeal to a heritage that prefigured the current missional church movement's interest by its drive toward full engagement with God's purposes in the world.

Various chapters in this volume bear testimony instead that contemporary Anabaptists recognize the compromises that have been made with Christendom and the slide into greater cultural captivity, which requires conversion. As a number of the essays suggest, the journey toward a lively missional consciousness will require a profound transformation that will lead to significant changes in our orientation and actions.

## Coming home to the missional message and methods of Jesus

This shift begins with a more profound adjustment in the way we see our world through the lens of God's purposes and what the Spirit is already doing. The recalibration we are seeking will return us to our roots and allow us to disengage from the world's values and its idols for the sake of engagement with the world in the way of Jesus. Against this backdrop, embarking on the journey toward becoming a missional people had the effect for many of "coming home," or perhaps reconnecting, with our truest identity, which had become increasingly blurred and in danger of being lost.

At the very heart of Anabaptist belief is the unquestioning centrality of Jesus, who is understood as the clearest reflection we have of God's purposes for the world. Matched with the conviction about the centrality of Jesus is a resolute commitment to follow Jesus in life. Jesus and the reign he announced as inaugurated—given life and form in his life, ministry and teaching, death, and resurrection—are seen as the embodiment of God's purposes for the world.

## Rooted in Scripture, lived in community, enunciated in word, enacted in deed

In this commitment Anabaptists find the mandate and imperative for taking the gospel seriously, since the story of God's unfolding purpose is rooted in the biblical text. Read in community, the text is foundational for discipleship formation. Moreover, the community itself, shaped by discipleship values, becomes an "interpretation" of the text. As some of the essays in this volume show, our engagement with the missional process is helping modern-day Anabaptists to learn anew the discipline of reading the Scripture in context.

The recovery of this discipline is consistent with a primary persuasion that Anabaptists share: to follow Jesus truly means to live incarnationally. The gospel enunciated in *word* is also enacted in *deed*. Faith is shared through our *verbal witness* and it is made visible and credible through our *actions*, which are in alignment with what Jesus modeled.

We have always understood that sharing our faith can never be coercive. Furthermore, the early circumstance of Anabaptist witness from within a cauldron of suffering made it difficult for that witness to be manipulative. In this new era of missional engagement, we are learning that being invitational means more than inviting persons to come to our churches. As reported in various case studies in this book, serious efforts are being made to equip and encourage people in our churches to engage the world outside our walls with the gospel so that God's healing and hope is advanced in situations of hurt, alienation, and brokenness.

In Anabaptist missional engagement, the centrality of Jesus makes a commitment to reconciliation, nonresistance, and peacemaking nonnegotiable. Several chapters here address this core Anabaptist distinctive, suggesting that our missional engagement requires a commitment to seeing the church as a contrast society. In the context of the endemic conflict and violence that have perennially plagued our world, Anabaptists understand that the gospel's call is to follow the example of Jesus in confronting the idols of the reigning worldview and in modeling the forgiveness and reconciliation with enemies that he witnessed to in his life and death. As many of the writers here attest, Anabaptists see the imperative for the church to resist the temptation to live in comfortable cohabitation with the powers of violence, hatred, and warring, which contradict the peaceable reign of God that is grounded in the love and reconciliation made visible in the cross.

# PART 1

# Roots and Foundations

# 1

# Why Missional and Mennonite Should Make Perfect Sense

*Wilbert R. Shenk*

Say "DNA" and it is assumed everyone knows what you are talking about. Try starting a conversation about "deoxyribonucleic acid" and you'll be met by blank stares. Fortunately, "DNA" is the shorthand for "deoxyribonucleic acid." The discovery of DNA as the basis of the genetic code that is unique to each human being is a relatively recent scientific breakthrough. But it has already made a substantial difference in various fields.

For example, DNA testing has largely replaced the older method of fingerprinting and other means of establishing a person's identity. DNA samples are used to trace the identity of persons who have died, leaving little or no information on themselves. Criminals are being apprehended by matching the physical evidence—including body fluids, skin, or hair unintentionally left on a victim—with samples taken from their own bodies. Persons who have served long prison sentences on death row are being released because DNA evidence shows that the accused person's DNA does not match the evidence collected by detectives twenty or more years before. DNA testing is a reliable tool used to establish true identity and relationships.

The power of DNA is that it identifies the most basic components of an individual. Yet the individual fits within a certain pattern that is shared by the kinship system of which the individual is a part. What light might the DNA metaphor throw on the present genealogy of Mennonite Church USA in relation to its genetic code?

Mennonite Church USA in 2015 is made up of diverse historical, cultural, and theological strands that have been added, especially since 1800. Twenty-first-century Mennonites have difficulty imagining the circumstances that gave rise to the several sixteenth-century reformations, including the Protestant, Roman Catholic Counter-Reformation, and Radical Reformation of the Anabaptists. While the roots of Mennonite Church USA can be traced to the Radical Reformation of the sixteenth century, multiple cultural currents have left their marks on the descendants of the Anabaptists. Some of these influences have enriched MC USA; others have seriously undermined crucial Anabaptist convictions.

## Anabaptist genius

The genius of the sixteenth-century Anabaptists was to recognize that the Christendom concept of the church was at odds with the apostolic vision. Christendom's DNA was formed by its imperial origins in the fourth century. The Anabaptists felt compelled to recover the apostolic understanding of the church. This put them at odds with both Roman Catholics and the Protestant Reformers who accepted Christendom, the powerful governing system based on the alliance of church and state. This system left no doubt that it was prepared to use whatever force was necessary to maintain social and political order, starting with the mandatory baptism of all infants. To insure that every person born in Christendom, except Jews, would be both a member of the church and a compliant citizen, it was required that the child be baptized soon after birth. These were inseparable requirements: citizenship and church membership must be synonymous.

By the sixteenth century this church-state alliance had been in place for more than a thousand years. The fruits of the system were plainly visible. The church was corrupted by its entanglements with the state.

Cardinals, bishops, and monastic orders were preoccupied with amassing political power and wealth. But for the peasant masses it was an oppressive system. They burned with resentment at the way they were exploited. The situation was like a volcano waiting to erupt. The masses were *Christian* in name only.

The Anabaptists rejected the entire system and called for the separation of church and state. The first article of the 1527 Schleitheim Confession denounced infant baptism as "the greatest and first abomination of the Pope." Instead, "Baptism shall be given to all those who have been taught repentance and the amendment of life and who believe truly that their sins are taken away through Christ . . . and desire to walk in the resurrection of Jesus Christ." The new birth is the only valid basis for becoming a member of Christ's body, the church.

A key text for the Anabaptist movement was what we call the great commission, in Matthew 28:19-20 and Mark 16:15-16. This clashed with the interpretation of the Protestant Reformers. Opponents such as Julius Mencius and Heinrich Bullinger brusquely dismissed the Anabaptist appeal to the great commission on grounds that this threatened the stability of the local parish system. Rather than answering the Anabaptist critique, they argued for maintaining the status quo on the ground that Jesus gave this instruction only to the original twelve apostles.

Intimately acquainted with the spiritual plight of the people of Christendom in the sixteenth century, the Anabaptists held that everyone urgently needed to hear the gospel. In August 1527 a group of Anabaptist leaders met in Augsburg, southern Germany, to discuss the evangelization of Europe. Although historical evidence is meager, it is believed some sixty persons representing the scattered Anabaptist congregations were present. Whereas the meeting at Schleitheim was concerned with formulating a statement of doctrine and practice, at Augsburg the delegates focused on a strategy for evangelizing Europe and beyond. The threat of persecution, and possibly death, was no deterrent to these leaders. This has been called the Martyrs' Synod because many of the delegates died within a short time as martyrs. S R: O'reach

For the next sixty years, hundreds of Anabaptist evangelists, often at great sacrifice and constant risk, fanned out across the European continent sharing the gospel wherever they could gain a hearing. By 1550 Anabaptist evangelists were active in every German state, Austria, Switzerland, Holland, France, Poland, Galicia, Hungary, and Italy. Some had made forays into parts of Scandinavia. Balthasar Hubmaier was reported to have baptized three hundred persons at Waldhut in a single day, and Melchior Hoffman did the same thing at Emden five years later. Between 1551 and 1582 Leenaert Bowens baptized 10,378 converts in the area between Emden and Kortrijk.

Anabaptist laypeople were full participants in this extraordinary evangelizing movement. They used natural relational networks—family, vocational, social—to reach people. Women and men alike engaged in evangelization. All members were expected to participate. South German Anabaptist leader Hans Hut included in his charge to those he baptized the phrase that they should obey the commandments along with the great commission, preaching the gospel and baptizing those who believed.

## From mission to survival

The transition from Anabaptist dynamism in the sixteenth century to *die Stillen im Lande* ("the quiet in the land") quietism in the seventeenth century was the defensive response of a people struggling for survival. Intense and sustained persecution had taken a terrible toll. Some two thousand Anabaptist martyrs are known by name. By the end of the sixteenth century surviving Anabaptists were seeking safe havens. The missionary impulse became blunted, and descendants of the Anabaptists either retreated to the margins of a hostile society (south Germany, Switzerland) or entered the mainstream of an increasingly tolerant environment (the Netherlands).

Seventeenth-century Europe was a miserable place. The collapse of the Spanish empire early in the seventeenth century meant the loss of its dominance in Europe. This left a power vacuum that opened the way for continual military conflict. The Thirty Years' War, 1618–1648, essentially a series of religious conflicts, resulted in the deaths of thousands of people. Political instability and constant wars kept the Continent unsettled. The Little Ice Age in Europe during the 1600s took a terrible toll. Crop failures, massive food shortages, and large-scale outbreaks of disease resulted in the deaths of large numbers of people.

In the late seventeenth century migration became a defining characteristic of the Anabaptist-Mennonite churches. The first of multiple waves took place within Europe. After intensifying its efforts to get rid of all Anabaptists in the 1660s, in 1671 Switzerland made an all-out effort. Some seven hundred Anabaptists fled. At the invitation of Count Karl Ludwig the majority went to the Palatinate. The count sought Mennonite help in recovering farmland devastated during the Thirty Years' War. The rest went to Alsace and Montbeliard. But wherever they went in Europe, the state churches made sure the Anabaptists were not allowed to own land or evangelize and baptize outside their own group. Even burial of their dead was often a contentious issue. In 1683 the first group of Mennonites arrived in Germantown, Pennsylvania. But large-scale emigration to North America did not begin until after 1710.

In 1660 Dutch Mennonite pastor T. J. van Braght published his massive compilation, the *Martyrs Mirror*. He was disturbed by what he observed to be growing spiritual complacency among his people. The Netherlands had emerged as the leading naval power in Europe and its economy expanded rapidly. Dutch Mennonites benefited from the growing tolerance in Dutch society toward minority groups, on the one hand, and the fine reputation of Dutch Mennonite bankers and businessmen, on the other. Dutch Mennonites intervened with the Swiss government in the seventeenth century on behalf of their Swiss sisters and brothers, repeatedly coming to the aid of Swiss and German Mennonites who were migrating to escape persecution.

As a result of these sustained hostile forces, the original Anabaptist evangelizing impulse was curbed by the unrelenting persecution of the state churches. The Anabaptist-Mennonite DNA was decisively altered in the seventeenth century. Mutual aid, relief, and service have remained defining characteristics ever since.

## Sources of renewal

Van Braght was not alone in his concern for the spiritual health of his people. A young German Lutheran pastor, Philipp Jakob Spener, was similarly disturbed by the spiritual lethargy he observed in the state churches. In 1675 he published a pamphlet calling for renewal of spiritual life. Spener's pamphlet was influential in sparking what became the Pietist movement. Essentially a lay movement, Pietism emphasized the importance of the new birth, spiritual practices, discipline fostered by cell group meetings, and actively engaging in witness and service.

Unlike Anabaptism, Pietism did not address the nature of the church directly. It stressed personal faith and practice. Pietist influence quickly spread across Europe and North America, touching all varieties of Protestants. It spawned other renewal movements, especially the Evangelical revival and Moravian Brethren in the eighteenth century. These currents brought new vitality to mainline Protestants as well as believers church groups such as the Quakers and Mennonites that, under intense external pressure, had turned inward.

One fruit of the Pietist/Evangelical revival was the modern mission movement. As early as the mid-1600s several missions were organized, all without support from the churches. The modern mission movement emerged around 1800. It, too, lacked the official backing of any church. The first Mennonite support for "foreign" missions came from Dutch Mennonites. The Baptist Serampore (India) Mission developed a support network in Great Britain and on the Continent in the early 1800s. A group was organized in the Netherlands, in which Dutch Mennonites were active. They also participated in the nondenominational Réveil, a European renewal movement patterned on the classical Pietist model.

The Great Awakening in North America and Great Britain, starting in the early eighteenth century, emphasized both personal conversion and social transformation. Out of this came various social reforms and mission initiatives: antislavery, education of children, child labor laws, prison reform, Bible societies, and home and foreign missions. This *whole gospel* vision continued into the nineteenth century. But with the rise of premillennialism and dispensationalism, especially after 1870, a narrowing of focus emerged. Since the return of Christ was imminent, it was argued, personal salvation was the priority. Every effort must be focused on "winning souls."

Across the eighteenth and nineteenth centuries Mennonites were interacting with these revival and renewal movements. Inevitably, tensions arose between those who welcomed renewal and those who did not. Traditionalists feared change. They correctly sensed that renewal threatened the status quo. Those who welcomed the message of renewal recognized that the church must find in the gospel the resources to engage the changing culture.

For example, Mennonites who had settled in Ukraine in the eighteenth and nineteenth centuries had become ingrown. Young people were not attracted by a religiosity that was not life-giving. Through the ministry of itinerant Pietist evangelists from Germany, many of these people experienced renewal. But the message of revival also brought conflict and schism. Similarly, in North America repeated schisms occurred across the nineteenth century as the message of revival influenced traditional Mennonite piety in rural communities that did not welcome change.

The contrast between the evangelizing fervor of sixteenth-century Anabaptists and nineteenth-century traditional Mennonites could hardly be sharper. Traces of the Anabaptist DNA remained in nineteenth-century Mennonite piety in terms of ethical values, but the instinct for world-avoidance drilled into the Mennonite subconscious by generations of persecution and migration retained a powerful grip on the Mennonite view of the world.

## Twentieth-century transformations

The tumultuous twentieth century affected all dimensions of life. These are key defining developments that continue to shape life globally:

- The birth of the atomic age
- The rise—and fall—of powerful new ideologies dedicated to world domination
- Two world wars, plus endless regional wars
- In the aftermath of World War II European colonial empires collapsed and independent new nations emerged throughout the world
- A Cold War that dominated world affairs for more than forty years, 1947–90
- The profound transition from modernity to postmodernity

- The ending of historical Christendom and the shift of the center of Christian vitality to Africa, Asia, and Latin America
- Resurgence of major world religions and emergence of many new religions and spiritualities
- Growth of world population from 1.6 billion in 1900 to 6 billion in 2000
- An increasingly interdependent global system: communications, economy, transportation, political

The two centuries of world-avoidance that had marked Mennonite piety and practice and defined the Mennonite DNA since the seventeenth century began to dissolve. Two developments played major roles in fostering this reorientation from an inward to an outward focus. Indeed, these engines of change moved in tandem: education and world mission.

## The role of education

In 1868 a group of visionary Mennonites founded the Wadsworth Seminary in Ohio. One of the teachers was C. J. van der Smissen, a German Mennonite pastor who received his training at the Basel Mission's training school, the leading Pietist mission society. Van der Smissen shared his passion for missions with his students. Wadsworth was soon followed by similar schools in Kansas, Indiana, and Ohio. Their main goals included preparing teachers, training church workers, and training missionaries.

Evangelist Dwight L. Moody sponsored a summer retreat for students in the 1880s. The Student Volunteer Movement (SVM) was founded at the 1888 student conference. By 1920 some twenty thousand students had offered themselves for missionary service. Noah E. Byers, first principal of Elkhart Institute (later president of Goshen College), had been associated with the Young Men's Christian Association, which was closely linked with SVM. The SVM student groups on Mennonite college campuses held weekly study and prayer meetings in support of the "foreign missions movement." The SVM influenced many of the young Mennonites who began to offer themselves from the 1890s on, in the words of the SVM pledge, "if God permit, to become a foreign missionary." Over the next century several thousand young North American Mennonites joined this extraordinary movement.

## Engagement in world mission

In his 1968 presidential address to the American Historical Association, John King Fairbank, eminent Harvard sinologist, observed that the modern Christian mission movement has been the most significant experiment in intercultural cooperation in human history, for it has been sustained over several centuries and extended to all corners of the globe. Fairbank understood that such interaction was multidirectional. While the missionary assumed that the people to whom mission efforts were directed would be influenced by the Christian message and the services the missionary offered, no missionary returned to the homeland unchanged. The process of learning another language and adapting to another culture was life-changing for the missionary as well.

Dutch Mennonites were the pioneers in Mennonite and Brethren in Christ cross-cultural mission. Some of those who had been supporters of the Baptist Serampore Mission in India decided in 1847 to form the Dutch Mennonite Sending Society. DMSS sent their first missionary couple to Indonesia in 1851. In the 1890s Mennonite Brethren from the Ukraine joined the Baptist Mission in Andhra Pradesh, India, and the first three missionaries from the (Old) Mennonite Church went to Central Province, India in 1898. In the early twentieth century, each decade saw several more Mennonite mission initiatives begun in Asia, Africa, and Latin America.

At the 1978 assembly of Mennonite World Conference it was reported that world membership stood at 613,600 baptized members: Europe and North America totaled 409,100, and Asia, Africa, and Latin America reported 204,500 members. In percentages, 67 percent of total membership lived in Europe and North America, 33 percent lived in other continents. Thirty-four years later MWC's 2012 Global Summary pictures a remarkable reversal. The historical heartland of the Anabaptist-Mennonite churches is steadily shifting from Europe and North America to other continents. World membership is reported to be 1,774,720 baptized members. Churches in Asia, Africa, and Latin America comprise roughly 60 percent of the total Mennonite and

Brethren in Christ membership, while Europe and North America account for some 30 percent.

| MENNONITE/BRETHREN IN CHRIST WORLD MEMBERSHIP | | | |
|---|---|---|---|
| Year | Total | Europe, North America | Asia, Africa, Latin America |
| 1978 | 613,600 | 409,100 | 204,500 |
| 2012 | 1,774,720 | 593,683 | 1,181,037 |

## Missional and Mennonite

If we inquire as to the DNA of twenty-first-century Mennonites, we quickly find it is not easy to describe it. The process of cross-fertilization over the generations has produced new hybrids. These tend to coexist uneasily under the Mennonite "tent." Focusing on the growth of the Mennonite faith family globally can divert attention from the fact that decline has also been a part of the story. Dozens of Mennonite congregations have disappeared in Europe and North America over the past two centuries. Some of the oldest and largest groups are stagnant or declining. The key observation is this: growth of Mennonite churches the past century on all continents has occurred where there has been *intentional* evangelization.

SR    To be *missional* is to be attuned to God's passion to redeem the world. God's yearning for the world's redemption is the golden thread running throughout the Scriptures. This is the "gospel" of which the first apostles were "not ashamed" (Rom 1:16). This was the anchor for the sixteenth-century Anabaptists. This gospel was the motive for Mennonites who since 1851 have been engaging in cross-cultural witness in many countries. Already the Mennonite and Brethren in Christ churches in Asia, Africa, and Latin America are sending people from their ranks as ambassadors of the gospel to other continents. This is the essential Anabaptist DNA.

# 2

# From Engagement to Preservation and Back Again

*Stanley W. Green*

Conrad Grebel, Felix Manz, and George Blaurock baptized each other on the twenty-first day of January, 1525, in Zurich, Switzerland. With that action, the Anabaptist movement was born, emerging from the stream of the so-called radical wing of the Protestant Reformation.

The movement was birthed with a strong missional consciousness. These early Anabaptists were convinced from their reading and study of the biblical text that a living vital relationship with Jesus Christ, not mediated by sacraments or ecclesiastical orders, was possible. That conviction issued in an irrepressible excitement to share this good news with their neighbors.

The Anabaptist movement, which usually traces its beginnings to that simple act of baptism in Zurich in January 1525, has experienced three distinct phases that preceded the current fourth phase in which we find ourselves.

## Phase 1. Courageous witness: Glimpse of a missional church

The initial phase in the Anabaptist movement was one of rapid growth spurred by the fervent and unflinching witness that was characteristic of the early believers. This witness was met by brutal attempts at repression. An effort was made to silence the witness of these earnest believers who claimed devotion to Christ before allegiance to civil or state authorities. Literally thousands of Anabaptist believers were killed, beginning with the martyrdom by Protestants under Zwingli. Felix Manz became the first martyr in 1527.

The *Martyrs Mirror* describes the persecution and execution between 1524 and 1660 of thousands of Anabaptists in the Low Countries—as well as Germans, Swiss, Austrians, and other Europeans—who refused to be silent about their faith. Living almost five centuries ago, these people typified a wing of the Radical Reformation that questioned literally every human tradition that had propped up the state church for a millennium and a half. Moreover, by their verbal proclamation and witness, they repudiated the silence of most Christians with regard to the gospel of salvation, reconciliation, and peacemaking through Jesus.

Refusing to defend themselves with political or military power, their influence spread even in the face of persecution and martyrdom. Perhaps one-tenth of the inhabitants of the Low Countries—now the Netherlands and Belgium—came to believe as the Anabaptists did, despite mass tortures and executions. While other less blatant forms of persecution continued, following the Inquisition by the Spanish rulers in the later sixteenth century, the executions and tortures gradually ceased by the late seventeenth century, bringing an end to phase one.

## Phase 2. From engagement to quiescence: Martyrs become the "quiet in the land" and a movement becomes a culture

During this second phase, those whose voices previously could not be silenced despite great privation and suffering came to be known, almost affectionately, as those who just wanted to be left alone to do their own thing. Continuing harassment and intimidation in Europe during the eighteenth century caused some of the most earnest followers of the Anabaptist dream to migrate to North America in that century and the following one.

These dynamics led to a period of quiescence among Anabaptists. During this time a shift was made from the zealous missional fervor of bearing witness to Jesus to a yearning for preservation and peace. In many communities the focus shifted from courageous, unflinching witness to a desire to secure space for adherents to practice their beliefs and to deepen cultural practices—practices that would later transmute into markers of an ethnic identity.

Desiring only to be left alone, Mennonites became known by the moniker "the quiet in the land."[1] It was during this period that Mennonites who had formerly been known by their notoriety for "troublemaking" became distinguished by identifiable last names. A once vibrant movement imbued with evangelistic fervor and courageous zeal ended up being transformed into an ethnic identity. With the progression of this phase, it had become possible to be "born" a Mennonite. Conversion had to do with another, different reality.

## Phase 3. From insular communities to cross-cultural engagement: Becoming a missionary people

The migrants to North America settled mostly in rural communities or on the edge of cities where they could practice their faith undisturbed. It was not until the mid-nineteenth century that the impact of

---

1. It should be noted that while the "quiet in the land" moniker came to be broadly accepted as an apt descriptor of Mennonites for two centuries from the midpoint of the eighteenth century onward, some have strongly contended that, with particular reference to the Dutch-Russian Mennonite experience, a different reality pertained. So, in an article entitled, "The Inter-Relationship between Mennonites and Slavic Evangelicals in Siberia and Central Asia," Walter Sawatzky observes: "Generally speaking, the Reformation traditions (Reformed, Anabaptist, Baptist and Hussite) . . . were not spiritual escapists, but sustained a lively emphasis on social ethics, on a social vision. It is in fact this social role of the protestantizing sects that has been their major contribution to the modernization processes of Russia, in particular in Siberia and central Asia. . . . Wherever the Mennonites or Moravians settled, they were quick to establish schools [and] to organize social/economic relations within their communities." See: http://mennonitestudies.uwinnipeg.ca/events/siberia2010/siberia-abstracts.php (accessed January 20, 2015).

the missionary zeal of the Protestant and evangelical churches began to influence Mennonite communities. It was during this time that mission to Native Americans, mission to the cities, and African American mission churches were started. By the end of the century this missionary energy expanded to include foreign missions, starting in India. This was a time when the new Mennonite heroes and heroines were those who volunteered to serve across the oceans in far-off lands. Disproportionate to their small numbers, Mennonites made an enormous investment in mission that saw the church planted in more than sixty countries on all continents. In the process a North Atlantic peoplehood of Dutch-Russian and Swiss-German ethnicities was transformed into a truly global family.

## Phase 4. Recovering our roots: Becoming a "missional" people

There was an unparalleled outpouring of missionary zeal during the twentieth century. During this era, missionaries were seen as heroic individuals who crossed the oceans, or who went to Native American reservations and African American communities in urban contexts. Mission meant geographical relocation and encounter with persons of other than European ancestry.

In the economy of God, the end of the twentieth century brought Mennonites, through a denominational merger, to a place of imagining a preferred, faithful future. The last half decade of the twentieth century was a time of liminality for North American Mennonites. During these years it seemed a door was opened to allow the church to imagine new possibilities. Who we could become as we took responsibility for the opportunity to shape the future of our church and our identity presented itself as an intriguing possibility. The trajectory within which the merging communities—comprised in the main of Dutch-Russian/General Conference Mennonite Church and Swiss-German/(Old) Mennonite Church—were evolving seemed to be leading in the direction of an embrace of a generic white North American identity accommodated to the impulses of Christendom. Instead, the new Mennonite Church at its 2001 Assembly, by unanimous consent of the delegates present, committed itself to a missional future with the promise of "finding a usable future in our past." We resolved together to embrace the identity of becoming a missional people in the twenty-first century.

## The journey toward full engagement—*again*

The journey toward becoming fully engaged has initiated some important insights and critical shifts. Some of these are the following:

*Centrality of vision.* Defining a clear vision for where we wanted to go was indispensable for securing the accompaniment of churches, conferences, and individuals on the journey toward fuller engagement. When we gathered in Nashville, Tennessee, in July 2001 and the vote was to be taken about becoming one new church, there were many disagreements from polity disputes to controversies surrounding theological convictions. These conflicts, compounded by perceptions and stereotypes that ran deep, threatened to fracture the church even before it was born. Critical to the consideration of how people would vote was the question on everyone's mind—What would be the driving force that would shape the identity of this new church? The threat of competing or of disparate visions was averted when the delegate assembly agreed that the vision for becoming a missional people was the most compelling narrative to undergird the birth of the new church.

*Redefinition of mission.* The transformation that is underway is grounded in a new way of thinking and speaking about mission. We are learning that how we talk about God, mission, and the church is formative for our identity and has profound impact in shaping our actions. We had been used to talking about our obligation in mission, about what we needed to do for the mission to be accomplished. We began a journey of learning instead to talk about God's mission and to observe what God was doing in the world. The terminus along this road we learned was not more or even yet better programs, but an alignment with God's purposes in the world rather than our carefully crafted plans for the church.

Furthermore, we began to understand that mission was not something that one part of the denomination—the mission agency—did for or on behalf of the church. Mission needed to be the very essence and lifeblood of every congregation. Consequently, this meant a shift in how we understood missionaries. Previously, missionaries were seen as heroic individuals employed by the mission agency and consecrated to cross the oceans. Rather, we were coming to understand that each individual participant in every congregation is a missionary and must be equipped to cross the boundaries in their current context—likewise a mission field—to share the good news about Jesus.

*Spirituality for missional engagement.* Another primary learning for us was that the journey we were embarking on was not merely, or even primarily, about the acquisition of new skills and competencies. It was about personal, communal, and ecclesial transformation. It was a journey whose success is predicated upon the conversion and renewal that each individual believer must undergo. It is, as such, a work of the Spirit of God.

The key prerequisite for this journey is a willingness to create space for God and an openness to the Spirit in our individual and church lives. To this end the primary introduction of the missional church vision to the delegates at the 2001 Mennonite Church USA Assembly was accompanied by a set of six spiritual exercises entitled "Habits of a Missional Church." Nurturing a spirituality to counter the self-absorption tendencies that churches and individuals constantly need to struggle against is critical. Such a spirituality must take for granted the commitment to creating space for listening to God, without which alignment to God's purposes is improbable.

## Conclusion

Just over a half millennium ago earnest Christians discovered the promise and imperative of being fully engaged with God in witness to Jesus Christ. Our Anabaptist forebears evinced a consuming desire to recover the unreserved missionary engagement of the New Testament church. It has been a number of years now since Mennonite Church USA set out in a pursuit to recover the vision that animated our Anabaptist forebears. It is clear for Mennonite Church USA that the journey has really only just begun.

Furthermore, plenty of distractions threaten to derail us. The vision demands radical transformation, even for a people whose roots were anchored in powerful missional impulses that defined the Anabaptist movement. Clearly, achieving the goal will require divine intervention among us and presume our openness to the renewing work of the Holy Spirit. Yet the promise is so tantalizing, we dare not lose heart.

# 3

# Tongue Screws and Testimony

*Alan Kreider*

Several years ago, at the seminary where I taught, our class talked about evangelism.

I gave a lecture, after which a student raised her hand. "Well, I think St. Francis got it just about right: 'Go into all the world and preach the gospel; use words if you must.'" There was a general murmuring of assent.

But another student raised her hand. "Look, I was raised a Mennonite," she said. "And I've been in seminary for several years. But I'm still uneasy talking about my faith. I know that how we live is important, but I think talking's important, too. Last year I was in a group that went to Fort Benning, to the School of the Americas, to protest the way the U.S. Army trained Latin American soldiers to suppress political opposition. Before we went to Fort Benning, the leaders carefully prepared us. 'Here are some of the questions that people are likely to ask you,' they told us. 'How are you going to respond?' So we worked together on how to give good answers, and then we tried them out on each other. We did a lot of role playing. It was really helpful. But," she said, "we've never done anything like this about Christianity.

I'm uncomfortable talking about my faith—you know, to outsiders, to people who don't go to church and have questions."

This student got me thinking. Here we were, in the middle of a course on mission and peace, and a student confessed that her articulacy hadn't kept up with her discipleship. She was silenced, but not by tongue screws.

Allow me to explain. This student, as a good product of a Mennonite seminary, knew Anabaptist history. So she knew about Maeyken Wens, who in the 1570s was so eager to give testimony at her execution that the authorities clamped an iron device in her mouth that would literally screw her tongue down. Nobody was putting a tongue screw in my student's mouth, but she was finding it very hard to talk. Why? What is it that makes it so hard for her—for *us*—to talk about our faith, not only in our conversations with each other, but with non-Christians? Let me suggest four things: Christendom, Mennonite Christendoms, the Enlightenment, and postmodernity.

## Christendom

In the first three centuries of the Christian movement, the church was a counterculture, a marginal religion that grew because it was interesting. Christians came across as attractive and question-posing, and many of them seem quite naturally to have offered verbal explanations of their lifestyles. But in the fourth century, the Christian church's position in the world changed, and most Christians lost their voice. By the end of Constantine's century, Christians had political power and were forcing pagans to become Christians. The advent of Christendom silenced most Christians in three ways:

- *Christendom made everyone Christian.* In Christendom, with the exception of a small minority of Jews, everyone was a Christian. In pre-Christendom, some people were Christians, but most people were in what the Christians called "the world." Now, in Christendom, people assumed that everyone was a Christian. Indeed, in Christendom, being a Christian was unavoidable. By the sixth century the law required the baptism of all, including newborns. So Christians became conventional, for example, in their approach to war. Christianity had become an unremarkable part of ordinary life and locally there were no non-Christians for Christians to talk to about their faith.

- *Christendom professionalized articulacy.* In Christendom, it was mainly the clergy who had a voice. In Ephesians 4:11-12, Paul had said that the ascended Christ gave gifts to people—"some would be apostles, some prophets, some evangelists, some pastors and teachers, to equip the saints for the work of ministry." But now that everyone was a Christian, Christ's *missional* gifts—apostles, prophets, and evangelists—no longer seemed necessary. So the church concentrated on the *maintenance* gifts—pastors and teachers. And the pastors and teachers performed the sacraments and spoke for the people instead of equipping them all for the work of ministry.

- *Christendom located mission on the periphery of the Christian community.* Christendom on occasion produced Christians who shared their faith. But they did so away from home; their missionary travels were to distant lands. And the Christendom missionaries were often associated with conquistadores and trading companies and imperial administrators. This intermingling of Christianity and violence has had disastrous effects. Many people today associate faith-sharing with coercion and cultural imperialism in which Christians *impose* something on other people.

Sixteenth-century Christendom was the setting in which Anabaptism was born, and the Anabaptists challenged the Christendom system. The Anabaptists asserted that not all Christians were Christian, that the gospel should be offered to all people, that the faith should not be territorially restricted or spoken about only by professionals. The Anabaptists, both men and women, were vigorously articulate. A wonderful example is Margaret Hellwart, from Württemberg, in the early 1600s, who was so intrepid in visiting neighbors to talk about God's love that the Lutheran authorities chained her to her kitchen floor. Nothing—neither tongue screws nor chains to the kitchen floor nor anything else—could keep Margaret from sharing her faith.[1]

---

1. See C. Arnold Snyder and Linda A. Huebert, eds., *Profiles of Anabaptist Women: Sixteenth-Century Reforming Pioneers* (Waterloo, ON: Wilfred Laurier University Press, 1996).

As the centuries went by, however, the various groups who descended from the Anabaptists inevitably changed. The Dutch *Doopsgezinde* were strongly affected by the Enlightenment and Pietism. Some became reasonable and culturally accommodated, while others, equally refined, became missionaries. In the mid-nineteenth century, it was the Dutch who were the first Mennonites to formally send missionaries abroad—to Indonesia. The Swiss Mennonites in Canton Basel chose a different route by cutting a deal with the Christendom authorities. In 1710, the Prince Bishop of Basel worked out a special arrangement for the local Swiss Brethren. In his Catholic canton he allowed Anabaptists to live in isolated enclaves, not in villages or in the valleys but in the uplands, over 1,000 meters (3,280 feet). And he forbade them to share their faith with others.

So the Christendom Catholics granted the Anabaptists a place of inconvenient safety, but this was the deal—they had to be silent. They were *die Stillen im Lande* (the quiet in the land). Of course, there were many places where people in the Anabaptist traditions didn't have arrangements this propitious. Many groups experienced discrimination and persecution. Some migrated and constructed impressive Mennonite communities that in time also experienced persecution. But in many places, as the centuries went by, and as the Mennonites migrated, the Christians of Anabaptist extraction became *still*, inarticulate. Some of them made a virtue of their silence, calling it *humility*.

## Mennonite Christendoms

The values of Christendom are not strange to us as Mennonites. Over the centuries we have created our own Christendoms. How did this happen?

Sociologically, Anglo Mennonites in North America became homogeneous. So today, we often spend a lot of time with people who are very much like us. There are good reasons for this homogeneity. We are a communitarian movement and our churches are, comparatively speaking, time-intensive. So we Mennonites have fellowship primarily with other Mennonites. Our friends tend to be Mennonites. We often choose to live near other Mennonites. We do business with other Mennonites. In a Mennonite Christendom, most of the people we relate to are Mennonite.

Some Anglo Mennonite churches—like churches in other Christian traditions—have grown by attracting Christians who belong to other churches who are drawn to our vision or to aspects of our life. These people from other Christian backgrounds resonate with Mennonite theology. They are attracted to a church that has no flags in it but supports Christian Peacemaker Teams and Ten Thousand Villages, a church in which it is normal to be pacifist. I am grateful for this growth. New Mennonites bring us great strength. And, together, we Mennonites—new and old—are finding our voice and making an important contribution to the Christian church in North America and beyond.

But there is a danger. If our growth occurs primarily by radicalizing people who are already Christian, it is arguable that we Mennonites are parasitic. Other groups *convert* people; we *correct* them! Where, then, do most Mennonites come from? Our historic means of recruitment has been the bedroom. But since the 1960s the birth control pill has made bedroom evangelism less effective. So many North American Mennonite churches are graying and decreasing in numbers, with relatively few members who come from non-Christian backgrounds.

As we know, new converts are eager to bear testimony about their newly discovered faith. Christendom Mennonites need these new Christians desperately. Of course, a healthy church needs the deep traditioning, the virtue and communal character, that is built up across the generations and that produces Mennonite saints. But a healthy church also needs new blood—people who naturally give testimony because they are joyful at the new life and liberation from sin and addiction that they have found in Christ and his community.

## The Enlightenment

The Enlightened philosophers of the eighteenth century hated Christendom. They despised most Christians, but some of them liked the Anabaptists. Voltaire, for example, made the one decent human in his *Candide* an Anabaptist named Jacques. The Enlightenment brought a measure of toleration for Mennonites that Christendom had never allowed. I'm grateful for that. Nevertheless, I believe that the Enlightenment has helped screw our mouths shut. How? The Enlightenment's advocates wanted to privatize Christianity and to saturate the public sphere with their own rhetoric. In reaction to Christendom, they made Christianity personal and rendered its story unacceptable as a part of social discourse. The Enlightenment's advocates affirmed things like these:

- Religions are human constructs, attempts to cope with the unknown and mysterious.
- All religions are the same. They are morally equivalent and very subjective.
- Natural law is immutable. Even if God exists, God doesn't matter because God can't change anything.
- Miracles do not happen, therefore, and prayer changes nothing.

Note that the Enlightenment thinkers consistently emphasize rationality and control. They align this emphasis upon control with technology and technique. Their worldview is mechanistic and has no room for a God who makes a difference, a God who acts spontaneously, a God who responds to prayer, a God who stirs up new initiatives and new hope. The Enlightenment, in short, tempts us to assume that we can micromanage our lives and ultimately leaves nothing to which we Christians can bear testimony. The Enlightenment, like Christendom, makes Christians inarticulate.

## Postmodernity

The same can also be said for postmodernity, which has added an attractive note of playfulness to our way of thinking. Postmodernity enables Christians to be less certain and less tense. Its rhetoric appears to be modest:

We live in a world of many narratives. You Christians have one metanarrative, the Enlightenment has another metanarrative, the Sufis of Turkey and the Jains of India have still other narratives, and so forth. Look, let's rejoice in this multistoried reality and delight in quilts made up of differing kinds of cloth.

Let's recognize the importance of spirituality. All humans in their more sensitive moments have encountered mystery. We all have experiences that we can't explain.

Let's not forget that spirituality is a matter of individual decision. Religion is my business, a taste choice. I'll choose my form of religion and you choose yours. Please don't talk to me about your choices and I'll not impose mine on you.

Many of us Mennonites are attracted to this approach, and there are things in it that we can greet, particularly the renewed openness to spirituality. But there are problems as well. We are embarrassed when people talk about Jesus, for this sounds particularistic and proud. So some of us embrace theocentrism and reject the heart of our Anabaptist tradition that is passionately Christocentric. And there are so many questions: What about the atonement, Christology, other religions? Who are we to talk to others about Jesus when we don't know what we think?

We defend our reluctance to talk with a rationale that is typically Mennonite—we're being humble! After all, shouldn't we be learning from other traditions? Shouldn't we be exploring the wisdom of other religions? So in our humility we don't bear testimony to God's saving work in Christ because we have nothing to say.

A world that is post-Enlightenment and postmodern is a difficult place for Anglo Mennonite Christians to bear testimony. Few of us are new Christians. We are repelled by Christendom and yet often live in Mennonite Christendoms. We are deeply shaped by the Enlightenment and postmodernity. We are afraid of giving offense, of not knowing how to answer questions. And we are softhearted, beneficent people who want to do good in the world. So we support digging wells and micro-enterprise and are ouchy about verbal testimony. As a result, it is hard for us to talk about Jesus. We are suspicious of mission. And we are even more suspicious of evangelism, which has a bad reputation for poor taste and manipulation.

## "Humble evangelism"—a way forward for Mennonites?

Should Mennonite Christians, then, stop giving testimony to outsiders? "No," says Stuart Murray, "Christianity is at heart a missionary faith."[2] But if we are to share good news with others, we must reconfigure the way we speak. Maybe we Mennonites should no longer talk about evan-

---

2. Stuart Murray, *Post-Christendom* (Milton Keynes, UK: Paternoster, 2014), 227.

gelism. Instead, we could imitate the Sri Lankan missiologist Vinoth Ramachandra, who always speaks of "humble evangelism."[3] And humble evangelism involves two ingredients—*incarnation* and *explanation*.

## Missional approach 1: Incarnation

SR

How we live matters. What we believe determines how we live. And how we live speaks. Most Mennonites know these things. But if the incarnational approach is to work, four things are necessary:

- *Nonconformity.* If our lives are to speak, they must be question-posing. We must know deep down that the ultimate purpose of life is not "to move from birth to death as comfortably as possible."[4] Instead, as individuals and communities we will live differently, more oddly, more interestingly than our neighbors. The way we handle issues of security, comfort, and consumption will speak and elicit questions.

- *Collaboration.* We will learn to know people who may or may not be churchgoers but who seek God's kingdom and its justice. We live near them, share food with them, get involved in local projects with them, and go fishing with them. We become friends. And we get out of our ghettoes.

- *Living out of control.* This is at the heart of a life that leads to testimony. For our lives to speak, it is important that we, in some area of our lives, intentionally live by faith. It is essential that we do something that requires us to take risks and relinquish control. We then pray, "God, it's up to you. We can only make it if you answer prayers, if you do miracles, if you make impossible things possible." It's only then that we have anything to say. And to live this way our lives must be rooted in prayer and worship.

- *Expressing hope.* When we live interestingly, out of control, we express hope. It is hope in God who works through Christians who are trusting enough to be odd, and to act oddly, because God's story is odd—and God's character is odd—and it's only through oddity that there is room for creative solutions to

3. Vinoth Ramachandra, *The Recovery of Mission: Beyond the Pluralist Paradigm* (Grand Rapids, MI: Eerdmans, 1996), 273.
4. Jonathan J. Bonk, *Missions and Money*, rev. ed. (Maryknoll, NY: Orbis, 2006), 107.

intractable problems. Conventional panaceas lead to despair, but the way of Christ leads Christians to "overflow with hope" (Rom 15:13 NIV). And the presence of hope always elicits questions. The New Testament writers don't tell their readers to "evangelize" others. They tell them to live with hope. And if we have hope, and express that hope in deviant behavior, people will ask questions that lead to testimony. Peter puts this in classic form when he writes, "Always be ready to make your defense to anyone who demands from you an accounting of the hope that is in you" (1 Pet 3:15). It is *hopeful incarnation* of the way of Christ that leads people to ask questions and demand explanation. If we act hopefully, people want to know why.

## Missional approach 2: Explanation

When we live hopefully and interestingly, then we can talk. Verbal articulacy explains what we are doing by bearing testimony to what God has done in our lives in Jesus Christ. Why is this verbal explanation necessary? Because unexplained actions allow people to draw all kinds of explanations. And if people are impressed with our unexplained action, they will glorify us!

A friend of mine recently spent time in Calcutta serving at one of Mother Teresa's hospices. As he reflected later on his experience there, he noted, "It struck me that without a knowledge of Bengali, I could only point to *myself.*" Words without action are hollow. But actions without words are either incomprehensible or only glorify ourselves. As disciples of Jesus, we want to point away from ourselves to God. We see our lives in continuity with God's story that begins with Abraham and Sarah, that courses through the history of the Jewish people, that culminates in the life, death, and resurrection of Jesus, and that through the Holy Spirit has been opened up to "all flesh"—to *everyone*! The story is continuing throughout the world today. Christianity is not a *Western* faith. It is worldwide and growing rapidly. So in order to explain the incarnational style of Jesus' disciples, what is necessary?

- *Relationships.* Building friendships with neighbors and colleagues is essential—not to convert them, but because we want to be in genuine, reciprocal relationship with them. For this to happen, love is indispensable. Love can grow where people live in stability, rooted in a place, enabling friendships to grow across time. When as a church of "resident aliens" we commit ourselves to a geographical place, we encounter a wide variety of real people. Gradually, we learn to know them and discover that we and they, as neighbors, share common concerns. We share with them the routines of neighborly existence. We learn to know their struggles, and we and they talk about our problems and local challenges. We support each other, have good times together, and lament with them about misfortunes, both theirs and ours. We engage, as Mark Gornik suggests, in the "daily improvisational practices of neighboring, prayer and social commitment that establish signs of God's reign and hints of the pattern of the city to come."[5] As we engage in these practices and manifest fidelity in our relationships, we and our neighbors will talk about our deepest convictions and about what or in whom we trust.

- *No formulas.* Formulas can't determine what will happen here. How we speak will depend on the person with whom we are talking and the nature of our relationship. It will depend on the depth and transparency of our friendship. Missiologist Art McPhee has observed, "Jesus' model was . . . inductive, spontaneous and natural, and most importantly Spirit-led."[6] As congregations, we can study how to bear testimony. We can be for each other like the trainers who prepare people for conversations outside Fort Benning. With each other, we can develop disciplines of talking truthfully about God and of listening well. We can do role plays, and after the conversations we can meet to profit from our experiences. Talking about our faith might be a useful topic to discuss as we prepare candidates for baptism. In catechesis (instruction) we can prepare them to think about their own questions and talk about their faith in response to those questions.

- *Hope.* When we converse with non-Christians, we discover that many people are full of despair. The news is bad. Healthcare

---

5. Mark Gornik, *To Live in Peace: Biblical Faith and the Changing Inner City* (Grand Rapids, MI: Eerdmans, 2002), 114.

6. Email from Art McPhee to Alan Kreider (Dec. 12, 2007).

is unaffordable and the climate is in trouble. The future looks dangerous. And yet we Christians have hope—hope that is question-begging.

» "Why do you have hope?"
» "Why do you think it's worth campaigning for undocumented immigrants or tutoring children in a local school?"
» "Why are you pouring your life out for people even when you've retired?"
» "Why are you not afraid to die?"
» "Why do you think God is going to bring God's reign of justice, peace, and joy?"

The answer is simple: Because God has given us forgiveness, joy, and that most countercultural commodity—hope. And hope, as Paul says, "does not disappoint us, because God's love has been poured into our hearts through the Holy Spirit that has been given to us" (Rom 5:5).

# 4

# Keeping Good News and Good Works Together SR

*Ronald J. Sider and Heidi Rolland Unruh*

We believe Christ our Lord longs for his community of disciples to weave together a seamless garment of active peacemaking, authentic compassion, and pursuit of justice together with winsome, passionate evangelism. And we believe Anabaptists ought to be the leaders in that kind of holistic mission.

## Anabaptists should be leaders in holistic mission

The first reason for this is how holistic mission is rooted in Anabaptist history. When our movement began in the sixteenth century, early Anabaptists combined evangelism, peacemaking, and a concern for economic justice. Our spiritual forebears lived and preached peace, rejecting the sword and modeling economic sharing. They also sent passionate evangelists all over Europe, inviting people to a vibrant personal faith in Christ and baptizing those who embraced their message. Early Anabaptists were so eager to proclaim the good news about Jesus that their persecutors would forcibly prevent them from speaking.

Second, understanding Jesus' gospel as the good news of the kingdom—beyond solely the forgiveness of individual sins—is a central theological foundation for holistic mission. Jesus' in-breaking kingdom brings not only a new forgiven relationship with God but also transformed socioeconomic relationships in Jesus' new messianic community—and this transformation spills over and improves surrounding society. Mennonites have had this understanding of the gospel for many decades in a way that has been deeper and more widespread than in many other parts of the Christian church.

Third, there is a deep longing in our world for an end to the pervasive violence and injustice that devastates so many lives. Our Anabaptist understanding of Christ as the Prince of Peace who calls everyone to peace and justice speaks to that longing. That message is intertwined with the good news that when persons place their faith in Christ, his Spirit lives in them and empowers them to become self-sacrificial agents of change. Thus holistic mission offers a transformative and appealing hope in a violent, unjust world.

Finally, we Anabaptists say we want to imitate the biblical Christ. We look to the stories of what Jesus did and taught as a model for what it means to live as a follower of Jesus. And the Gospels show Jesus loving the whole person, body and soul. He healed sick bodies, called people to compassion, challenged prevailing ideas about violence, confronted the unjust acquisition of wealth, and offered forgiveness of sins. He sent out his disciples to share in his work: "Cure the sick who are there, *and* say to them, 'The kingdom of God has come near to you'" (Luke 10:9, emphasis ours).

## Why are so many Mennonites hesitant about evangelism?

Why then are so many Mennonites today—particularly in white, middle-class churches—so hesitant to practice evangelism?[1] Why do

---

1. We note that Mennonites in predominantly non-Anglo churches are more likely to practice vibrant evangelism. For example, in a national survey of Mennonites, respondents in the "racial/ethnic" category were three times more likely to regularly invite non-Christians to church activities than other Mennonites. See Conrad Kanagy, *Road Signs for the Journey: A Profile of Mennonite Church USA* (Scottdale, PA: Herald Press, 2007), 72–73.

only half of Mennonites speak regularly about their faith to people outside their church and family? Why are only 2 percent of Mennonites new believers, versus those born to Mennonite families or denominational transfers?[2] Again, there are many reasons.

Centuries of persecution have certainly helped to make us the "quiet in the land"—people who just want to be left alone to follow Jesus. The stream of Mennonites who immigrated to Russia made a pact with Catherine the Great to abstain from proselytizing in return for land and security. While Mennonites living in the West today rarely face persecution or overt restrictions on evangelism, hesitancy to verbally share our faith has become embedded in our identity.

Secondly, Mennonites react against the imperialist, destructive way evangelism has sometimes been practiced. Historically, Christian mission too often went hand in hand with colonization and suppression of indigenous cultures. Evangelism was used as an instrument of coercion rather than liberation. Today, we observe some Christians engaging in aggressive techniques to "win souls" while ignoring the rest of people's lives, tangling up gospel proclamation with a political agenda, or manipulating converts for financial gain. Because we value peace and justice, Mennonites tend to toss out the evangelism baby with the dirty bathwater that has too often accompanied it.

A third factor is cultural assimilation. Many Mennonites living in the West like to think of themselves as distinct, but research shows that our worldview and lifestyle largely mirror the secular culture around us.[3] Our culture tells us that religion is a private matter and that sharing personal faith is inherently offensive. Social justice is trendy; talking about Jesus is not.

Finally, some Mennonites have embraced a theological stance that undermines the call and commitment to evangelism. This group is relatively small when compared to the whole Mennonite body, and our official theological statements are still those of historic Christianity. But there is an influential minority of Mennonites who question traditional claims about the deity of Christ, his bodily resurrection, and his uniqueness as the way to salvation. Their focus is on peace and justice. They

---

2. Ibid., chapter 3.
3. Ibid.

advocate choosing a nonviolent lifestyle and working toward ending war and injustice in the name of Christ. But this group is disconnected from the calling of Christ to "Go and make disciples of all nations." Their sense of mission is vital, but incomplete.

The following story illuminates the problem. I (Ron) spoke a few years ago to the seniors at Taylor University, an evangelical school in Indiana. One senior introduced herself to me as a Mennonite, the daughter of missionary parents. She told me that as a junior, she had done a semester in Israel. She was thrilled to visit all the places where Jesus walked, but slowly became aware that her class was meeting almost exclusively with Israelis. They were not engaging with the Palestinians. Then she met the Christian Peacemaker Teams in Hebron. She was delighted with what they were doing. In fact, she said, she believed she had found her calling for life. The next fall, she had attended Christian Peacemaker Teams' national conference. Sadly, she told me how terribly disappointed she was because the conference had very little about Jesus and nothing about inviting others to follow him.

Let us be clear. CPT is a very important movement. We want it to multiply exponentially in size and impact. We have respect and gratitude for the teams who courageously embody their faith by demonstrating the power of nonviolent action. But we also believe it is a loss when Christian activists who seek peace and justice do not also embrace publicly the power of personal transformation through Christ. What might have happened if top Mennonite leaders had dared to wholeheartedly endorse CPT while helping CPT to integrate word and deed in their witness to Christ?[4]

## Keeping evangelism, peacemaking, and the work for justice together

The central tenets of historic Christianity are an essential foundation for evangelism. We believe they also provide crucial grounding for peacemaking and work for justice.

---

4. We realize that verbal witness to Christ is not possible or appropriate in every context where CPT and other Christian groups are involved. What we yearn for is more intentional grounding of the work of peacemaking in God's unique work of reconciliation through Christ, and the passionate desire to plant seeds of this reconciliation throughout the world.

In Jesus' day, messianic pretenders got crucified. The only conceivable conclusion on the day after Jesus' crucifixion was that the Nazarene prophet of peace and justice was a fraudulent failure. Yet when Thomas met the risen Jesus, he said, "My Lord and my God!" The early church, comprised overwhelmingly of strict Jewish monotheists, dared to call a backwater carpenter not just Messiah but Lord—*kurios*, the Greek word used in the translation of the Hebrew word *Yahweh*. It was only because they met the risen Jesus that they dared to believe again that his kingdom of peace and justice was actually breaking into history.

If Jesus is only another great prophet, then there is little compelling reason to go around the block and the world inviting others to believe in him. But if the carpenter from Nazareth is both true God and true man, then we have an urgent incentive to tell others. If his resurrection on the third day was a powerful demonstration of his claim to be the Son of God, then believing that he is the only way to salvation is not presumptuous.

In fact, the deity and resurrection of Jesus is central to peacemaking. Loving one's enemies, daring to forgive and confront rather than kill even the worst tyrants, laying down one's life to overcome evil with good, is a very difficult path to walk. While Christians are not the only ones who choose this path, knowing that the God-man Jesus modeled this by suffering for our sake offers a powerful motive and guide. The one who calls us to sacrificial love for enemies is the Creator-of-the-universe-made-flesh who offered forgiveness even to his murderers.

Furthermore, it is Jesus' resurrection as the guarantee of our resurrection at his second coming that gives us the courage to risk death to love enemies. Death does not mark the end for those who believe in Christ. Knowing that we will be raised with him to live forever powerfully emboldens us to stand up for peace and justice in this violent world.

As noted earlier, Jesus' gospel of the kingdom leads inevitably to combining word and deed. The prophets had predicted that the future Messiah would bring forgiveness of sins as well as peace and justice. Jesus claimed to be that long-expected Messiah. Central to his ministry was the message, "Repent, for the kingdom of heaven has come near" (Matt 4:17). Jesus described God as a father who longs to forgive prodigal daughters and sons. Equally central was the claim that the messianic time of peace and justice was actually breaking into the present in Jesus and his new community. He validated his messianic claim by pointing to both his restorative deeds and his transformative preaching (Matt 11:2-6). And he sent out his disciples to do the same as they preached and lived the gospel of the kingdom.[5] As followers of Jesus, we cannot pray, "Your kingdom come" (Matt 6:10) and then do only evangelism— or only social action.

Other significant theological themes also provide a foundation for holistic mission. Since God created persons with both a physical and a spiritual dimension, God values both social action that secures material necessities and evangelism that leads to spiritual renewal. Since Scripture condemns sin that is both *personal* (e.g., lying and adultery) and *social* (e.g., political corruption and economic oppression), righteousness demands both discipleship that transforms personal character and advocacy that creates more just, peaceful social structures. Since biblical eschatology indicates that at the end of history this broken world will not be destroyed but renewed, Christians anticipate that Christ's return will herald a restored creation where the best of human civilization will be taken up into the New Jerusalem. We trust that both evangelism and social action have eternal consequences. Thus by leading people to Christ and improving society, we work toward that partial transformation that Christ will complete at his return.[6]

## Evangelism and social action are inseparably connected, but not identical

Our Anabaptist faith leads us to see evangelism and social action as essential and intertwined—but not identical. Social action is that set of activities whose primary purpose is improving the physical, socio-economic, and political well-being of people through relief, development, structural change, and the reduction of violence. Evangelism is

---

5. See Ronald J. Sider, *Good News and Good Works: A Theology for the Whole Gospel* (Grand Rapids, MI: Baker, 1999), especially chapters 3 and 4.

6. For a fuller statement of these points, see Sider, *Good News and Good Works*; see also Ronald J. Sider, Philip Olson, and Heidi Rolland Unruh, *Churches That Make a Difference: Reaching Your Community with Good News and Good Works* (Grand Rapids, MI: Baker Books, 2002) for descriptions of how this theology looks in practice.

that set of activities whose primary intention is to invite non-Christians to embrace Jesus' gospel of the kingdom, believe in Jesus Christ as Savior and Lord, undergo baptism, join Jesus' new redeemed community, and experience daily personal fellowship with the Holy Spirit, with the joyful anticipation of eternal life with God.

We can and must look beyond an individualistic approach to mission that only values counting souls. But in a similar way we should not neglect the spiritual needs of individuals. Persons can be regenerated only through the saving work of Christ. We cannot evangelize social structures—e.g., corporations, governments, and economic systems—though we ought to work to change them. In addition to advocating for reform, we can pray against evil spiritual forces that twist social structures away from the good that God intends. We can prophetically envision their transformation when Christ reigns victorious over all injustice. We can also seek opportunities to share Christ with people in positions of influence in these structures, as well as the people negatively affected by them.

Defining evangelism and social action as distinct though overlapping areas of focus is important if we are to fulfill the full scope of our mission. Though evangelism has socially beneficial consequences, we cannot claim that just telling people about Christ constitutes social action. This gives Christians an excuse to neglect the deliberate, costly acts of service, organizing, advocacy, and peacemaking required to truly love our neighbor. Conversely, if everything Christians are sent into the world to do is called evangelism, then people may focus exclusively on social action and peacemaking while claiming to be sharing the gospel—though they never invite a single person to accept Christ. The special task of communicating the gospel with the prayer that others will accept Christ and become his followers tends to get lost.

Can our good deeds attract people to Christ? Is the Holy Spirit active in drawing hearts to God even before we say a word? Certainly. But at some point, to be faithful to the Lord of the harvest, Christians must explicitly speak the good news. We must give attention to telling our faith story, inviting people into our church or spiritual community, offering to study the Bible together, to pray intercessory prayer, and to do other activity intended to encourage individuals to accept and follow

Christ. This doesn't mean pushing the gospel message on people who don't want to hear it or pressuring people before they are ready to accept it. We must listen before we speak, look for appropriate times and ways to share, respect people's right to reject our message, and depend on the Holy Spirit to do the convicting and converting. We can admit to not having all the answers. But we need to recognize that our love for our neighbor is incomplete unless we share Christ in word as well as in deed.[7]

While good news and good works are not identical, they are inseparably connected and mutually reinforcing.[8] In practice, evangelism has a social action dimension and social action has an evangelistic dimension. Biblical evangelism calls on people to embrace Christ, not just as a Savior who forgives sins, but also as Lord of every area of life including one's politics and economics. That means helping converts to repent of perpetuating systems of injustice and violence, as well as individual moral failings. Holy Spirit–transformed persons begin to live differently, and their transformed lives slowly make whole societies more just and peaceful. We see this in the example of the corrupt official Zacchaeus, who was so overjoyed by his encounter with Jesus that he made restitution to those he had defrauded and pledged generous support to the poor (Luke 19:2-10).

Biblical evangelism also draws people into a community of faith that engages their gifts in social action. Furthermore, just being the church—if our communal life truly follows Jesus' way—develops models of mutual caring and sharing that the broader society frequently is inspired to imitate. One example among many is the manner in which Christians have led the way in starting hospitals for the sick and schools for poor children.

Social action and peacemaking can also foster evangelism. Good works point to the goodness of the kingdom that is fully realized only in Christ. When people see Christians working to end violence and overcome poverty, they become more open to the gospel. If we communicate that we do these things because of the love of Jesus, others may

7. Sider, *Good News and Good Works*, chapter 9 and appendix.
8. Ibid., chapter 10; see also Sider et al., *Churches That Make a Difference*, chapters 1–5.

be more ready to hear about who this Jesus really is. Our actions make our words more credible and compelling.

Bernard Sejour's story demonstrates this powerful link. As a Haitian, Bernard wanted to make a difference for his country, so he became a human rights worker. He met Anna, a Mennonite Central Committee worker serving in his organization. He noticed something different about Anna and learned she was a Mennonite. Forced to flee to the United States because of his activism, Bernard tracked down other Mennonites, who explained the gospel more fully to him. He gained pastoral training at a Mennonite college and planted a church for Haitians in Philadelphia—right before the massive earthquake that hit Haiti in 2010. A grant from MCC helped Bernard to offer case management for newly arriving Haitians who had lost everything. His work helping immigrants access legal and social services has also given him opportunity to form relationships that lead to invitations to his church community, which is intentionally welcoming to "whoever wants to know who Jesus is."

## PRINCIPLES FOR KEEPING WORD AND DEED TOGETHER

*Love.* Both evangelism and social action should be motivated and guided by love, which always seeks what is best for the other person, even at a cost. We do not engage in evangelism or social action to enlarge our own, or our congregation's, "empires" (Mark 12:29-31; 1 Cor 13:1-3; John 3:16-18).

*Holism.* We minister to whole persons, recognizing that people are more than just souls or bodies. People need both spiritual salvation and tangible acts of mercy and justice. We also are all called to repent of both personal sins and participation in systemic evils (Ps 107:5-9; Matt 9:35; 3 John 1:2).

*Relationships.* Making the good news real requires incarnational involvement. Both good news and good works are most effective, and have the most integrity, in the context of authentic, bridge-building relationships that reflect the reconciling work of Jesus Christ (2 Cor 5:18; Col 1:15-22; Eph 2:13-19).

*Respect.* We affirm the dignity and worth of each individual regardless of religious or economic status, grounded in the imago Dei (image of God). This includes respecting each person's God-given right to religious freedom, so our ministry methods are never coercive or manipulative (Gen 1:27; Prov 14:31; James 2:1-5).

*Special concern for those who are poor and marginalized.* In both evangelism and social action, we can emulate God's attentive care for those who are poor and vulnerable throughout Scripture, and Jesus' intentional ministry of reaching out to those on the margins of society (Deut 15:4-11; Luke 4:18-19; 7:18-22; 1 Cor 1:26).

## Let's end the scandal!

Our dream for the Mennonite church is that every congregation would continually be engaging non-Christians "to know who Jesus is," inviting them to accept him as Savior and Lord, and throwing their arms around these new Christians, helping them to become the whole persons God desires. And every Mennonite congregation would also be actively engaged in ending poverty, correcting injustice, and reducing violence in our world. Think of the impact if this is what non-Christians experienced with their local Mennonite congregation. Think of the impact if everyone connected with agencies like Mennonite Central Committee, Mennonite Disaster Service, and Mennonite Economic Development Associates were daily praying for the right opportunity to gently, winsomely tell of their love for Christ and share the gospel. Think of the impact if everyone connected with agencies like Mennonite Mission Network and Eastern Mennonite Missions were regularly asking for divine guidance on how their church planting activities can promote peace and justice.

Let's end the scandal where some of our churches primarily do evangelism, others primarily do peace and justice, and far too many do neither. Let's love whole persons the way Jesus did.

5

# God's Shalom Project

Why Peace and Mission Are Inseparable

*James R. Krabill*

In a survey conducted among a group of North American high school seniors, the students were asked what they believed would be the greatest challenge their graduating class would face in their lifetimes. Not surprisingly, the challenges identified were almost as numerous and as varied as the students themselves. They ranged from world poverty, societal trends—divorce, suicide—and distressing diseases—like AIDS—to growing materialism, climate change, terrorism, family crises, and the quest for personal happiness and fulfillment.

## We live in a messed-up, broken-down world

These graduating seniors have it right. The issues they will face are both local and global, societal as well as personal. As the students have correctly noted, *no part of the human condition* remains untouched by the deep sin and consequent brokenness our world is experiencing at every level. This is no piddly problem we've got on our hands. For brokenness, as it turns out, is a *universal* phenomenon. It is *comprehensive* in nature and scope. And it *runs deep*—far, far back and beyond our current reality into the near-mythical past of the human experience.

*Brokenness runs deep.* Many cultures of the world have within their collective memory stories of a "paradise lost"—an original state of harmony and bliss disturbed and destroyed when something went drastically wrong. These stories take us back in time, back beyond the actual memory of clan historians, back to the earliest days of the human experience when, out of deceit, arrogance, jealousy, or some other kind of disruptive or disobedient behavior, brokenness entered the world and changed the human story forever. Though these ancient accounts vary greatly in detail, they share this lesson in common: The world has been living in brokenness for a mighty long time—so long, in fact, that we can't even imagine what our existence would be like without it. Brokenness runs deep. It's a fact of life. The way things are. And, for all practical purposes, the way they've always been.

*Brokenness is universal.* The specific shape of brokenness is determined in part by the culture or society in which it finds expression. In some cultural contexts, this translates into alienation or loss of meaning in life. In other settings, it takes the form of materialistic obsession, political oppression, or evil spirit possession. Whatever the particulars of brokenness in any given place and among any people, it is clear that no culture or society can claim immunity to the problem. For in every human setting, there are those who lie and deceive. Those whose lives are filled with hate talk and acts of violence. Those who wrongfully take things belonging to others. Who cheat on their spouses. Beat their children. And treat both friends and enemies in ways that defy all sense of human dignity.

*Brokenness is comprehensive.* The problem is not only deep within the human past; it is deep within each human being. And no part of that being—body, soul, or mind—has emerged unscathed from the effects of sin's devastating blow. Healing is needed all around—healing that alone can bring peace of mind, soundness of body, and true joy in the heart.

## For such a very big problem, an equally big solution is required

The Scriptures are clear that God is on top of the situation, very much aware of our sad state of affairs. And it is for this precise reason that God has devised a plan—a plan to come to our rescue, to heal our brokenness, to bring peace out of conflict and strife, and to make things right once and for all with the world.

In the pages to follow we will examine ten points highlighting the main features of God's plan, God's mission, to put the universe with its fallen structures and inhabitants back on track. This essay is about God's *mission*. But in every one of the ten statements, the word *peace* will appear. *Really?* you might wonder. *Mission and peace inextricably interwoven into the same text?* Well, yes. Because for followers of Jesus, the two can't be separated. The gospel just won't let us do it.

Not that the church hasn't tried to keep the two apart! We have created our fair share of evangelism committees and peace clubs. And unfortunately, many of the people making up these two groups rarely speak to each other. Some of them downright wouldn't want to. Others simply see no need for it. "We're just not on the same page," is the reason given for their separate agenda.

But Anabaptist Christians—by our history and theology—should know better, even if we have often not done much better than anyone else. Maybe the time has come for us to examine this matter once again. And the following affirmations could help us to do just that.

So, here then are ten statements to help ground us and guide as we live and share the good news of God's-Shalom-Project-in-Jesus with friends and neighbors in today's broken world. They are not the only statements that could be made. But they will get us started on the journey.

## 1. Origins: Mission originates in God's loving, comprehensive plan to restore peace to the universe

Mission is not a human invention. It was God who started it. The God we encounter in the Bible is, above all, a missionary God. From the earliest pages of human history when men and women turned their backs on God's love, it was God who took the initiative to pursue them, coming into their world, seeking, wooing, calling, and restoring them.

God does this not because rebellious men and women deserve to be delivered from their brokenness and sin, but because this is in the very nature of the Creator's love. And so, God has put in motion a comprehensive, long-range plan to "bring everything together in Christ, everything in deepest heaven, everything on planet earth." The rest is history—the history of God continually breaking into the human experience to offer peace, forgiveness, liberation, and hope.[1]

## 2. Means: Jesus is the means by which God intends to restore peace

The biblical witness is abundantly clear on these two points: that Jesus is, and has always been, God's "big secret"—at the very heart of God's plan to save the world; and that Jesus' earthly life and ministry, ending with his death and resurrection, together constitute the single most important event of all time—the event by which all history is divided and all other events are defined and understood.

It is in Jesus, the Scriptures tell us, that God intends to make things right with the universe. It is in Jesus that everything will be "brought together" and "summed up." In Jesus that "all creation will be set free from its slavery to decay" and "brought back to God." That past sins will be forgiven and forever forgotten. That the walls of anger and hostility between countries, clans, and classes will be broken down. And that races living in conflict will be formed into one new people and enter together into God's presence "by Christ's atoning death on the cross."

There are those throughout history who have sought to "complete" the work of Jesus by adding on to what he has already accomplished. Early Jewish Christians wanted to have Jesus . . . *and* the Law. Others spoke of Jesus *and* angels. Or again, Jesus *and* the old sacrificial system. In our day, we hear of Jesus *and* Buddha, Muhammad, or Krishna.

But time and again, God's people have reaffirmed that, next to Jesus, there *is* none other. Jesus, the Christ, is All-Sufficient. He is All-in-All. He alone shows us the *Truth* about God, provides access for us as the *Way* to God, and makes it possible for us to experience most fully *Life* with God.[2]

## 3. Message: The message of Jesus is the gospel of peace

The Old Testament prophesied it—God's suffering servant would be called the Prince of *Peace*. The angel choir proclaimed it—*Peace* on

---

1. To pursue more fully the points presented in this section, see the following biblical passages: Ps 51:1-15; Ezek 36:16-38; John 3:16-17; Rom 3:10-26; 5:6-8.
2. Biblical passages expanding the points here include Isa 9:2-7; Luke 2:8-14; John 14:1-7; Acts 10:34-36; Eph 1:3-10; 2:14; Col 1:19-22; 2 Cor 5:15-17.

earth! A Savior is born! Jesus himself pronounced it—the blessed ones are those working for *peace*. And the first Christians preached it—in Christ, we have *peace* with God and with each other. Making peace through Jesus has been central to God's salvation plan from the very beginning.

Behind much of God's peacemaking intentions for the world is the Hebrew idea of *shalom*. The noun *shalom* occurs some 235 times in the Old Testament and more than one hundred times in its Greek translation, *eirene*, in the New Testament. Shalom is a broad concept for the Hebrews. It is "human well-being in all its dimensions." Personal and social. Physical and spiritual. Inward, outward, and upward.

That is why words like *peace*, *justice*, *righteousness*, and *salvation* are often used interchangeably in the New Testament. They are all different aspects of what Jesus came to bring, to be, and to do.

In God's grand plan for making things right, Jesus not only *restores* peace. Jesus *is* our peace. And his peace is much bigger than we usually imagine. It is all-encompassing. Comprehensive. As grandiose as the universe. As up-close-and-personal as any single one of us. It is good news. The gospel. Or, as Peter would call it, the "good news of peace" (Acts 10:36 RSV).[3]

## 4. Messenger: The primary messenger of the peace plan is the church

Amazingly, and for some reason not fully explainable, God has chosen the church—those "believing followers of Jesus" who were and forever will be the undeserving recipients of God's grace and peace in their own broken lives—to be the primary instruments through which that same grace and peace are extended to others.

Why God—from the very outset of the Christian movement—should have decided to entrust this enormous assignment to a smelly pack of fisherfolk, tax collectors, and women with checkered pasts is beyond human imagination. And why God should be willing to continue making use of the likes of us is no easier to comprehend. Yet this is precisely the strategy God has chosen to employ and for which no apparent backup plan has been put in place.

---

3. Corresponding scriptural texts include Matt 5:9-12, 38-47; Luke 19:41-44; Acts 10:34-36; Rom 5:1, 9-11; Eph 2:11-18.

The church's calling to be God's collaborators and key carriers of the peace plan goes back to God's promise to Abraham and Sarah: "By you all the families of the earth shall bless themselves." The Bible emphasizes repeatedly that the principal means by which God is reaching out to the world is through the people of God. It is through this people-in-mission that God's love is to be most visibly demonstrated and most clearly made known to those who have not yet seen and heard. God's people are, in short, the primary *model* and *messengers* of God's plan.[4]

### 5. Task: The church's task is to announce Jesus, the one God has sent to restore peace

Throughout the years, God has communicated at various times and in numerous ways with humanity. But it is in *Jesus* that God gets through most directly and with greatest clarity. For it is in Jesus that God takes on human form, walks our streets, eats our food, and washes our feet to show us, at long last, God's will and ways.

What God did in Jesus is unique and unrepeatable. Yet Jesus challenges us to follow him into the world as he was in the world, identifying at the deepest level with the human experience in order to witness to God's new order of grace, peace, and salvation.

For all these reasons and more, the church must keep focused on Jesus. Any other focus ultimately results in deviation, distortion, distraction, or delusion. When God's people are faithful, they are *working diligently* to continue the mission that Jesus himself began during his earthly ministry. When they are faithful, they are *witnessing joyfully and unapologetically* to the healing and hope that only Jesus can bring.

Witness and work. Word and deed. The faithful church preaches what Jesus practiced and practices what he preached. And in so doing, she announces the *whole gospel* of Jesus to the broken world he so loved and for which he died.[5]

---

4. See Gen 12:1-3; Matt 28:18-20; John 17:13-19; Acts 1:6-8; Eph 3:10, 20-21; 2 Cor 5:18-20.
5. See 1 Cor 2:1-2; 2 Cor 4:1-6; 5:18-20; Eph 6:14-15; Heb 1:1-3.

## 6. Goal: The goal of announcing Jesus is to gain ground for God's peace plan in the world

Mission is the means by which God's peace plan in Jesus is modeled, made known, and embraced throughout the world. This happens as increasing numbers of people are invited to participate in the plan by accepting for themselves the grace and peace offered in Jesus, and then joining in the formation of faith communities committed to living out and promoting to others the good news of God's desire to make things right with the world.

We come closest to understanding God's desire for humanity when we give special attention to Jesus' own earthly life and ministry, following along after him as he walks around the towns and villages of his homeland, entering broken lives and offering forgiveness, new beginnings, healing, and wholeness to all those he encounters.

The brokenness of people in Jesus' time runs parallel in most instances to that experienced by many today. Then, as now, we find physical infirmity, social inequality, religious impurity, intellectual inadequacy, emotional instability, and spiritual captivity. Then, as now, Jesus comes into the human situation, encounters and confronts people in their area of deepest need, and invites them to embrace God's liberating, saving grace in their lives.

When the church, empowered by God's Spirit, faithfully does now what Jesus faithfully did then, we "gain ground" for God's peace plan in the world.[6]

## 7. Strategy: The methods used in announcing Jesus must be consistent with the gospel message of peace

Among the most tragic moments in the life and history of the Christian movement are those times when zealous people resort to methods and strategies that are in basic contradiction to God's peacemaking initiatives in Jesus. Violence, manipulation, bribery, imposition, coercion, insensitivity, lack of respect, attitudes of triumphalism or superiority—whenever these tactics are employed by Christians in their life and witness to the world, good news turns quickly into bad news and the gospel message of peace is distorted and betrayed.

---

6. See Matt 9:35-38; Luke 4:16-21; 10:1-8; Acts 8:4-8; Rom 12:14-21.

Jesus told his followers he was sending them out in the same manner that he himself had been sent forth by God. And we know plenty about how Jesus went forth—in loving compassion, willing service and faithful obedience to God's plan, even unto death.

If the church is to have any integrity in her witness to the world, then Jesus' way must become our way. His manner, our model. His service, our style. His loving compassion, our lifelong commitment.[7]

## 8. Scope: God's peace plan in Jesus is comprehensive, encompassing "all things" and all people in the world that God has created

It is central to God's peace plan in Jesus that "all creation be summed up" and "brought back to God." Now, admittedly, *all creation* is a vast reality, representing infinitely more than we humans can begin to comprehend. Yet *all creation* it is and must remain, because "God so loved the *cosmos* (κόσμον)," we are reminded in John 3:16. And *that* is why God "gave his only Son" to redeem it and offer it new life.

Participating in God's Shalom Project, then, means doing what God does, loving the world—*all* of it—as much as God does, caring deeply for its welfare and working to set right what has gone wrong. This includes, of course, extending God's love to the totality of individuals, societies, and cultures that inhabit God's world—all these, the Scriptures tell us, are dear to the heart of God. All these are recipients of divine care and affection.

✳ No individual on the face of the earth is omitted from the list of God's unfailing love. No culture is excluded from God's embrace. No society is disqualified from God's big plan to make things right. The world is, in fact, so loved by God that he has offered Jesus—the very best—in order to restore it and put it back on track.

The challenge for God's people is to learn to love the world with the depth and passion that God does. To see in each individual—however helpless or hopeless—a person created in God's image with the full potential of becoming God's child. To see in each culture—however decadent or destructive—the capacity to find fulfillment in the creator God, who alone gives meaning and life.

---

7. See Isa 52:13–53:12; John 15:1-17; Phil 2:1-11; 14-16; 1 Pet 2:18-25; 3:8-16.

It is true that God's people must convert "from the world to Christ." But it is equally true that they must be prepared to convert back "from Christ to the world"—becoming in the process "all things to all people" so that the world might hear and know of God's grace and peace.[8]

## 9. Risks: Announcing God's peace plan in Jesus will not always be well received

By coming to earth and taking on human form to live as one of us, God emphatically affirmed human culture and society, and the created physical order of the universe as we know and experience it.

Yet it is this very world so dearly loved by God that finds itself in the tight grip of the evil one. It is this same world that minimizes the need for God, that mocks God's peacemaking initiatives as irrelevant and unrealistic, and that promotes values other than those making for wholesome living, healthy relationships, and human dignity.

In such instances, the gospel finds itself no longer *affirming* culture, but rather *challenging* and *critiquing* it. No longer embracing that which is, but rather pointing prophetically to that which *could* and *should* be. Not surprisingly, conflict and outright opposition arise when cultural norms and societal standards are put into question and threatened by a new set of values, understandings, and priorities.

The first followers of Jesus were warned by Jesus himself that suffering would likely accompany them in their witness to the world. And all too often throughout church history, Jesus' words have proven true: "If they persecuted me, they'll persecute you, too. The servant is no greater than his Master."[9]

## 10. Power: God has promised Holy Spirit power to the church to strengthen and sustain her in faithfully announcing the peace plan until Jesus returns

The church finds itself today "between the times"—between Pentecost and Christ's return; between the old order and the new; the "already" and the "not yet"; the promise of Christ's ultimate victory

---

8. See Matt 11:25-30; Acts 15:6-11; Eph 4:19-22; Rom 1:16-17; 3:21-30; 1 Pet 3:9; Rev 5:1-10; 7:9.
9. See Mark 8:34-38; John 15:18-21; 16:2-4; Acts 5:17-42; 2 Cor 4:7-12; 11:16-33; 1 Pet 4:12-19; Heb 11:35-38; Rev 6:9-11.

and the current reality of a sinful, suffering world held hostage by the evil one.

Fortunately, God's people are not expected to serve as messengers of the gospel peace plan equipped only with the human energy and resources they can manage to muster. Were that the case, the whole good news project would have failed and folded long ago.

"You will receive Holy Spirit power for this assignment," Jesus assured his frightened disciples. "And I will be with you to the very end." These promises have strengthened and sustained the church for now almost two thousand years. And it is this same Spirit presence and power that will fill and follow God's people into the future as newer, younger generations choose to become instruments of God's peacemaking initiatives in the world.

It will take Spirit-gifted people of every kind to complete the unfinished task still ahead. Men and women. Younger and older. The skilled and the schooled. The weak and the strong. All God's people are called to be sent. To the ends of the earth. Till the end of the age.[10]

---

10.  See Matt 28:18-20; John 15:26-16:1, 4-15; Acts 1:2-8; 2:1-42; 1 Cor 12:4-11, 27-31; 1 Pet 1:3-12; 2:9-10.

PART 2

# Context and Perspectives

**6**

# Developing and Sustaining the Vision in Mennonite Church USA

*Ervin R. Stutzman*

> **Vision: Healing and Hope**—God calls us to be followers of Jesus Christ and, by the power of the Holy Spirit, to grow as communities of grace, joy, and peace so that God's healing and hope flow through us to the world.

Helen Keller was once asked what would be worse than being blind. She responded, "To have sight and no vision." Born in 1880, Keller lost the ability to see and hear because of illness when she was nineteen months old. Yet when her parents found the right teacher for her some years later, she blossomed into a prolific author and campaigner for woman's suffrage, as well as other social causes. Although blind, she became a visionary person who motivated others to make a difference in their world.

On several occasions, Jesus addressed the problem of sight. When he looked at the people who crowded to him, he saw them as sheep without a shepherd, a harvest to be gathered for the kingdom of God

(Matt 9:36). Others could look at the same crowds and see only trouble-makers and indigents. He once told his disciples, "Do you not say, 'Four months more, then comes the harvest'? But I tell you, look around you, and see how the fields are ripe for harvesting" (John 4:35). Again, in the account of the man born blind, Jesus showed that physical sight is secondary to spiritual vision (John 9:1-41).

## Spiritual advances are shaped by vision

Every spiritual advance is shaped by a vision in someone's mind and heart. Our spiritual lives have been significantly shaped and formed by the lives and writings of people in Scripture. What if Nehemiah had not been obedient to the vision from God to rebuild the Jewish temple? What if the twelve disciples had not heeded the call of Jesus? What if the apostle Paul had not heeded the vision he received on the road to Damascus? How different our spiritual lives and our world would be!

It takes people with vision to see or discern God's actions and plans for the world. That was the role of prophets or seers in Bible times. In our day we sometimes call them visionaries. It is both a gift of the Spirit and an ability one can develop. Perhaps we could use the analogy of a jigsaw puzzle, like the one laid out at our annual congregational retreat. It lay on the table, inviting people to assemble it. While it's quite pos-sible to assemble a jigsaw puzzle by simply looking at the individual pieces, it's far more exciting if there is a picture of the finished puzzle on the box to go by. There's a sort of magic to discovering the part that each piece contributes to the finished product. Each piece counts, espe-cially at the end. There's nothing more disappointing than to find that there is one piece missing. The missing part, however small, mars the entire picture.

In the same way, painting a verbal picture of what God desires can help people to find their place in the overall scheme of things. That's what the apostle Paul portrayed with his analogy of the church as a body. He shared the vision of a well-ordered and healthy body, made up of members—or parts—that each contributed to the whole. One of these parts, or spiritual gifts, as Paul envisioned them, was the visionary role of the prophet.

While not all Christians are called or equipped to be prophets or visionaries, all have been gifted with the ability to see beyond what is visible with the human eye. This gift is called faith. "Now faith is the assurance of things hoped for, the conviction of things not seen" (Heb 11:1).

When we falter in our spiritual lives, a conviction born of faith can propel us forward with new hope and determination. That's why it's important, in the case of a denomination, to keep the vision clearly before us. It provides:

- a unifying point of reference
- an island of clarity in a sea of confusion
- a mental picture of what God wants to accomplish in and through our church
- the destination toward which we intend to travel together
- a guide for the process of discernment and decision making as a church

The Mennonite Church USA statement of "Vision: Healing and Hope" is widely used across the church. It has been printed on banners, bookmarks, flyers, and many publications. Whenever the Executive Board meets, it displays a banner of the statement in at least two languages. As executive director for the denomination, I often refer to the vision statement and repeat it when I bring greetings to groups of people or speak in congregations. I often quote it in the columns or articles I write. The vision statement provides a point of commonality and reminds us of the goal we are pursuing together.

## The "Purposeful Plan" provides members of MC USA with specific priorities and plans

The vision statement, however, is simply the beacon that shows the way for ensuing action. Vital churches build on the vision by praying fervently and planning diligently for ways to bring it to pass. In the case of Mennonite Church USA, the vision has been enlivened through the development of a mission statement and made concrete by a specific set of priorities and outcomes, or plans. These form the heart of the paper called "Desiring God's Coming Kingdom: A Missional Vision and Purposeful Plan for Mennonite Church USA," or "Purposeful Plan" for short. The following mission statement explains our specific calling as a community: *Joining in God's activity in the world, we develop and nurture missional Mennonite congregations of many cultures.*

If we accept our identity as the sent ones of God, we will be compelled to discern the places in our church and world that await the transforming power of Christ's kingdom. We will ask ourselves where God is calling us to go. That is the basis of the purpose statement for Mennonite Church USA, shown above.

## Seven priorities enable us to align our work with God's purposes

We believe that in the pursuit of this purpose, God is calling us to pay attention to seven priorities in the life of our church over the next decade. As we attend to these priorities, the Spirit will enable us to align our work with God's purposes so that we may become an effective sign, instrument, and foretaste of God's kingdom.

### 1. Christian formation

This first and highest priority commits us to fashion and mold our lives after that of Jesus Christ. As the Sent One of God, Jesus sends us into the world. As missional communities, our congregations, conferences, and agencies will ensure that people are invited to make a commitment to Christ, discipled in the way of Christ, taught to engage with the Scriptures, helped to develop Christian identity from an Anabaptist/ Mennonite perspective, and given the capacity to cultivate their vocational calling.[1]

### 2. Christian community

As a sign and foretaste of God's coming kingdom, our church communities serve as a vital part of our witness in the world. As communities in God's mission, we will strengthen the loving interaction within the body of Christ and enhance our witness through worshiping

---

1. See Matt 28:18-20; Rom 8:28-30; Col 1:28-29; 2 Tim 1:5; and Articles 17 and 18 in the *Confession of Faith in a Mennonite Perspective* (Scottdale, PA: Herald Press, 1995).

together, extending hospitality, practicing scriptural discernment, cultivating Christ-centered unity, and learning to agree and disagree in love.[2]

### 3. Holistic Christian witness

The church exists for the task of bearing witness to the coming of
Christ's kingdom in the world. As missional communities we will share
the good news of Jesus Christ in word and deed, help birth new communities of faith, and reflect the reign of God by striving for peace and
justice. Our allegiance to Jesus Christ calls us to pacifism, being willing
to die rather than to kill even our enemies. The witness of congregations
and the broader community of faith is expanded through institutional
ministries that carry a shared and specialized mission on a collective
basis beyond the capacity of any one congregation.[3]

### 4. Stewardship

In his words and practices, Jesus modeled an understanding that
God is the Lord of all life. Thus, we are called to be stewards of all that
God has generously entrusted to us for the sake of God's purposes in the
world. As missional communities we will assist every participant in our
congregations to cultivate a healthy whole-life stewardship, to care for
creation, to practice mutual aid, and to be generous in ways that reflect
the generosity of God.[4]

### 5. Leadership development

The church calls forth leaders as prompted by God to inspire the
congregation for its evangelizing mission in the world and to ensure that
every member and participant in the faith community is empowered,
equipped, and supported for their unique vocation in witness. As missional communities we will develop leaders at all levels of the church,
helping every member to reach their God-given potential as they follow
Christ's call.[5]

---

2. See 1 Cor 12:12-14; Col 3:12-17; Phil 3:7; and Articles 14 and 16 in the *Confession
    of Faith*.
3. See Matt 12:15-21; Luke 4:18-21; John 20:21-22; and Articles 10 and 22 in the
    *Confession of Faith*.
4. See Ps 24:1-2; Prov 22:6-7; Luke 19:1-10; 2 Cor 8:5-7, 13-15; 9:6-15; and Article 21
    in the *Confession of Faith*.
5. See Exod 18:13-23; Eph 4:7-16; and Article 15 in the *Confession of Faith*.

## 6. Undoing racism and advancing intercultural transformation

Racism, antipathy, and alienation among different cultural groups stand in the way of Christ's kingdom of love, justice, and peace. As missional communities we will seek to dismantle individual and systemic racism in our church. We will also seek to develop intercultural competence, which means that we intend to heal racial divisions, learn to live and work in a multicultural context, and value all the gifts of God's diverse people. We envision people of many nations, tribes, people, and languages as participants in the kingdom of God. We believe it is Jesus, pictured as the Lamb, who calls people together from all nations.[6]

## 7. Church-to-church relationships

The unity of Christ's church is hindered when any particular communion remains disengaged and isolated from others who belong to the same body of Christ. In a world of global economic disparity and vast cultural differences, our unity in the church bears witness to an alternate reality where we share each other's pain and rejoice when others rejoice. As missional communities we will learn and grow through interaction with other Christian fellowships. We will cultivate a particularly close relationship with Mennonite Church Canada, since we share a common confession of faith, a common ministerial polity, and many joint ministry ventures.[7]

# From each of the seven priorities come specific goals and plans of action

While it can be quite challenging to agree upon the priorities for the church, it is even more difficult to agree on specific plans. In the case of Mennonite Church USA, we linked each of the outcomes to one of the seven priorities, as listed below. Along with the list of outcomes, I have listed one specific, measurable goal designed to express that outcome. Note that each outcome and goal relates in some way to the more general vision statement.

---

6.  See Acts 10; Gal 3:25-29, Eph 2:15; Rev 7:9; and Article 9 in the *Confession of Faith*.
7.  See Eph 4:4-6; Rev 5:9-10; and Article 9 in the *Confession of Faith*.

## Priority 1: Christian formation

To increase our capacity as a community of faith to be and make disciples of Jesus Christ.

- Goal: Produce an evangelical/Anabaptist discipleship training resource in English and Spanish called *Begin Anew* (written by Palmer Becker) in cooperation with Mennonite Church Canada (2014).

## Priority 2: Christian community

To deepen our capacity to engage in biblical/communal discernment and deal with our differences in a Christlike manner.

- Goal: Develop resources for biblical/communal discernment to be used in congregations, area conferences, and other settings where believers seek to discern God's will regarding important matters as a church (2015).

## Priority 3: Holistic witness

To deepen engagement across the church in service, peacemaking, evangelism, witness for justice, and helping to birth new communities of faith.

- Goal: Convene a church planting summit to enable practitioners, area conference leaders, historians, missiologists, and theologians to explore what we can learn from our past experiences in church planting and to discern God's calling for the future (2015).

## Priority 4: Stewardship

To reflect God's abundance through our generosity as God's stewards, in order to achieve missional goals across all parts of the church.

- Goal: Provide stewardship training and education for immigrant congregations that are relevant to their context (2013-15).

## Priority 5: Leadership development

To call, train, and nurture church members with leadership gifts in Anabaptist theology and practice, and work together in various teams so that both credentialed and lay leaders can be empowered to fulfill the church's missional vocation.

- Goal: Revise the Mennonite ministerial polity handbook, in collaboration with Mennonite Church Canada, to reflect both current practices and aspirations of the church we are being called to become (2014).

## Priority 6: Undoing racism and advancing intercultural transformation

To overcome antipathy and alienation among different cultural groups through dismantling individual and systemic racism in our church, making a way for people of every racial/ethnic group to have just and equitable access to church resources, positions, and information as manifestations of the one new humanity we have in Christ.

- Goal: Coordinate a "Hope for the Future" event for people of color and guest leaders from the dominant culture in the church to discuss aspirations for the future of people of color leadership in the church (2014).

## Priority 7: Church-to-church relationships

To give and receive gifts within the broader body of Christ as a witness to the unity to which God calls us and to help us be more faithful to God's mission in the world.

- Goal: Respond to the queries from the Evangelical Lutheran Church in America about how we see our relationship to each other in the body of Christ, and to affirm the Mennonite World Conference/Lutheran World Federation dialogue on baptism (2013–15).

# We make plans, all the while depending on God's grace and enablement

The outcomes listed above and the full range of goals in the "Purposeful Plan" can only be achieved by God's grace and the empowerment of the Holy Spirit. We do well to make our plans with the biblical admonition in mind: "Come now, you who say, 'Today or tomorrow we will go to such and such a town and spend a year there, doing business and making money.' Yet you do not even know what tomorrow will bring. What is your life? For you are a mist that appears for a little while and then vanishes. Instead you ought to say, 'If the Lord wishes, we will live and do this or that'" (James 4:13-15).

We acknowledge that the implementation of this plan depends on God's blessing and enablement and may take years to achieve, depending on the availability of resources. The dates in parentheses behind each of the goals indicate the period of time in which we intend to pursue that goal and report to the denominational delegate body on the progress or completion of it. Without this kind of specificity and accountability, plans often languish on papers in someone's desk or get lost in a virtual data file. An old saying goes says that "what gets inspected gets done, not what is expected." To really achieve a vision, you must set up the standards and measure the results to see if they are matching up. Effective missional churches learn to not only "talk the talk" but also to "walk the walk."

## Sustaining the vision beyond the developmental stages

How then is the vision of the denomination sustained beyond the developmental stages? In the case of Mennonite Church USA, the entire "Purposeful Plan" is subject to review at each biennial assembly of denominational delegates. The board and staff provide the delegates with a report on the progress toward or achievement of each specific goal. This is a powerful form of accountability that is too often overlooked in denominational assemblies.

Each goal that has been reached is considered a mile marker or milestone along the way to our ultimate destination—the fulfillment of "Vision: Healing and Hope." Keeping a record of milestones provides inspiration and motivation for continuing the journey, even when the road is steep.

A written statement of vision for a congregation or a denomination may serve well for many years, perhaps a decade or more. Beyond the vision from God, however, there are three additional ways of seeing that can bring about change in the plans designed to carry out the vision.

L ꟲ R

1. *Looking back.* The first way of seeing is to *look back* at the experience of pursuing the vision. This is the principle of assessment. One might ask: How well have these priorities and plans enabled us to achieve our stated vision? What might we change in order to increase our effectiveness for the future? In the case of Mennonite Church USA, delegates are invited to give feedback to the report of the goals that have been reached. Sometimes individuals write very specific suggestions for shaping future goals.

2. *Looking ahead.* A second way of seeing is to *look ahead.* This might be called an environmental scan. One might ask: What are the technological trends that will affect the achievement of our vision? What are sociologists predicting that will shape the people to whom we will minister?

3. *Looking around.* A third way of seeing is to *look around* at the demographics in your community. One might ask: How is our community changing? Who are the new people to whom we may be called to minister?

In sum, vision is essential to the spiritual life of a people. A common vision helps to draw people together in common purpose. Visionary leaders are called to pursue God's will for the people by developing and sustaining a vision that people can see in their mind's eye. In the case of Mennonite Church USA, "Vision: Healing and Hope" invites us to follow God's call for the ultimate purpose of bringing healing and hope to a broken world.

# 7

# *Missional*

## The Amazing Adjective That Changes Everything

*James R. Krabill*

My friend Doug has taught architectural acoustics at Columbia College in Chicago for many years. Not a very obvious place or profession, it would seem, for sharing one's faith. Yet Doug has seen it otherwise.

Most of Doug's students at this large liberal arts college are not really atheists, he has told me. Nor are they antireligious. They are simply *areligious*: possessing virtually no exposure to any form of organized religion. "These young folks are likely to believe that Joan of Arc was Noah's wife," he muses.

So imagine the students' surprise on the first day of class, when Doug asks if any of them hold any beliefs or values deeply enough that they'd be willing to die for them. For most of these students, having grown up in mainstream America where one is taught to avoid pain and suffering at all costs, Doug's question is a disorienting one and produces few takers. "Then you have a lot of homework to do," he tells them, "in understanding the history and worldview of many of your clients out there in the marketplace."

As it turns out, a class in architectural acoustics equips students to understand and manage issues related to space and sound design. And of course, some of the key clients for this kind of expertise are the synagogues and churches scattered across the land. "These people you will be dealing with," Doug tells his students, "come from a long history of passionate conviction, persecution, and spiritual strength. You will never be able to relate effectively to them until you take the time to understand them. The challenging task that lies ahead of you is not simply to improve sound quality in public meeting places but, from the user's perspective, to help people enter into the presence of God. So let's get started: learning about these people, their history, their faith, and the things that give them life, energy, and hope."

Doug balks at the idea of thinking of himself as a "missionary." But that is, in reality, what he is: someone who takes his personal faith commitment seriously. Someone who carries his passion out of the Sunday morning worship space into the Monday morning work place. Someone who is willing to apply his gifts to God's big project of "setting things right with the world." Who is constantly and creatively asking the all-important gospel communication question of how to build a bridge from the good news of Jesus to the context where God has planted him. Doug is not simply a professor of architectural acoustics. He is a *missional* professor of architectural acoustics. And that little adjective makes all the difference!

SR

## You are only missional if you are . . . *missional*!

The word *missional* in the English language has the capacity to get used, misused, and abused until it means everything at once, and finally, nothing at all. Our task as God's people is to continually monitor our vocabulary and to either reclaim important terms to their original intent or to replace them with expressions of equivalent meaning.

To focus and refocus the term *missional*, we will need to return to the big project God is working on and the role we are invited to play in it. Four central principles for understanding and embracing that project are the following.

## 1. God's project is cosmic

Our starting point is the big picture, the cosmic view, the "grand mystery of God's will" to "reconcile to himself all things, whether on earth or in heaven, by making peace through the blood of his cross" (Col 1:20; Eph 1:9, 22). "For God so loved the *cosmos* (κόσμον)," Jesus told Nicodemus, "that he gave his only Son" (John 3:16).[1] This unfathomable love for the entire created universe and the reconciling initiative God has undertaken in Christ to "set all things right" are where we begin in laying the foundation for missional understandings.

## 2. God's project is personal

It would be easy to imagine that a project of such grand scale would have little concern for the likes of you and me. But the biblical writers remind us over and over that we, too, are included in the "all things" being set right, that we, too, "have peace with God through our Lord Jesus Christ, through whom we have obtained access to this grace in which we stand" (Rom 5:1-2). The peace God offers us in Christ is not an *individualistic* one—despite how some Christians might perceive or describe it—but it is nonetheless a *personal* one. For we as persons created in God's image were separated from God. And in that sorry state of affairs, it was *God* who took the initiative to reach out and reconcile us in Christ. Our reconciled relationship with God is a key component of the good news we live, celebrate, and proclaim as God's missional people.

## 3. God's project is social

For some folks, that's the end of the story—personal, "vertical," reconciled relationships with God are all that matter. Except that the scriptural witness and the early church insist that there is more! The coming together of Jewish and Gentile peoples into a new family of faith was considered in New Testament times as nothing short of a miracle and an integral part and proof of God's reconciling project. For "now in Christ Jesus you who once were far off have been brought near by the blood

---

1. Replacing the NRSV term *world* here with *cosmos*—from the Greek κόσμον—is my choice, as is the italicization of the word.

of Christ. For he is our peace; in his flesh he has made both groups into one and has broken down the dividing wall, that is, the hostility between us. He has abolished the law . . . that he might create in himself one new humanity in place of the two, thus making peace, and might reconcile both groups to God in one body through the cross" (Eph 2:13-16). God's amazing creation through Christ of a new Spirit-filled and empowered people from former enemies, establishing new social and "horizontal" relationships, is another central feature of missional understandings and commitments.

### 4. God's project is invitational

So how was the world to find out about God's grand plan to "set all things right?" Throughout holy history, God has employed multiple modalities of delivery to communicate the message—dreams and visions, angels and prophets, and most importantly, Jesus himself, who both proclaimed and embodied God's reconciling good news for the world. As his ministry drew to a close, this same Jesus gathered together his petrified disciples and commissioned them by saying, "Peace be with you. As the Father has sent me, so I send you. . . . Receive the Holy Spirit" (John 20:21-22). The early church took this to heart and, in the afterglow of Pentecost, went to work as the primary *model* and *messengers* of God's cosmic project. "So if anyone is in Christ, there is a new creation: everything old has passed away; see, everything has become new! All this is from God, who reconciled us to himself through Christ, and has given us the ministry of reconciliation; that is, in Christ God was reconciling the world to himself, not counting their trespasses against them, and entrusting the message of reconciliation to us. So we are ambassadors for Christ, since God is making his appeal through us; we entreat you on behalf of Christ, be reconciled to God" (2 Cor 5:17-20).

## We are entrusted with God's cosmic project . . . you're kidding, right?

These statements require the church—the "ambassadors of Christ" entrusted with "the message of reconciliation" and through whom "God is making his appeal"—to ask a number of very sobering questions:

- Have we sufficiently rewired our brains and lives to understand and embrace the momentous calling that is ours as God's people?
- To what extent does this reality shape our core identity, our passion, and our priorities as a faith community?
- Are there things we should be reflecting about and acting on that we have totally overlooked or neglected as the body of Christ because of our preoccupation with ridiculously smaller, less significant matters?
- Which of our current activities should be scaled back, reconfigured, or abandoned altogether in order to liberate us to focus on making the main thing . . . the *main thing*?     C B ?
- When we gather for fellowship or worship, do we have a sense that what is happening in our meeting might actually qualify as one of the most important activities in the entire cosmos at that moment? Are we convinced that our gatherings are among the only real events of any current or eternal value because of their intrinsic connection to God's ultimate peacemaking initiative in Christ and the church's invitation to participate in it?
- Are we ready to reorder our lives as faith families so that:
  - » *every function* within our community—every softball game, Sunday school session, food pantry, English as a Second Language program—intentionally contributes to God's reconciling plan;
  - » *every structure*—age cluster, church committee, interest group—is grappling with its specific role in living out the church's divine calling;
  - » *every congregational purchase or expenditure* is prayerfully considered in light of its advancement of God's peacemaking purposes;
  - » *every discernment process* is lavishly marinated in a profound awareness of how it aligns itself with God's passion to "set things right with the world";
  - » *every worship experience* situates local concerns and personal needs in the context of God's desire that "all things" be made right; and

»  *every member of the body* is constantly reminded of God's cosmic intentions through the regular rhythm and diet of church
life and equipped to participate more fully and faithfully in
the reconciling project through roles within the church—
usher, mentor, décor facilitator—as well as neighborhood and
professional encounters—car mechanic, hospice caregiver,
school board chair?

## Which brings us to the part of speech we call "adjectives"

Most of us know what *mission* is: God's reconciling work through Christ
in the world. And we are acquainted with *missions*: the church's activities in response to God's invitation to serve as representatives of God's
mission. And finally there is *missionary*: a person participating in God's
purposes who is sent into an area, historically a "foreign field," to carry
out activities in the form of evangelism or ministries of service such
as education, literacy, social justice, healthcare, and economic development. Each of these three terms—*mission, missions,* and *missionary*—is
defined as a noun, a part of speech that names or identifies a person,
place, thing, quality, idea, or activity.

When we come to *missional,* however, we are dealing with an
adjective: a word that modifies a noun. Nouns are words that name
something. Adjectives are words that give *more information* about that
something. They are describing words. They are added to nouns to state
what kind, what color, which one, or how many. Adjectives are said
to "modify" nouns and are necessary to make their meaning clearer or
more exact.

So we all know what a youth sponsor is: a person who is asked and
sometimes employed by a congregation to concentrate on faith formation and relationship building with the church's youth population. This
might include facilitating Bible studies or discussion groups, providing pizza for late-night activities, attending local school activities where
youth are involved, and organizing group trips to concerts or amuse-
ment parks.

But suppose the youth sponsor were a . . . *missional* youth sponsor?
Hmmm! Not sure what that means. But one thing it likely implies is

that this person will be painting with broader strokes, reminding the youth how they fit into God's grander purposes in the world. A missional youth sponsor will care deeply about the young people of the congregation but will also challenge them to think beyond themselves to the needs of their friends, neighbors, classmates, and the larger world. Great care will be given to making group life not only a fun and safe space for the congregation's own youth but also an open and hospitable place for newcomers. Those newcomers will be warmly and intentionally invited to join, contribute, and begin shaping the life of the group. Missional youth sponsors long to see and work diligently to develop missional youth, which in time fosters missional consciousness and passion within the group itself, and eventually beyond that, to the congregation as a whole.

When that simple but creative adjective *missional* is placed before  every function in the congregation, every structure, every expenditure, every discernment process, every worship experience, and every member of Christ's body, the church will find itself transformed. It will find itself with a new identity, set of priorities, and passion to embrace its divine calling as reconciling ambassadors for Christ in the local community and the world.

Is there a manual or guidebook for congregations on how to do this? No, not really. But figuring this out as a local faith community should be the primary preoccupation and heartbeat of its life—in its worship, its small group conversations, its faith formation functions, and its budget considerations. The template has been provided for us—God is reconciling *all things* to himself in Jesus Christ and has invited us to participate in the project. Everything else is local and contextual— the neighborhood, the language, the obstacles, the gifts, the history, the personalities, the resources, the leadership, the partnerships, and the creativity necessary to connect all the dots of these various features and keep them focused on our primary calling as God's people.

## It was the pork roast that opened my eyes

Several years ago I was asked to spend a weekend with a small and dying rural congregation to explore how they might restore their life as a faith community and get it back on track. On Friday evening I met with members of the church's evangelism committee, who spent the time presenting an inventory of all the things working against them. They mostly focused on dwindling resources and their rural location—"Who would want to drive out here in the middle of nowhere to be a part of *our* group?" I had to admit that was a good question to be asking!

At the end of the meeting, one of the committee members added, "Oh, and by the way, tomorrow we are having our annual pork roast fundraiser to provide resources for our youth group to attend the upcoming denomination-wide youth convention next summer. You are certainly welcome to join us if you'd like."

The following afternoon, I made my way back out to the church. As I approached, I found myself impeded by a long line of vehicles parked a quarter mile out along the side of the road. I parked my car along with the others and completed the journey on foot. Arriving in the church parking lot, I was greeted by the frantically busy youth sponsor who informed me, "This happens every year at this point in the afternoon. People come from everywhere for our pork roast, and we get backed up in delivery. So we ask people to go and sit in the sanctuary until their row is called and their order has been filled. Do you mind having a seat in there? It shouldn't be more than a twenty-minute wait."

When I arrived in the sanctuary, I found five rows of benches on each side of the aisle, filled with eager but patient pork roast customers. For nearly twenty minutes we sat in total silence, waiting as attendees at a funeral ceremony, for our row to be called. Finally, our time came and we filed quietly out to receive our prize.

On Sunday afternoon, I was asked to meet again with the evangelism committee to pursue our conversation. I began my part of the discussion with these words:

> I'm a bit baffled by what I've experienced here this weekend. On Friday evening, I heard that your rural location makes it difficult for you to attract people to be a part of your community. But yesterday afternoon, I parked my car and walked a quarter mile because your parking lot and the surrounding roads were congested with people trying to get in here. Once I was ushered into the sanctuary, I sat in silence for twenty minutes waiting to receive my portion of pork.

So my question to you is this: What would have kept you from engaging all these friends and neighbors crowding into your space? Why wasn't it possible for someone to stand up and say, "Welcome to our faith community on a Saturday afternoon. We are sorry you need to wait for your order, but allow us to explain what's going on here. We have a vision in this congregation of equipping our young people to be engaged in God's work in the world. And so we send them to our churchwide youth convention to prepare them for this task. At that gathering they attend seminars, listen to inspiring speakers, and worship with thousands of young people from across the church. They come back to our congregation excited and inspired to continue their walk with Jesus. This fundraiser that you are participating in helps us to make this youth convention possible for our young people. And we want to thank you for this important contribution to our vision and God's work.

Oh, and by the way, we do more than pork roasts around here. It could be that you are not part of a faith community like this one and would like to learn more about us. We meet here every Wednesday evening for prayer and Bible study and on Sunday morning for worship and fellowship. You are more than welcome to join us at any time. Here is a brochure that gives you the contact information you might need to connect with us, if you are interested.

So thanks again for your time and support. We deeply appreciate it and want you to know how important this to us. It's been a pleasure to meet you and you are more than welcome back any time. Thanks for listening, and the next three rows can now go for their pork roast.

My experience that day on that rural county road reminded me that there are pork roasts and that there are *missional* pork roasts! *Missional*: that amazing and subversive little adjective that changes everything!

**8**

# Holy Spirit Empowerment

## What Mennonite Church USA Can Learn from the Global Faith Family

*Tilahun Beyene Kidane*

### The Holy Spirit in Scripture

The role of the Holy Spirit as a member of the Trinity is crystal clear and very evident throughout the Bible. Right from the very beginning of creation, the Holy Spirit was in attendance and at work: the Spirit "swept over the face of the waters" (Gen 1:2), drawing the line between light and darkness in preparation for filling the void and giving shape to the formless. The Holy Spirit was there when light was ordered into existence, when the waters and the sky were separated, vegetation was brought forth, and living creatures came into being by the command of the Almighty. Finally, the Holy Spirit participated in bringing human beings to life from the dust of the earth and breathing into them the breath of life (Gen 2:7).

From this act of creation until the great flood that wiped out nearly all humanity, there is no mention in the Scriptures of the Holy Spirit. People enjoyed extremely long lives, but when God was deeply grieved by the level of wickedness prevailing at the time, God declared, "My spirit shall not abide in mortals forever, for they are flesh; their days shall be one hundred twenty years" (Gen 6:3).

In subsequent portions of the Old Testament, we see the Holy Spirit empowering leaders and kings and inspiring prophets as God shepherded the nation of Israel, through whom the Messiah was destined to come and restore creation to its original relationship with God. Not only was the prophecy about the coming of the Messiah inspired by the Holy Spirit, but the Messiah was himself conceived of the Holy Spirit, who then raised and empowered by him—at *baptism* (". . . he saw the Spirit of God descending like a dove and alighting on him. And a voice from heaven said, 'This is my Son, the Beloved, with whom I am well pleased'" [Matt 3:16-17]); in *temptation* ("Then Jesus was led up by the Spirit into the wilderness to be tempted by the devil" [Matt 4:1]); and in launching his *public ministry* ("Jesus, filled with the power of the Spirit, returned to Galilee . . ." [Luke 4:14]). There, in his hometown of Nazareth, Jesus stood up in the synagogue, and identified himself with the prophecy of Isaiah (61:1-2):

SR
> The spirit of the Lord God is upon me,
>     because the Lord has anointed me;
> he has sent me to bring good news to the oppressed,
>     to bind up the brokenhearted,
> to proclaim liberty to the captives,
>     and release to the prisoners;
> to proclaim the year of the Lord's favor,
>     and the day of vengeance of our God;
>     to comfort all who mourn.

This clearly confirmed the role of the Holy Spirit as the sender and empowerer of Jesus the Messiah. As a result people immediately recognized that his teaching had authority (Luke 4:32), enabling him to teach, heal the sick, drive out demons, and demonstrate what God was like. Through the power of the Holy Spirit Jesus was able to withstand the rigors of living in the flesh and the extreme stresses of being abandoned by his disciples, friends, and even God, during his hour of suffering and death.

The awesome power of the Holy Spirit was ultimately manifested most visibly through the resurrection of Jesus Christ from the dead, as

Paul attests in Romans 8:11: "If the Spirit of him who raised Jesus from the dead dwells in you, he who raised Christ from the dead will give life to your mortal bodies also through his Spirit that dwells in you."

One of the most important things Jesus taught his disciples was about the role of the Holy Spirit in the ministry he was preparing them to assume after his departure. First, he told them that the Holy Spirit would convict the world and prepare hearts for the sowing of the gospel message. He also told them that the Holy Spirit would serve as their counselor, guiding them to the truth in a world where perception of truth is imperfect.

After his resurrection, Jesus commanded his disciples to stay in Jerusalem and "wait there for the promise of the Father. 'This,' he said, 'is what you have heard from me; for John baptized with water, but you will be baptized with the Holy Spirit not many days from now'" (Acts 1:4-5). The reason for these instructions becomes clearer a few verses later: "But you will receive power when the Holy Spirit has come upon you; and you will be my witnesses in Jerusalem, in all Judea and Samaria, and to the ends of the earth" (1:8). In this Jesus underscored the very important link between the power of the Holy Spirit and mission, implying that the work of transforming people's lives was beyond human capacity, initiative, and power.

At Pentecost the apostles and followers of Jesus received the baptism of the Holy Spirit and became effective witnesses of the good news of Jesus, preaching the Word boldly and drawing many into the kingdom. They gave priority to studying the Word, prayer, and walking in deep love for each other. They were uncompromising, ready to pay any price, even their lives, for their faith.

## The Holy Spirit in church history

The good news spread like wildfire across the wide expanse of the Roman Empire. But persecution also escalated as the followers of the Way refused to acknowledge Caesar as god and pay homage to him. Christians in the Roman Empire, especially during the reign of Nero, suffered immensely for their convictions. This was reversed, however, when Emperor Constantine embraced Christianity and legalized it in the Roman Empire. This eventually became a snare for the church in the

West, compromising its strong stand on many issues of righteousness and muzzling its prophetic voice.

From this point on we see a shift in the trajectory of the church as it moves from being a dynamic, Spirit-led movement to a highly structured institution with hierarchical leadership, leaving a reduced role for the Holy Spirit. Divisions and splinters occurred within the church, causing untold bitterness and pain in their wake. On occasion these divisions escalated to national and international levels, leading to protracted armed conflicts such as the Thirty Years' War (1618–1648). The failure of the church to follow scriptural injunction to "love neighbor" and "live peaceably with all" had a hugely negative impact on the propagation of the gospel.

God, of course, remained at work, sending revivals and renewals at different times throughout history. One such time was the sixteenth century, when our forebears, the Anabaptists, came on the scene. Anabaptists were radical in their discipleship, adhering to what was written in the Scriptures and fearlessly living out their faith by the power of the Holy Spirit. It appears that they followed in the footsteps of the early church, born at Pentecost with great results. They paid a heavy price, however, for standing on biblical teachings and truth, proving once again that "indeed, all who want to live a godly life in Christ Jesus will be persecuted" (2 Tim 3:12).

Subsequent revivals, like those in the twentieth century in both the United States and Wales, spread quickly around the world and ignited the fire of the Holy Spirit in Africa, Asia, and Latin America. Millions came to faith through deep conviction by the Holy Spirit. Others who had lived as nominal Christians for many years surrendered fully to the Lord and became powerful witnesses, ushering many into the kingdom.

Such Spirit-filled people are not afraid of persecution or the threats of the enemy. They are prepared and ready to go wherever and whenever the Spirit leads. The enemy, however, continues to sow tares to deceive those who are not yet strong in the faith. Yet even in this the Holy Spirit watches, guards, and nurtures believers all the time.

While many churches have benefited from the outpouring of the Holy Spirit, there are two—similar, though not identical—that have resulted from the mission outreach of Eastern Mennonite Missions

(EMM). These are the Meserete Kristos Church of Ethiopia (MKC) and the Amor Viviente Church of Honduras.

## The Holy Spirit in the life of the global faith family

*The Meserete Kristos Church (MKC) of Ethiopia.* MKC as a church came into existence in the early 1960s. At the initial stage of its formation, the missionaries served as the first wave of leaders alongside their Ethiopian counterparts. A youth movement soon started and was swept along by the wind of the Holy Spirit blowing into the country. Although MKC could not initially figure out what this initiative was all about, it did not try to distance itself from the movement and instead appointed an elder to monitor its activity.

As the movement gathered momentum, however, the youth did not feel comfortable associating so closely with the mother church. But through the leading of the Holy Spirit, coupled with patience and tolerance on MKC's part and the growth and maturity of the youth leaders, the Lord blended the two groups together. Both needed to learn valuable lessons—the youth to live within a structure and to test everything according to the Scriptures, and the mother church to open herself up to the move of the Holy Spirit. MKC's rapid growth, beginning already in the early 1970s and continuing to the present day, is none other than the opening up of the church to the leading of the Holy Spirit.

MKC was closed down by the government in 1982. At that time there were only fourteen congregations and an estimated membership of about five thousand. When the ban was lifted in 1991, the church had grown tenfold. Today, the membership stands at over 255,000 with about 822 congregations across the nation. In addition, there are also 1,012 church planting centers scheduled to become full-fledged congregations within a period of one to two years. As a result, MKC is today the largest member of Mennonite World Conference. No individual or group can take credit for MKC's phenomenal growth. It is the work of the Holy Spirit.

*Amor Viviente Church of Honduras.* The path through which Amor Viviente came into existence and grew is slightly different from that of MKC. The Lord used a missionary, Edward King, sent by EMM to initiate a Spirit-led ministry. King was himself significantly affected by the outpouring of the Holy Spirit at the beginning of the work in Honduras. He and his team then began to work with street kids and other marginalized people they encountered. Powerful things began to happen and transformed lives drew the attention of people outside of the faith community. Ed King taught, discipled, and empowered those he identified as potential leaders. Although Ed has passed on to glory many years ago, Amor Viviente continues to thrive and expand by the power and guidance of the Holy Spirit and under the leadership of those he selected, trained, and released. Today Amor Viviente has forty-two congregations within Honduras, seven in other Latin American countries, eight in the United States, and two in Spain, representing a total membership of twelve thousand.

## Conclusion

We have cited here only two examples. But many other churches and mission agencies around the world likewise understand the Holy Spirit to be the guide to all truth and the source of power behind missions and church planting. It is the Holy Spirit who convicts unbelievers, brings them to faith, and nurtures and enables them to live victorious, God-honoring lives. This is what we see in many parts of the world as the wind of the Spirit continues to blow.

Yet, could it be that we as Anabaptists have not given the right focus and emphasis to the role of the Holy Spirit in our lives and churches? In the words of the writers of *Winds of the Spirit*: "Perhaps, in our zeal to be Christocentric, we have minimized the Spirit who transforms us into Christ's image and who Christ himself sent to empower us to faithfulness. Perhaps, in our focus on a historic Jesus, we have rejected the present power of Jesus as manifested in his death, resurrection, and the sending of the Spirit at Pentecost. Embracing the work of the Spirit will not make Anabaptists less Christocentric, but rather will make them more so, as the life and teaching of Jesus find fuller expression in current realities and experiences."[1] If this in some way describes our current situation, could it be time to recalibrate our understanding of the role

---

1. Conrad Kanagy, Tilahun Beyene, and Richard Showalter, *Winds of the Spirit: A Profile of Anabaptist Churches in the Global South* (Harrisonburg, VA: Herald Press, 2012), 236.

of the Holy Spirit and change our orientation? We live in the era of the Holy Spirit. I humbly encourage us all to catch the powerful updraft of the Spirit in good time.

# 9

# Developing a Missional Culture within the Church

*David W. Boshart*

## Tending to the church's missional culture

The culture of any organization or living system has everything to do with whether that living system will die, survive, or thrive. Organizational psychologist Edgar Schein has made the bold statement that "the only thing of real importance that leaders do is to create and manage culture and . . . the unique talent of leadership is their ability to work with culture."[1]

In many cases organizational cultures are more "ecologies" than "machinery." Because most leaders are not founding leaders of a living system, the task of leadership is more focused on managing and working with cultures than creating them. Nevertheless, fostering the development of a missional church culture requires leadership. Unless church leaders tend to the missional culture of the church, as the church interacts with the wider culture, the church's culture will tend to regress toward reflecting the values of the surrounding culture, stagnate with little sense of purpose, or devolve into ministries of cloistered self-service.

---

1. Edgar Schein, *Organizational Culture and Leadership* (San Francisco: Jossey-Bass, 1985), 2.

Cultures emerge, evolve, and are sustained by complex interactions among many influences. So it is with the church. Because the Christian church exists as a living system of disciples who are following Jesus in the world, some kind of church culture exists. At times in history, the culture of the Christian church has been vibrant and faithful, acculturated and declining—prophetic or compromised. The culture of the church has evolved and will continue to do so. But as Jesus promised, the church will survive history. The question is: What is needed of leaders to constructively manage or influence the church's culture in order to embody the church's missional vocation?

## The *internal integration* and *external engagement* of missional church culture

According to Schein, organizational culture is defined as "a pattern of shared basic assumptions learned by a group as it solved its problems of external adaptation and internal integration."[2] The development of a culture is a learning process.

For a church that seeks to develop a missional culture, leaders will need to work with two broad facets of culture development. First, cultures are *evolving* as they interact with changes in the surrounding environment. Second, cultures are *self-reinforcing* as they organize around common affirmations, beliefs about the nature of reality, and practices that result in faithful or unfaithful witness. For the purposes of looking at missional church culture, these movements can be characterized in terms of *external engagement* and *internal integration*.[3] These two movements help us to explore what it means to develop a missional culture.

---

2. Ibid., 18. Schein's full definition is, "The culture of a group can now be defined as a pattern of shared basic assumptions learned by a group as it solved its problems of external adaptation and internal integration, which has worked well enough to be considered valid and, therefore, to be taught to new members as the correct way to perceive, think, and feel in relation to these problems."

3. Schein, *Organizational Culture,* 4th ed., 2010; use the 2000 edition, pp. 73–115. Schein refers to these movements as external adaptation and internal integration. For the purposes of this essay I will refer to the evolving movement as "external engagement" because the church, by its nature, is not assumed to *adapt* itself to every external circumstance it meets. The missional church will, in some ways, produce an alternative society within the external environment that is quite out of step with and puzzling to the external environment.

## Internal integration

First, let's examine some of the internal qualities of a missional church culture. The missional church will be *incarnational.* The church seeks not only to talk about the kingdom of God or forecast the kingdom of God. The missional church seeks to embody life in the kingdom of God now. The missional church seeks not only to offer good news, but seeks to *be* good news. If the church is *bad* news, for instance, what witness to God's reign can it hope to sustain?

The culture of the missional church is *cruciform.* In the life, death, and resurrection of Jesus, we see the fullest revelation of God we can know. We have seen the embodiment of God's reign. Through the cross and resurrection of Jesus, the outcome of history has already been decided. Through the cross of Jesus, God accomplished everything necessary to set all things right. In the missional church believers will be trained to conform to the way of the cross of Jesus, the path that leads to abundant life.

The culture of the missional church will be made up of people who are *reconciled* to God and one another. If reconciliation is the central work of God's mission in the world, then how can the church hope to sustain a missional culture if the internal life of the church is fractured and unreconciled? Of course, this doesn't mean that the church's life will always be characterized by agreement and sameness. But it does mean that to sustain a missional culture, church leaders will tend to "the unity of the Spirit in the bond of peace" as an essential priority. This reconciled unity that the missional church enjoys is understood as a gift from God through the death and resurrection of Jesus.

The culture of the missional church will be reinforced through *biblical imagination.* The biblical narrative is the trustworthy source for what the missional church *knows* as we live in the world. As Lois Barrett and others so eloquently stated about this commitment: "The Bible is normative in this church's life. It sets the standard for our life as a people. The church reads the Bible together in the light of Jesus Christ under the guidance of the Holy Spirit to learn God's good and gracious intent for all creation, the way of salvation, and the identity and purpose of life together."[4]

---

4. From "Our Purposeful Plan: Desiring God's Coming Kingdom—A Missional Vision and Purposeful Plan for Mennonite Church USA" (available at: http://mennonite

The understanding of Scripture means that leaders in a missional church culture will make a prior commitment to obedience when the church reads its central text. This is not the same as a literalist or wooden approach to the Scriptures. We can and do learn about our experience of reality through many sources. *But* a missional church culture will be reinforced by a hermeneutic of obedience where all "claims on our understanding of Christian faith and life, such as tradition, culture, experience, reason and political powers, need to be tested and corrected in light of Holy Scripture."[5]

In other words, the missional church sees reality from a particular perspective, from the perspective of a people whose citizenship is in, *but transcends*, the material world.[6] Rather than accepting reality based on what is presented materially or through empirical demonstration, believers in the missional church receive training to see reality in a different way. Believers in the missional church culture see reality through the lens of biblical imagination where all observable things are understood in relation to the power of God at work in the lordship of Jesus on the earth, above the earth, and under the earth (Phil 2:10).

The culture of the missional church will be *distinctive*. Throughout the New Testament, we are reminded that we have been called to be a peculiar people.[7] As kingdom citizens, our way of being is different from the world's way of being. This way of being is organized by abundant life as it is understood in the kingdom of God. If the culture of the missional church isn't distinct from the surrounding culture, if it doesn't cause the wider culture to raise questions, it is impossible to discern that a peculiar culture exists within the church at all.

Without leadership processes tending to these internal qualities, it will be impossible to sustain a missional culture in local, regional,

---

usa.org/purposeful-plan/, February 2014), 6; adapted from Walter C. Hobbes, "Indicators of a Missional Church," in *Treasure in Clay Jars: Patterns in Missional Faithfulness*, ed. Lois Y. Barrett (Grand Rapids, MI: Eerdmans, 2004), 160.

5. *Confession of Faith in Mennonite Perspective* (Scottdale, PA: Herald Press, 1995), 21–22.

6. Phil 3:20-21, "But our citizenship is in heaven, and it is from there we are expecting a Savior, the Lord Jesus Christ. He will transform the body of our humiliation, that it may be conformed to the body of his glory, by the power that enables him to make all things subject to himself."

7. See Luke 10:21-24; John 18:36; Rom 12:2; Eph 2:11-22; 1 Pet 2:9-10.

national, or global expressions of the church. Tending to these common internal qualities is as essential to the church's ability to bear witness to the reign of God as tending to the church's engagement with the external environment.

## External engagement

Second, we can examine some of qualities of a missional church culture as the church engages the external environment. Each of these external qualities can be seen in relation to their corresponding qualities of internal integration (see diagram at end of essay). While the missional church will seek to incarnate, or embody, the reign of God as revealed in the life, death, and resurrection of Jesus, this embodiment is not only for the church's own edification.

The missional church will understand itself as *sent* into the world. As Wilbert Shenk has written, "Mission requires deep penetration into the world—for the world, against the world."[8] The missional church will understand it has been sent into the world to bless the world, to proclaim and be a sign of the gospel. The missional church will also understand its vocation as having been sent into the world to confront the world where the world is broken, where injustice reigns, where sin persists. The church will be in constant training "to see where the sick are being healed, where the prisoners are being free. We will enter the world to, in fact, participate in the healing and the freeing."[9]

Formed in the way of Jesus' life, death, and resurrection, the culture of the missional church will, at the same time, be *contextual*. While the internal quality of a missional church culture will be distinctive or differentiated from the world, it is a community formed for the purpose of making the reign of God understood in the world. Rather than replicating the church in identical forms around the world, the missional church will adapt its forms to communicate the message of the gospel in the clearest terms possible.

---

8. Wilbert Shenk, *Forging a Theology of Mission from an Anabaptist Perspective*, Mission Insight series, no. 13, ed. James R. Krabill (Elkhart, IN: Mennonite Board of Missions, 2000), 4–14.

9. Harry Huebner, *Echoes of the Word: Theological Ethics as Rhetorical Practice* (Kitchener, ON: Pandora Press, 2005), 126.

Andrew Walls speaks of two principles that are simultaneously at work when the gospel is being introduced in any society. The first principle is the *indigenizing* principle. This principle suggests that "we are all conditioned by a particular time and place, by our family and group and society, by 'culture,' in fact."[10] The other principle is the *pilgrim* principle, suggesting that while God accepts people as they are, God "takes them in order to transform them into what God wants them to be." So the gospel both helps us feel at home and puts us "out of step with our society."[11] These principles represent a tension that requires diligence to maintain but also keeps the church from devolving into Christendom models of mission as colonial replication.

The culture of the missional church as it interacts with the external culture will be *reconciling*. Just as a missional church culture will be internally governed by a commitment to live as the reconciled people of God, the missional church will announce and model the hope of reconciliation in a world imbued with competitive hostility. The missional church culture is self-renewing as the church engages the world, announcing in hope that through the power of God all things are reconciled in the death and resurrection of Jesus.

The culture of the missional church will be *demythologizing*. In whatever temporal context believers finds themselves, the culture of the missional church will "unmask" the provisional powers of this age and point to the lordship of Christ and the promise that the kingdom of God will prevail.[12] Our common identity as the people of God is rooted in an understanding of a holy nation that transcends all temporal boundaries. It is a holy nation marked by the ingathering of all tribes, and peoples, and languages, and nations. A missional church culture will constantly "re-story" the world's nationalistic narratives. It will be a culture marked by people who are able to welcome—rather than live in mistrust of—the "Other."

Finally, a missional church culture leverages its distinctive quality and the practice of demythologizing so it is propelled into *engagement*

---

10. Andrew Walls, *The Missionary Movement in Christian History* (Maryknoll, NY: Orbis, 1996), 7.
11. Ibid., 8.
12. Huebner, *Echoes of the Word*, 103.

with the external environment. It will do this as witness. Church history offers many examples of underengaging the surrounding context. This leads to cloistered Christian communities marked by distinctive practices and forms but so disengaged that the world sees little relevance in what is modeled. Church history also offers many examples of overengaging the surrounding context, believing that the church is dutybound to solve all the world's problems.

A missional church culture will be formed in the understanding that "God is the primary agent of redemption, the world's and our own. We are but secondary agents. Our task is to point to the power of God's redemptive activity and to embody it."[13] As Alan and Eleanor Kreider and Paulus Widjaja write, "After all, our mission as Christians is not primarily to bring solutions to the world's problems, but to bring hope for redemption."[14] In this way, demythologizing is closely connected to engagement because the very nature of exposure to the *mythos* of the world makes the church vulnerable to absorbing wrong understanding about reality. Demythologizing is an essential discipline for distinctive engagement.

## Keeping the internal and external in creative tension

When the qualities of internal integration—incarnation, cruciformity, reconciliation, biblical imagination, and communal distinction—are placed in tension with the characteristics of external engagement—a sent vocation, contextualization, reconciling witness, demythologization, and contextual engagement—we discover the crucible in which leaders cultivate and manage a missional church culture.

It doesn't matter which comes first—internal integration or external engagement. The church in all times understands itself as part of the unfolding story of God's people beginning with Abraham and continuing until the bridegroom returns for the bride. So it is not a matter of finding *our* beginning point from which we ready *ourselves* adequately for mission. Jesus sent the seventy in Luke 10 believing that the context of mission was itself the platform for formation. The disciples had no

---

13. Ibid., 143.
14. Alan Kreider, Eleanor Kreider, and Paulus Widjaja, *A Culture of Peace: God's Vision for the Church* (Intercourse, PA: Good Books, 2005), 79.

idea what powerful outcomes God would bring out of their witness. In Mark 6:30-44, when the twelve returned from their missionary experiment, the gospel writer refers to the twelve in the same story alternately as apostles—those who were sent—and disciples—learners.

Conversely, we show up in the world that has its own long history. Many people are fond of labeling epochs in world history—the Dark Ages, the Enlightenment, the Gay Nineties, the Roaring Twenties, or our current Age of Anxiety. There is no objective beginning point in which a missional church culture begins engaging the world. The church's unfolding narrative always engages the world's story midstream.

Instead, wherever we find ourselves in the story of God's people and in the story of world history, when we place the basic questions of internal integration and external engagement in conversation we will naturally cultivate a missional culture. "How are we enlivened by the life, death, and resurrection of Jesus?"—internal integration—and "What is God doing in the world?"—external engagement. In this crucible we see that a missional church culture develops through a learning process that places internal integration and external engagement in a rhythm of action and reflection resulting in spiritual transformation. As we observe God's activity in the world, animated by the life, death, and resurrection of Jesus at work in our body/ies, making ourselves available to the Spirit's transformation in our lives, a missional church culture emerges reflecting the very nature of the trinitarian community.

## Developing an unlearning/learning process

As we place these two questions in an action/reflection learning process, a missional church culture will develop as we unlearn what we have wrongly absorbed through external engagement and learn the power of God at work in us through the life, death, and resurrection of Jesus as the Spirit transforms us "from one degree of glory to another."[15] To sustain this process, the teaching ministry of the church must be at the center of developing a missional church culture. Let's consider some examples of unlearning and learning that contribute to a missional church culture.

---

15. 2 Cor 3:18.

## Unlearning abstraction and learning participation

First, developing a missional church culture will require unlearning faith as conceptual abstraction. Memorizing a list of doctrines on a page, ascribing to the words of a written creed, for all their rich and dense rhetoric, will not align the church with the mission of God. The missional church will embody the ancient story. The church's life is formed in the world through ambidextrous observation of and dramatic participation in God's unfolding story of redemption from creation to Jesus' return. The preferred method of learning in the missional church is ongoing intentional catechesis (instruction) where believers submit themselves to the church's teaching in a context of external engagement and internal integration expecting that it will result in changed lives.[16]

## Unlearning "settledness" and learning "sentness"

Second, a missional church culture will develop as the church unlearns an imperial identity as "settled" and relearns its missionary nature. The mission of the *settled* church imposes its characters, forms, and script in every context. The missional church contextualizes and embodies the mission of God uniquely in every place. The missionary church is freed from its need to control the forms of the Christian community in every place. As Wilbert Shenk writes of this model, "The gospel message encounters a particular culture, calling forth and leading to the formation of a faith community, which is culturally authentic and authentically Christian."[17] In this endeavor, the church fulfills God's purpose, "that the *wisdom of God in its rich variety* might be made known to the rulers and authorities in the heavenly places" (Eph 3:10, emphasis added). In this way the church embodies her missional vocation to the enhancement of our collective internal spiritual vitality and increases our capacity for contextual engagement.

---

16. See Alan Kreider, *Patient Ferment: The Growth of the Church in the Roman Empire* (Grand Rapids, MI: Baker Academic, forthcoming in 2016). Kreider's chapter 6 offers a rich description of transformational catechesis in early church perspective.
17. Wilbert Shenk, *Changing Frontiers of Mission* (Maryknoll, NY: Orbis, 1999), 56. Shenk refers to this as the "contextualization" model.

## Unlearning exceptionalism and learning Spirit-dependency

Third, a missional church culture will develop as the church unlearns the Western cultural mythology of *exceptionalism* and learns *Spirit-dependency*. Western Christianity, wedded to powerful, imperial political systems, is always at risk of absorbing various forms of idolatry unawares. In our external engagement we risk absorbing the illusion that the supreme nationalistic power is perpetual rather than provisional. Western Christianity has been lulled into a false assumption that through the powers of effectiveness, efficiency, innovation, the unprecedented power of the industrial military complex, we will be able to overcome every obstacle to our success. We can fix every problem and order the world as we want it to be. Yet the foundation of this thinking is crumbling even now. Western empires are mortgaging their future to preserve this false sense of security in the present. Exceptionalism is the great idolatry of the Western world and it, too, will come to an end.

Instead, a missional church culture will be a training ground to learn how to depend on the power of the Holy Spirit to strengthen us to face every challenge in this age—not to conquer—but to meet every challenge with faithfulness. Developing a missional church culture requires an intentional catechesis that assumes a prior commitment to obedience and repentance as first steps of faith in Jesus. This catechesis then patiently walks believers in trust and dependency through the paths of obedience, patience in adversity, life in reconciled community, and yieldedness in communal discernment. Rather than insisting that a secure present needs to be preserved and protected, this catechesis imbues the church with a missional culture that lives by a robust eschatology. The missional church harmonizes itself to a groaning creation while we wait in patience for redemption (Rom 8:18-25).

To do this will require keen attention to where all members of the community are in their own formation story. All human communities include novices, practitioners, and elders in some form. So it is with the church. Without overt recognition of elders who model the way of the Jesus joyfully and faithfully over a long time, we diminish one of the most important influences in the development of a missional culture. Without this recognition, novices are easily overwhelmed in their opening journey or they prematurely adopt an authoritative voice to paper over their insecurities. The vitality of practitioners is allowed to stagnate in mediocrity where there is little inspiration to really "know" Christ.[18] Naming our elders provides novices a place to securely submit themselves to transformative teaching. The modeling of elders provides a goal toward which practitioners of the Christian faith can aspire.

## Unlearning anxiety and learning joy     S R

Finally, as we answer the questions posed by external engagement and internal integration, we will need to unlearn *anxiety* and learn *joy*. It has been said that when historians look back on the epoch that began after September 11, 2001, they will refer to the ensuing period as the Age of Anxiety. Much of our external engagement with the world reinforces a sense of anxiety, fear, and insecurity. This anxiety is a symptom that we are absorbing a new experience of reality, one in which ordering the world as we want it to be is no longer in our power, as though it ever was. So what are our choices? Shall we concede to the power of anxiety, which makes our fears more real? Or shall we unlearn anxiety and learn a new level of Spirit-dependency for the outcome of everything, believing that God is at work? By doing so we can grow in hope-filled joy. As Harry Huebner writes, "We praise God for transformations, including of our minds; transformations we can see and ones we know are taking place which we cannot see. After all, we know that Christ, the one who has already come, is also the one who is to come."[19]

Perhaps this last point can become a sort of litmus test in the action/reflection learning process of spiritual transformation in developing a missional culture. As we place external engagement and internal integration in conversation with each other, surely the best test of whether the learning process is cycling in the right direction is if the character of the missional church culture is reducing in anxiety and increasing in joy. May it be so.

---

18. "For though by this time you ought to be teachers, you need someone to teach you again the basic elements of the oracles of God. You need milk, not solid food; for everyone who lives on milk, being still an infant, is unskilled in the word of righteousness. But solid food is for the mature, for those whose faculties have been trained by practice to distinguish good from evil. Therefore let us go on toward perfection" (Heb 5:12–6:1). The word *perfection* here is from the Greek word *telos*, which refers to moving toward one's intended purpose or full realization.

19. Huebner, *Echoes of the Word*, 127.

## DEVELOPING A MISSIONAL CULTURE
## WITHIN MENNONITE CHURCH USA

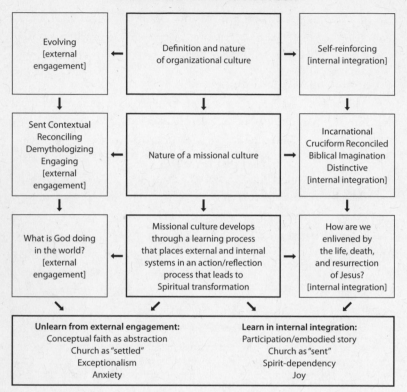

Evolving
[external
engagement]

Definition and nature
of organizational culture

Self-reinforcing
[internal integration]

Sent Contextual
Reconciling
Demythologizing
Engaging
[external
engagement]

Nature of a missional culture

Incarnational
Cruciform Reconciled
Biblical Imagination
Distinctive
[internal integration]

What is God doing
in the world?
[external
engagement]

Missional culture develops
through a learning process
that places external and internal
systems in an action/reflection
process that leads to
Spiritual transformation

How are we
enlivened by
the life, death,
and resurrection
of Jesus?
[internal integration]

**Unlearn from external engagement:**
Conceptual faith as abstraction
Church as "settled"
Exceptionalism
Anxiety

**Learn in internal integration:**
Participation/embodied story
Church as "sent"
Spirit-dependency
Joy

10

# Eight Characteristics of Successful Mennonite Urban Ministry

*Glen Guyton*

Urban ministry can be rewarding, but it comes with its own unique set of challenges. In urban areas you have a critical mass of people, cultures, and customs coming together. This does not mean they are coming together in synergetic harmony. You have class extremes—the rich and poor living in close proximity. Doctors and lawyers may live a few blocks from dock workers and bricklayers. There are also issues of communication. One neighbor may speak Korean; another may speak Spanish; and still another, Sudanese.

In addition, issues of social and religious heterogeneity need to be addressed before any relevant ministry can occur. While many churches need to learn how to preach the gospel to first-time seekers, can you imagine needing to do this in a room filled with former Catholics, Muslims, Hindus, and Buddhists?

Yes, the density, diversity, and heterogeneity of the urban setting can be challenging, but there is an upside—namely, people. In the urban setting, there is never an absence of people. There are thriving multigenerational homes and people living on top of other people in an amazing amalgamation of cultures and understandings that form something distinct and new. Often, because of the great needs and scarcity of resources in urban communities, there is a hunger for good news—a hunger for the gospel of peace. Urban dwellers understand that in order to survive, everyone must find common ground and develop new ways to live in harmony as one.

Successful, thriving urban churches all possess several similar characteristics.

## 1. Identity

First and foremost, successful urban churches *know their identity*. In the midst of diversity, the church has to know its primary mission and the vision God has given it for the community. First Chronicles 12:32 illustrates the impact that wisdom has over brute force and power. When facing a time of war, two hundred unarmed leaders with their relatives of the Issachar tribe were singled out from David's army. This small group of people understood the signs of the times and knew the best course for Israel to take. They are mentioned not because of their ability to fight, but due to their understanding of context. The successful urban church can clearly articulate its vision for anyone who asks. It is a prophetic vision that the community can identify with.

## 2. Spirituality

Successful urban churches have a *missional spirituality*. The missional church is not a theoretical concept to be discussed; rather, living and sharing one's faith are necessary tools for survival. The denseness of urban settings forces the church to reach out and touch the community. Leaders must rely heavily on the Holy Spirit to translate and interpret the gospel message in a way that transcends language and cultural barriers. In successful urban churches, missionality must manifest itself via a relevant word that fits the needs of the people. Talk is cheap, as some would say, but the Word of God is transformative. The successful urban church must be able to share the gospel in meaningful and tangible ways.

## 3. Discipleship formation

Successful urban churches focus on *discipleship* and *Christian formation* for new believers. There is a strong relationship between evangelism and social connections in the urban context. Why? You need look no further than situations like Ferguson, Missouri. People in poorer urban areas need hope and positive role models. How do you end racism, the poverty mentality, and fratricide in the urban community? You end it through education and the gospel of peace. The message of Christ is necessary to combat the lies and unhealthy paradigms of pop culture and the world. Discipleship is by its very definition synonymous with discipline and self-control. Successful urban churches seek change, not from the Oval Office, but from helping new believers see that despite their flaws they are imago Dei—created in the image of God. Through discipleship and healthy role models, people are equipped for leadership within the community.

## 4. Diversity

Unlike homogeneous communities, successful urban churches *develop and relate to a diverse Christian community*, facilitating an intercultural fellowship of believers. The urban church is often an amalgamation of people with different expectations. Getting along under a single umbrella is not always easy, but successful churches figure it out. The church as a whole gains a shared sense of grace and works on developing intercultural competences. Competences that can help dismantle systemic, cross-cultural, and intracultural racism. One key is that the diversity of the leadership of the successful urban church is typically a reflection of the people in the pews.

## 5. Interchurch partnerships

This goes hand in hand with successful urban churches developing *strong interchurch partnerships*. With so much diversity in the urban context there is little time to focus on the many differences between groups. To quote from *Star Trek*, "The needs of the many outweigh the [selfish desires] of the few." To quote from Scripture, "The harvest is plentiful, but the laborers are few" (Matt 9:37). Meeting great needs takes a number of great partners and a strong network of churches all working together—Anabaptists, evangelicals, independents, and others.

## 6. Holistic witness

Successful urban churches understand *holistic witness* in their respective context. For the church to survive, the people must survive. Better yet, when the people thrive, the church thrives. So ministry is not limited to preaching and teaching Scripture. The urban church ministry models the holistic ministry example set by Christ. Many urban churches, either alone or as a part of a network, are involved in the feeding and healing of the body through various programs. They are centers of social and political reform in the community. And they are often places that provide educational opportunities to help people climb the socioeconomic ladder, providing them with a sense of dignity. In addition, the urban church is a place of refuge for people when violence, disaster, and injustice infringe upon the community.

## 7. Stewardship

Successful urban churches have sound *stewardship practices and knowledge*. They understand how to manage money and inspire good stewardship in the community. The successful church and its leaders put into place sound financial practices, operate with a measure of faith, and teach the principle of reaping and sowing. The church can help its members in practical living and education on how to manage personal finances, moving people in the community from a mentality of poverty and consumerism to one where needs are met with generosity. Successful churches can thrive even in an impoverished context because transformation begins to happen in the minds of the people. As the apostle Paul counsels, "Don't copy the behavior and customs of this world, but let God transform you into a new person by changing the way you think. Then you will learn to know God's will for you, which is good and pleasing and perfect" (Rom 12:2 NLT).

## 8. Leadership development

Finally, successful urban churches have a plan for *leadership development*. Through mentoring, education, entrepreneurship, and sound management practices, the successful urban church continues to grow and thrive. In the garden of Eden, God told Adam and Eve to be fruit-ful and multiply. Successful ministry recreates itself. It multiplies and expands its reach within the community. New leaders are trained and there are healthy opportunities for leadership internships and succes-sion. The tools of success are not consolidated in one person or person-ality, but dispersed throughout the congregation. The leadership knows and understands how to utilize the gifts of others to maximize the effec-tiveness of the organization.

Every successful urban church may not possess all of these character-istics, but the majority of churches will be working towards efficacy in most of the categories listed. People often think that the miracle of the loaves and fishes is about making a bunch of fish sandwiches out of a few items. The miracle is actually in the preparation:

- Jesus evaluated the resources at hand.
- He got the people to sit down and organize themselves to prepare for the miracle.
- He trusted God to make it happen.
- And he had trained disciples in place to meet the needs of the people once God had delivered.

That is urban ministry at the core. If nothing else, the successful urban church understands that before God will take you to the next level, you have to be prepared for the journey.

## 11

# Inspiring the Next Generation for Involvement in God's Mission

*Faith: passing it on*

*Nelson Okanya*

Born and raised in a Mennonite home in Kenya, I watched my parents closely. As a family, we gathered every night before bedtime and sang a popular chorus or one or two hymns from *Tenzi Za Rohoni*—the Swahili songbook in frequent use among Mennonites. The singing was followed by a sermonette from my father and a prayer from either parent referencing each of us children by name and various needs—the widows, orphans, and needy—in our immediate community and the world.

Faith was clearly important to my parents. My dad's sermonettes sometimes seemed like overkill to us kids. But as I look back now, I marvel at how much these regular nightly routines, prayers before meals, prayers when leaving and returning home, and church practices of footwashing, communion, sermons, songs, and testimonies were formative in my faith and life journey.

There are troubling signs in the North American church today. Of particular concern is the seeming erosion of the Christian faith and the increasing difficulty we are facing in passing on that faith to the next generation. Many alternative stories and practices are forming and shaping us and quickly replacing the Christian story and its practices. I am alarmed at this current state of affairs and would like therefore to reflect in this essay on what the church might be and do to become a community that nourishes and nurtures the faith of its young people to live as God's missional people in the world.

## Teaching about Christian religion doesn't necessarily produce disciples of Jesus

About four decades ago, John H. Westerhoff III, an educator and professor of theology and Christian nurture at Duke Divinity School, posed a haunting question to the American public in his seminal book entitled *Will Our Children Have Faith?* Westerhoff was concerned by the paradigm shift in Christian education and the seeming lack of alternative to it. He wrote,

> Since the turn of the century, in spite of nods to other possibilities, Christian educators and local churches have functioned according to a schooling-instructional paradigm. That is, our image of education has been founded upon some sort of a "school" as the context and some form of instruction as the means. . . . Attempts to broaden that perspective, while intellectually acknowledged, are functionally resisted. . . . The schooling-instructional paradigm isolates us from new possibilities while continuing to occupy most of our attention in teaching, research, practices, and resource development. To compound our difficulties, we find it functionally difficult to imagine or create any significant educational program outside it.[1]

He rightly contends further that "education correctly understood is not identical with schooling. It is an aspect of socialization involving all deliberate, systematic and sustained efforts to transmit or evolve knowledge, attitudes, values, behaviors, or sensibilities. . . . The history of religious education, therefore, needs to include the family, public schools,

---

1. John H. Westerhoff III, *Will Our Children Have Faith?* (Harrisburg, PA: Morehead Publishing, and Toronto: Anglican Book Centre, 1st ed., with Seabury Press, 1976; quotations used here taken from the revised and expanded edition, 2000), 5–6.

community ethos, religious literature, and church life."[2] Then, in his weighty judgment of the new paradigm, Westerhoff concludes,

> It appears that as Christian faith has diminished, the schooling-instructional paradigm has encouraged us to busy ourselves with teaching about Christian religion. As our personal commitment to Christ has lapsed, many church persons have turned for solace to teaching children what we believe, and what is right and wrong. . . . There is a great difference between learning about the Bible and living as a disciple of Jesus Christ. Faith is expressed, transformed, and made meaningful by persons sharing their faith in an historical, tradition-bearing community of faith.[3]

Therefore, the result of the instructional paradigm of education and its focus on the school as context of education has led to a diminished faith because formation takes more than literacy; it encompasses one's entire life.

## Recent research on religious trends among American youth is sobering

Did Westerhoff miss the mark in being overly critical of a solution that was meant to save Christian education? Or did the church ignore his concerns to its own peril? Forty years later, a 2007 survey by the Pew Forum on Religion and Public Life discovered that one in four young adults is unaffiliated with any religious tradition.[4]

In another recent survey, published under the title *Soul Searching: The Religious and Spiritual Lives of American Teenagers*, researchers for the National Study of Youth and Religion concluded that there now seems to be an "alternative faith" among American youth today. The researchers call it "moralistic therapeutic deism." This faith describes God as

> one who exists, created the world, and defines our general moral order, but not one who is particularly personally involved in one's affairs, especially affairs in which one would prefer not to have God involved. In this faith, God wants people to be good, nice, and fair to each other (as taught in the Bible and by most world religions); the central goal of life is to be happy and

---

2. Ibid., 14.
3. Ibid., 18–19.
4. See the Pew report at http://religions.pewforum.org/reports.

feel good about ourselves; and God is not involved in our lives except when we need God to solve a problem.[5]

It is common knowledge that parents are the primary faith trainers for their children. The question that begs an answer is: Where did these teenagers get the named faith from?

In her book *Almost Christian: What the Faith of Our Teenagers Is Telling the American Church*, author Kenda Creasy Dean attempts to interpret these findings and suggests a way forward for church youth ministry. Dean is perplexed that "we 'teach' young people baseball, but 'expose' them to faith. . . . [We] blithely assume that religious identity will happen by osmosis, emerging 'when youth are ready.'"[6] More relevant to this article is Dean's major finding that Mormons top the charts when it comes to integrating their faith as teenagers. She writes,

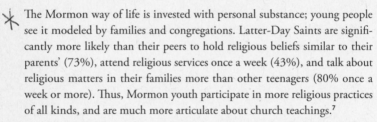

The Mormon way of life is invested with personal substance; young people see it modeled by families and congregations. Latter-Day Saints are significantly more likely than their peers to hold religious beliefs similar to their parents' (73%), attend religious services once a week (43%), and talk about religious matters in their families more than other teenagers (80% once a week or more). Thus, Mormon youth participate in more religious practices of all kinds, and are much more articulate about church teachings.[7]

Carlton Johnstone is the national youth ministry development leader for the Presbyterian Church in New Zealand. In a recently published work, *Embedded Faith: The Faith Journeys of Young Adults within Church Communities*, Johnstone—unlike Dean—focuses on a generational unit *within* the church. He examines various aspects of the faith journeys of twenty- and thirtysomethings, including the phenomena of changing churches, choices of churches, choices to engage and disengage in church life, life transitions, church practices, and other topics.

Johnstone examines similar young adults who share a particular kind of faith—one that is owned and embedded in a community of faith. He finds that rituals play a critical role in embedding faith among young

5. See Christian Smith and Melinda Lundquist Denton, *Soul Searching: The Religious and Spiritual Lives of American Teenagers* (New York: Oxford University Press, 2005), 164.
6. Kenda Creasy Dean, *Almost Christian: What the Faith of Our Teenagers Is Telling the American Church* (New York: Oxford University Press, 2010), 15.
7. Ibid., 51.

adults. Families and the church pass on the faith by embodying the faith to their young ones.[8]

A study done specifically among young Anabaptists by their peers discovered the inability of youth and young adults to articulate their own faith. This inability is, of course, not unique to young Anabaptists. The *Soul Searching* study reveals that this is characteristic of young adults in mainline Protestant and Catholic churches as well.

But equally if not even more troubling in the Anabaptist study was the finding about how young Anabaptists understood missions. Here the researchers discovered that their peers had reduced missions to acts of service, while conversion as the goal of missions had receded almost entirely into obscurity.[9] This understanding was likewise reflected in the attitudes of denomination-wide delegates at the 2011 Mennonite Church USA convention in Pittsburgh, when many resonated with the statement that as Mennonites, "we love service, flirt with peace and are allergic to evangelism."[10]

The lack of faith formation among our youth and young adults, coupled with the larger socioeconomic shifts in our culture today, continue to have a negative effect on the next generation and their capacity for or interest in missional involvement. As the American church experiences a large exodus of eighteen- to thirty-five-year-olds, we must wake up to these troubling dynamics.

## Mennonites reflect broader trends

Mennonites are not exempted from surrounding cultural realities. Conrad Kanagy's 2006 research shows that the Mennonite church, like most of the American ecclesial reality, is losing a generation and becoming increasingly older. Kanagy found that "Mennonites between the ages of 18–35 are less engaged in the church than older members. While 86 percent of older members—age 36 and above—consider

8. Carlton Johnstone, *Embedded Faith: The Faith Journeys of Young Adults within Church Communities* (Eugene, OR: Wipf and Stock, 2013).

9. This research was conducted by students Matthew Krabill (Fuller Theological Seminary) and Jamie Ross (Anabaptist Mennonite Biblical Seminary), who presented their findings at the Council of International Anabaptist Ministries in Chicago, January 2012.

10. Mennonite Church USA Summary of Delegates responses at Pittsburgh 2011 (Attachment 3).

themselves 'active' members of their congregation, only 69 percent of young members do so." Kanagy also found that younger members attend both church worship services and Sunday school less often than older members, and fewer young members say their relationship with their congregation is very important to them.[11]

Where do these young adults go? The *Wall Street Journal* reported a few years ago that 88 percent of the millennial generation—those born in the 1980s–90s and early 2000s—prefer to live in cities. "Automakers like Toyota and GM are alarmed that millennials are choosing to live in places where walking, biking, and mass transit can take the place of driving," says Joe Showalter, president of Rosedale Mennonite Missions.[12] If the church neglects these findings and realities, it does so to its own detriment.

A majority of young people go to urban locations for higher education and other opportunities. But unlike their parents, they choose to stay in those locations. Tim Keller, a pastor and church planter in New York City, has reflected on this migration to urban settings and concluded that "if the church in the West remains, for the most part, in the suburbs of Middle America and neglects the great cities, it risks losing an entire generation of American society's leaders."[13]

From my observations of Mennonite churches in Lancaster County, Pennsylvania, and the research done by Conrad Kanagy, it is clear that in traditional Mennonite communities we are losing a generation of youth and consequently the church is increasingly becoming older. If it is true that our young people are relocating to urban centers, might it be that Mennonites are losing a generation in part because of the church's largely rural presence? Are there new opportunities for Mennonite/Anabaptist witness and influence in urban settings?

---

11. Kanagy states that 68 percent of young members attend church weekly compared to 83 percent of older members, and 39 percent attend Sunday school compared to 57 percent for older adults. Forty percent of younger members say that their relationship with their congregation is very important to them while 57 percent of older Mennonites affirm that statement. See Conrad Kanagy, *Road Signs for the Journey* (Scottdale, PA : Herald Press, 2007), 59.

12. Joe Showalter, "RMM in the City: An Open Letter about Office Relocation," *Rosedale Mennonite Missions News and Stories* (May 20, 2014), http://www.news.rmmweb.org/2014/05/rmm_in_the_city.html.

13. Timothy Keller, "The Call to the City," *Anthology* (April 2014): 31. *Anthology* is published by Missio Nexus.

I believe that older Mennonites who have grown accustomed to rural and suburban realities may need to become more flexible in their understandings of church and ministry. Just as Paul's strategy for multiplying church movements was to minister in major urban centers, we too may need to do the same if we want to have growing, vibrant Anabaptist churches. Engaging the younger generation of Anabaptists will, however, take a much more profound commitment than simply moving from rural to urban localities.

## It is time to regain our missional imagination

Let me suggest that as Anabaptists in North America, we ought to be compelled to action by these discoveries. Let us return to teaching our children the Christian story from an Anabaptist vantage point and embodying that story through spiritual practices such as communal Scripture reading, footwashing, and regular communion. It is essential that we share our faith by both verbal proclamation and through acts of service, practicing hospitality, and sharing our testimonies as followers of the living risen Lord to reinforce that story in our homes and churches.

This engagement in forming our youth is one way to regain missional imagination as our children grow and develop with an embedded faith that helps them assess and reject other competing stories. I believe that such a step will lead to our young people being inspired by the heart of God and the biblical story. Authentic, passionate teaching and practice is how the church can ensure the next generation's involvement in God's mission.

Individual congregations and church agencies should collaborate with the Mennonite Church to find relevant ways of telling God's story, embedding it in our identities, and embodying it through various formative practices that help young people develop spiritual muscles. This will nurture, inspire, and enable them to live as God's missional people in a world marked by formative stories that compete with the biblical narrative and ultimately offer little hope.

Carlton Johnstone's observation is instructive when he notes that "our biography, our sense of identity, is formed through telling our stories which are embedded in the story of the communities in which we participate."[14] He goes on to apply Stanley Fish's theory of interpretive community to the church when he writes, "Fish's concept of interpretive communities helps us to see that how the biblical Christian story is told is an extension of community perspectives. . . . By combining Bellah and others' notion of communities of memory with Fish's notion of interpretive communities, it is possible to develop an understanding of churches as 'interpretive communities of memory.'"[15]

The church tells us what to believe and why. While we add our own contributions and interpretations, the church interprets both the Scripture and the world for us. This is why for nearly five centuries, the stories, practices, and traditions that were distinctive to the Anabaptist faith—albeit in varied forms given the context—have by and large formed and shaped Anabaptist communities around the globe.

I grew up in Kenya knowing that Mennonites as followers of Jesus did not baptize infants, nor did they kill their enemies. Unfortunately, without intentionally and continually telling our stories, like those found in the *Martyrs Mirror*, and teaching and demonstrating practices and rituals like footwashing central to our faith, key aspects of Anabaptism are being lost. Beliefs and practices regarding mission, discipleship, love of enemy, and the centrality of Jesus Christ will become memories that recede into a distant past. These features of our faith community are already competing with other powerful and seemingly relevant stories, making it a challenge for the church today to inspire the next generation for involvement in God's mission.

## "From barrenness issues a new generation"

There is one other reflection that needs to be added to this conversation. One decade after John Westerhoff posed the haunting question, "Will our children have faith?," Walter Brueggemann, Old Testament professor at Columbia Theological Seminary, gave that question an intriguing twist by reversing the emphasis and asking, "Will our faith have children?" Readers could surmise that he was concerned about a seemingly practical atheism on the rise that might overtake the church's story about a God. Brueggemann demonstrated a critical awareness of the

---

14. Johnstone, xv.
15. Ibid.

God of impossibilities by asking whether we are open enough to receive a future from God that will surprise us. For "it is assumed in evangelical faith," he wrote, "that any real future is given us underived, unexpected, ex nihilo, by the mercy of God" (cf. 1 Cor 4:7).[16]

Brueggemann makes an excellent point because ours is a faith that does not really depend on us, but on God. As Mennonites—and as part of the larger American culture—we are good "doers," and we draw our sense of accomplishment through our work. We have been deeply influenced by the narratives of both the Protestant work ethic and the more secular narrative that one's identity should be based on what one does and accomplishes. Our Christian faith story, however, is given to us by God and does not depend on us.

I believe that equally if not more important than a focus on the questions of our children's faith should be questions about *our own* faith. It was my parents' lived faith that impressed me and spurred me on my own individual faith journey. I was challenged and encouraged by their love and trust in God. My parents related differently than most families in our village. There was gentleness in their relationship, a respect for each other, and a deep sense of relational obedience to God.

Unlike many men in our community, my dad's interaction with us his children and with the other children in the village spoke to us more loudly than his words. Together with the lived and practiced faith in our home, my fascination with Scripture and my mother's and grandmother's evening singing, the faith modeled by my parents became embedded in my life. Though I wrestled with it through my teenage and young adult years, I gradually becoming more and more convinced it was the path I was to choose.

With time I made this faith my own and this is the reason I am serving the church today in my role as a mission agency president. Now that my wife, Jessica, and I are raising two young boys of our own, it is our prayer that we will faithfully live out our convictions in such a way that will inspire our sons to make faith their own and be involved in God's mission. We hold this hope humbly, however, trusting God and in agreement with Brueggemann when he writes, "Precisely to the

---

16. See Walter Brueggemann, *Hope within History* (Atlanta, GA: John Knox Press, 1987), 92–93.

barren one is the promise made (Isa 54:1-3), 'Sing barren one, you who have not yet been in labor.' Rejoice because from barrenness issues a new generation which will outreach the married, full, affluent, technologically secure Babylon. The statement is nonsensical unless it is taken as evangelical, i.e., hope against the reason of the day."[17]

17. Ibid., 94.

12

# The Impact of Immigrant Churches on Mennonite Church USA

*Nehemiah Chigoji, Matthew Krabill, and Sunoko Lin*

It is no secret that post-1965 non-Western migration to the United States has had a profound impact on the American religious landscape. Despite the fact that three in four new migrants to the United States self-identify as Christian, very little attention has been given to the presence of immigrants within traditional European denominations. This chapter uses Mennonite Church USA—a denominational home to an increasing number of immigrant congregations—as an arena to explore issues of multiethnic identity, theological orientation, and mission.

Specifically, the reflections here illustrate the encounter between non-Western immigrants and Mennonite Church USA through the experiences and vision of two southern California immigrant Mennonite pastors. In his reflections, Pastor Nehemiah Chigoji describes the shifting cultural and theological attitudes and convictions within the denomination by focusing on the issue of sexuality. Using Maranatha Christian Fellowship's vision of becoming a multiethnic church, Pastor

Sunoko Lin reflects on the journey of living into that missional reality. Lin hopes that his congregation's experiences can help others in the denomination embark on a similar journey, and he suggests key practices for others desiring to embrace a multiethnic identity.

## Nehemiah Chigoji—"For such a time as this . . ."

In recent years, immigrant churches have had an interesting and profound effect on Mennonite Church USA. When I first became familiar with the denomination, the relationship between immigrant churches and the rest of the church shared similarities to that of the Jews and Gentiles in the early Christian movement. While we did not hear anyone proclaiming that immigrant churches should not be allowed in MC USA, we certainly heard from white Mennonites who believed that immigrant churches needed to become more "Mennonite"—that is, assimilate to white ethnic Mennonite culture—as a necessary step for membership in MC USA. This situation seemed comparable to the Jewish leaders in the first century AD who expected Gentiles to become outwardly Jewish through circumcision prior to becoming Christian.

In the nearly sixteen years since I have been in the United States and have increasingly become more active in MC USA, I have observed changes in cultural attitudes among both the immigrant churches and white American Mennonites. Both have come a long way in recognizing the value of the other's worship and cultural styles. This is due in large part to the denomination's recognition of the importance of diversity in the leadership of the broader church, resulting in a significant effort to include people of color from immigrant churches in national leadership.

In MC USA the practice of discussion and debate—rather than expulsion and exclusion—is utilized for those who do not conform to established church theology. While immigrant churches may generally embrace this practice, they tend to believe that adherence to biblical mandates is more important than the need for ongoing discussion on certain issues. As a result of creating space, immigrant churches have increasingly voiced their opinions and beliefs to the broader church. This has often empowered the less vocal majority in MC USA to speak up when in agreement with the immigrant churches.

One current example of this approach to theological disagreements is the issue of human sexuality. Most immigrant churches believe that issues concerning this matter have profound theological implications and understand that there will always be points of conflict between any culture and the claims of the culture. Many conservative Christian churches in the Global South have had to face the issue of Christian sexuality in dealing with cultures that allow polygamy. For immigrant churches, behaviors that are seen as deviating from a biblical view of marriage and sexuality cannot be allowed within the church. For most of them, active LGBTQ persons may not be ordained, married, or become church leaders.

While there is widespread agreement with Article 19 of the church's *Confession of Faith*—that marriage is between one man and one woman—there is less consensus about what sanction should be applied to persons who allow or perform same-sex marriages. A majority of immigrant churches believe that the credentials of a pastor who officiates at a same-sex union should be withdrawn from MC USA.

The theological issue at stake here, according to most immigrant congregations, is balancing the concern for keeping the leadership of God's church pure (1 Tim 3:2—"Now a bishop must be above reproach . . .") with the concern of the grace the Lord Jesus showed (John 8:7b—"He . . . said to [the Pharisees], 'Let anyone among you who is without sin be the first to throw a stone at her.'")

While I do not know how the Lord will work out this significant difference of opinion within the denomination, I do strongly believe that "immigrant churches may have been brought to MC USA for such a time as this" (Esther 4:14b, loosely paraphrased by author). In other words, the immigrant Mennonite churches may challenge the broader church to think beyond an insular, culturally captive theology to take a fresh look at what the Bible may be trying to tell us in new ways.

## Sunoko Lin—Maranatha's multiethnic missional journey

Over the last couple of decades, the ethnic and cultural landscape in America has dramatically changed. In the 1970 U.S. census for example, 23 percent of California residents were considered people of color.[1] Three decades later, in the year 2000, Hispanics alone comprised 40.3 percent of the southern California population while 39.9 percent were of white descent; 11.3 percent were of Asian background, and 7.6 percent were African American.

The dramatic shifts in California are indicative of larger national trends, as is evident by the fact that the census projects white Americans will no longer be the majority by 2050.[2] How will churches in Los Angeles respond to this reality of changing ethnic dynamics? Will they embrace a multiethnic identity? How will they do so? I believe that churches in Los Angeles need to embrace ethnicities beyond their own if they want to become missional churches. That includes Maranatha Christian Fellowship—a member congregation of Pacific Southwest Mennonite Conference—which I have pastored since April 2006.

Located in Northridge, California, about twenty-five miles north-east of Los Angeles, Maranatha is an ethnic Indonesian church that has missional aspirations of becoming a multiethnic church. This aspiration came to me after reading the book *Asian American Evangelical Churches.*[3] The author writes, "It is important for the (Chinese) church to minister to Chinese Americans, but it is also important for us to reach non-Asians, non-Chinese, because Christianity is for everyone, not just for Asians."[4] This is consistent with New Testament Scripture where Jesus commands the disciples, saying, "Go therefore and make disciples of all nations . . ." (Matt 28:19). Applied to our contemporary context, Jesus' "all nations" must include both Asians and non-Asians.

## Incarnational living

Our missional journey began in 2011 following our decision to hold two services, one in Indonesian and one in English. The English service enables us to reach non-Indonesians in our community. Specifically,

1. Kathleen Garces-Foley, *Crossing the Ethnic Divide* (New York: Oxford University Press, 2007), 58.
2. See "A Milestone En Route to a Majority-Minority Nation," Pew Social Trends, http://www.pewsocialtrends.org/2012/11/07/a-milestone-en-route-to-a-majority-minority-nation/.
3. Antony W. Alumkal, *Asian American Evangelical Churches: Race, Ethnicity, and Assimilation in the Second Generation* (New York: LFB Scholarly Publishing, 2003).
4. Ibid., 82.

we intentionally want to reach the international student community at California State University Northridge (CSUN) because it is in our neighborhood and its student body is comprised of eighty different nationalities.

Launching two services was not easy. In the beginning, we experienced strong resistance from our first-generation Indonesian adults. They were afraid to lose their identity. Relating to like-minded people is much more comfortable after all. It took several years of educating our first-generation members about the necessity of *incarnational living*— the desire to invite everyone, regardless of their background, to follow Jesus. We do so by modeling the life of Jesus for others in a very tangible way so that they will discover the redemptive work of God in Christ.

Being a missional church is about witnessing and inviting. Rather than asking people to "come to us," we follow Jesus' example by scouting our neighborhood and actively engaging the community. Following Jesus means we become seekers just as "the Son of Man came to seek out and to save the lost" (Luke 19:10).

## Communal and generous living

Despite the challenges confronting us, we proceeded on our missional journey. Another characteristic of that journey is what we call *communal and generous living*. One major strength at Maranatha is its conviction that church is a family. As a family, we understand that church is about people and not programs. Relationships and commitment are important values for us. We gather as a community not because we like the programs or ministries, but because we make ourselves available for one another.

We have been practicing this value in our church. Not long ago, for example, one of our members had legal problems and could not afford a lawyer. In response, everyone helped contribute to pay for the member's legal fees. Another instance involved a single mother. When her husband died, we grieved with her. We cooked for her, took her children to school, and suffered with the family. When one suffers, all of us suffer.

Our care for others, however, is not limited to those inside the church. Following the Haiti earthquake in January 2010, we asked our congregation how we could respond to the tragedy. Maranatha responded positively by setting aside significant financial giving for Haiti relief. I was deeply touched when one of our Sunday school children gave 50 percent of her birthday gift towards Haiti relief. While this might seem like a small gesture, I believe it is the kind of practice that we need to encourage so that thinking beyond ourselves—our own ethnic identities—becomes a natural part of our everyday life and witness.

# PART 3

# Tools and Applications

13

# What Is an Anabaptist Christian? *Serm & SR*

*Palmer Becker*

## Introduction

Christians with an Anabaptist perspective on faith and life have existed from the very beginning of the Christian era. Anabaptist is a way of being Christian. Just as there are Anglican, Baptist, and Lutheran Christians, so there are Anabaptist Christians.

*Anabaptist* is an invented name meaning "rebaptizers." It was given to sixteenth-century Christians who saw little value in infant baptism and, therefore, baptized each other as adults upon confession of faith. These Anabaptist Christians were the forerunners of today's Mennonite Christians and many others in the Free Church tradition.

Anabaptist/Mennonite Christians hold many beliefs in common with other believers. But they often hold these convictions somewhat differently than others.

Anabaptists are sometimes identified as the left wing of the Protestant Reformation. They rose up in a time of social and economic upheaval and were intent on carrying further the Reformation begun by Martin Luther, Ulrich Zwingli, and John Calvin. Christians of an Anabaptist perspective have throughout history placed strong emphasis on following

Jesus in daily life, being covenanted with each other in Christ-centered community, and seeking to overcome conflict in nonviolent ways. Are you a Christian with an Anabaptist perspective?

While programs and goals may change, the unique core values that bring an organization into being are sometimes said to be "sacred" and should not be changed. What are the "sacred" core values of Anabaptist Christians? This essay will explain them in the form of three key statements. They are:

1. Jesus is the center of our faith.
2. Community is the center of our lives.
3. Reconciliation is the center of our work.

These three core values had multiple beginnings. We will try here to describe how they developed in history and suggest how they apply to today's world. We readily recognize that the positive contributions of the early Anabaptists are emphasized in this essay and that more negative features are minimized. Our purpose here is to give inquiring persons an opportunity to ask and respond to the question, "What does an ideal Anabaptist Christian look like?"

## Core Value 1: Jesus is the center of our faith

> [Let us fix] our eyes on Jesus, the pioneer and perfecter of faith (Heb 12:2 NIV).

Jesus began his ministry in approximately 30 CE by gathering together a group of disciples. For three years these disciples lived, ate, and worked with Jesus. They observed how he cared for the poor, healed those who were ill, gave sight to the blind, forgave sinners, and taught the multitudes. During these years of ministry, and also in the days after his resurrection, Jesus became central to their faith and life. They came to believe in him as their Teacher, Savior, and Lord in contrast to the teachers, saviors, and masters of their time.

To be a Christian meant more to these early disciples than being a believer or worshiper. It also meant being a Spirit-filled person who was obeying Jesus in daily life. Because of their commitment to Jesus and the ongoing presence of the Holy Spirit in their lives, people noticed that they were being transformed to become Christlike in their attitudes and lifestyles. If you had asked those first disciples, I believe they would have said with enthusiasm, "Jesus Christ is the center of our faith!"

For 250 years, the first Christians continued to experience the Spirit of Jesus in their midst. But then over the next centuries, so many changes were introduced to the Christian faith that it nearly became another religion. While early Christians were a persecuted minority worshiping in secret, now they met in ornate buildings. While new converts in the first centuries underwent significant training, received adult baptism, and joined an alternative community, now infants were baptized and all citizens except Jews belonged to a church aligned with the government. Whereas the early church emphasized following Jesus, now the focus was on correct doctrine, elaborate ritual, and defending themselves against enemies. While members of the early church had shared their faith daily with their neighbors, now evangelism meant primarily extending the boundaries of the "Christian" empire. While the majority of early Christians had rejected military service, by the time of Augustine's death, only Christians were permitted in the Roman army.

Between the years 1200 and 1500 CE, a variety of concerned persons and groups began to realize that there were serious inadequacies in widely accepted understandings of salvation and the church. Martin Luther, a German monk, who was thoroughly schooled in Augustinian theology, was one of these reformers. Ulrich Zwingli, a Swiss pastor, and John Calvin, a reformed theologian, were others. They came forward to introduce significant changes.

Several students of Ulrich Zwingli, including Conrad Grebel, Felix Manz, and George Blaurock, gathered regularly for Bible study in Zürich, Switzerland. Hans Hut, Hans Denck, Pilgram Marpeck, and Jakob Hutter were on a similar pilgrimage in south Germany and Moravia. Somewhat later, Menno Simons, a former Catholic priest, taught and coordinated groups that were emerging in the Netherlands.

While these first Anabaptist Christians affirmed the Apostles' Creed and much of what Luther and Zwingli were preaching, they wanted to go further. They preferred to talk about being "born again" rather than about being "justified by faith." While salvation was indeed by the grace of God, they called for a more radical response of obedience on the part of believers. They insisted that salvation, made possible by Jesus and the power of the Holy Spirit, should lead to the transformation of a person's moral, social, and economic life. Adult baptism became a sign that this salvation and transformation had taken place. If you had asked those first Anabaptist Christians, I believe they would have joined with the first disciples in saying, "Jesus Christ is the center of our faith!"

What does this mean for us today? Christians from an Anabaptist perspective seek to apply their understanding of Jesus in three important ways.

## 1. Jesus is to be followed in daily life

Salvation, in the Anabaptist tradition, emphasizes being transformed from an old way of life to a life that exemplifies the Spirit and actions of Jesus. Salvation is not merely a change of God's attitude toward us. It is a change in our attitudes and actions toward God, toward people, and toward the world. This change is made possible by the indwelling presence of the Holy Spirit, who empowers disciples to follow Jesus in daily life.

## 2. The Bible is interpreted from a Christ-centered point of view

While Christians from an Anabaptist perspective see the Scriptures as the ultimate source of information about God's purposes in the world, they see Jesus as the final authority for faith and life. Jesus the Christ is Lord of Scripture and is normative for both personal and social ethics. Thus, when Anabaptist-minded Christians face an ethical question, they go first to Jesus for their primary guidance and then to additional Scriptures for further background and understanding. If two passages of Scripture seem to disagree on the matter, they let Jesus be the referee!

## 3. Jesus is accepted as both Savior and Lord

Many Christians affirm Jesus as their personal Savior from sin, but place less emphasis on following him as Lord in daily life. They look to Jesus as Savior from personal bad habits, but when they face larger social or political problems, they give their obedience to an employer, civic leader, military general, or president. As a result, many Christians today are more obedient to the commands of earthly leaders than they are to those given by Jesus. Christians from an Anabaptist perspective believe that authorities need to be obeyed to the extent that Christian discipleship will allow. Government's purpose is to preserve life and create order in a secular world. Obedience to laws does not mean that we give blind obedience to all things commanded. Since our highest loyalty always belongs to Jesus and the kingdom of God, we may on occasion need to disobey an order because it is contrary to the teaching and spirit of Jesus. When there is a conflict between the ways of Jesus and the ways of Caesar, we say with the early disciples, "We must obey God rather than any human authority" (Acts 5:29).

| MANY CHRISTIANS EMPHASIZE: | ANABAPTIST CHRISTIANS EMPHASIZE: |
| --- | --- |
| **1. Christ's death**<br>Many Christians focus primarily on the holiness of God and the need for personal salvation. They emphasize that "Christ came to die" and focus less on the life, teachings, and empowering Spirit of Jesus. Christianity is primarily about forgiveness. | **1. Christ's life**<br>Anabaptist Christians affirm the holiness and forgiving grace of God, but also emphasize that "Jesus came to live." His death resulted in part from the way he lived. Jesus as risen Lord empowers us to follow him in life. Christianity is primarily about discipleship. |
| **2. A "flat" Bible**<br>Many Christians tend to see the Scriptures, rather than Jesus, as their final authority. Guidance for daily living comes from various Scriptures that seem to fit the situation. All decisions do not need to coincide with the teachings and Spirit of Jesus. | **2. A "Christ-centered" Bible**<br>Anabaptists affirm that while all Scripture is inspired, Jesus is the fullest revelation of God and the final authority for decision making. Jesus fulfills the Old Testament and is the norm for both personal and social ethics. |
| **3. Government as final authority**<br>Many Christians believe that since government leaders are ordained of God, they must be obeyed even if their demands are contrary to the teachings of Jesus or the dictates of conscience. | **3. Jesus as final authority**<br>Anabaptists recognize that government is ordained of God to preserve life and maintain order in a secular world. However, the demands of government shall not overrule the lordship of Jesus. |

## Core Value 2: Community is the center of our life

> Every day . . . they broke bread in their homes and ate together with glad and sincere hearts, praising God and enjoying the favor of all the people (Acts 2:46-47 NIV).

By referring to his followers in family terms, it became evident that Jesus wanted his followers to not only believe in him, but also to have a strong sense of belonging to each other. Observers were amazed at what God did in and through these groups of early Christians. They had the gifts, insights, and courage to continue doing what Jesus had begun to do while he was with them. If you would have asked those first followers of Jesus, I believe they would have said, "Christ-centered community is the center of our life!"

Over time, the idea of belonging to Christ and to each other in close-knit community was largely lost. Those who wanted to follow Jesus obediently and to experience close community chose to become monks and nuns who lived in monasteries and convents. This gave the impression that following Jesus in daily life and living relationally in Christ-centered community was impossible for common people.

Martin Luther and other reformers originally intended to reform the church to its biblical origins. Luther and Zwingli were prevented by the Peasants' War and other political circumstances from implementing many of their intended reforms. They continued with the basic structures of Constantine and the theology of Augustine, retained the state church as the polity of the church, the sanctuary as the structure of the church, infant baptism as the introductory rite into the church, the use of the sword by government as the tool for discipline, and the interpretation of a "flat" Bible as the primary way of knowing God's will.[1]

Early Anabaptists, including Menno Simons, were disappointed with the incompleteness of the Reformation. They did not want merely to reform the church back to the structures set in motion by Constantine and the theology of Augustine. They wanted to restore the church to its original New Testament pattern and form. They believed that the church needed to be an independent and alternate society in the world.

The Anabaptists saw the church as being composed of transformed believers who were committed to Jesus and each other in covenant communities. Both Protestant and Catholic leaders viewed this as a threat to the established church. As a result, they imprisoned and severely persecuted many Anabaptists. More than four thousand were drowned, beheaded, or burned at the stake as martyrs for their faith.

---

1. A "flat" Bible means reading and applying the Scriptures from the Old Testament to the New, with no authoritative priority given to the life and teachings of Jesus.

The early Anabaptists' strong sense of belonging to Jesus and their loyal support of each other helped them to live devoted ethical lives in the context of a hostile world. If you would have asked them, I believe they would have said with the first disciples, "Christ-centered community is the center of our life!"

In today's world, Christians with an Anabaptist perspective understand and practice Christ-centered community in three distinct ways.

## 1. Forgiveness is essential for community

Jesus came that we might have life and have it more abundantly. He prayed fervently that we would be one with each other even as he is one with the Father. A warm sense of community and all the benefits pertaining to it emerge when members of the body of Christ are committed to asking each other for forgiveness. Confession and forgiveness remove the barriers that prevent fellowship with God and with each other. Anabaptist Christians believe that forgiveness is essential for creating and nurturing community.

## 2. The Scriptures are interpreted in community

Christians from an Anabaptist perspective believe that the Scriptures need to be studied both privately and in the context of a Spirit-guided community where fellow believers give and receive counsel. Generally, community members who come together in small groups, classes, and conferences in the Spirit of Christ can best determine what a Scripture is saying to them about a particular situation.

## 3. Community is experienced in face-to-face groups

Some aspects of Christian living happen best in relational groups of twelve or fewer people. This is often true as we give and receive counsel, discern gifts for mission, and have fun and fellowship. Healthy congregations are structured for community. They are often networks of small groups. Some would go so far as to say that the small group is the basic unit of the church. Christians from an Anabaptist perspective experience Christ-centered community as the center of their life.

| MANY CHRISTIANS EMPHASIZE: | ANABAPTIST CHRISTIANS EMPHASIZE: |
|---|---|
| **1. Vertical forgiveness**<br>Many Christians focus more on vertical forgiveness from God than on horizontal forgiveness from each other. Forgiveness is seen as a means for receiving individual salvation and eternal life. | **1. Horizontal forgiveness**<br>Christians need both vertical forgiveness from God and horizontal forgiveness from each other. Forgiveness builds community and is a means to peaceful relationships with each other. |
| **2. Individual interpretation**<br>Many Christians seek to interpret the Scriptures out of their own understanding and experience. On the other hand, some rely almost totally on trained teachers or pastors to interpret the Scripture for them. | **2. Corporate interpretation**<br>Anabaptists believe that individual study of Scripture must be combined with group study. Group members commit themselves to giving and receiving counsel from others in the Spirit of Jesus. |
| **3. Meet in sanctuaries**<br>Many Christians tend to think of the worshiping congregation as the basic unit of the church. Often, the church is seen as a structure, an organization, or as a Sunday morning performance. | **3. Meet in small groups**<br>Anabaptist Christians tend to see the church as a family. While corporate worship happens, healthy churches, it is believed, are often those organized as networks of small groups who fellowship, study, share, and pray together. |

## Core Value 3: Reconciliation is the center of our work

> All this is from God, who reconciled us to himself through Christ, and has given us the ministry of reconciliation (2 Cor 5:18).

God sent his Son, Jesus, as the solution to the problem of sin. Jesus came to reconcile all those who would respond to God and to each other. He addressed brokenness and injustice of all kinds and trained a group of followers who became ambassadors of reconciliation.

Jesus outlined specific steps for reconciliation within the faith community as recorded in Matthew 18:15-20. Offended persons and groups are to go to each other one-to-one to seek a solution to the presenting problem. If the injustice or offense remains unresolved, further steps are to be taken enlisting more community members.

At the end of his ministry, Jesus said, "As the Father has sent me, so I send you" (John 20:21). "Go therefore and make disciples of all nations, baptizing them in the name of the Father and of the Son and of the Holy Spirit and teaching them to obey everything that I have commanded you" (Matt 28:19-20). As a result, the early disciples went throughout the known world preaching, teaching, and practicing a new way of life so that people everywhere might be reconciled to God and to each other. If you would have asked the first Christians, I believe they would have said, "Reconciling people to God and to each other is the center of our work!"

When Constantine began to merge church and state, major changes came to the church. Some within the church became rich, and others, poor. Christians became persecutors as former peacemakers went to war. And instead of spending their energies on evangelism, peacemaking, and ministry, enormous amounts of energy were given to constructing great cathedrals in nearly every province of Europe. Constructing these buildings became the center of their work.

Early Anabaptist Christians under the leadership of Menno Simons and others struggled to find common understandings on how to live as the body of Christ in the world. They came to believe that due to the work of the Holy Spirit and their commitment to each other, followers of Jesus could become Christlike and behave in a Christlike way.

The Anabaptist movement was in some ways the charismatic or Holy Spirit movement of the Reformation era. Anabaptist leaders spoke more about the transforming power of the Holy Spirit than did the other reformers. They believed that the Holy Spirit empowered them for discipleship, evangelism, peacemaking, and living the simple life.

The Anabaptist movement was also the evangelistic movement of the sixteenth century. With persistence and passion, key leaders—often at the cost of their lives—went throughout Europe seeking to reconcile people to God and to each other. By the thousands, people came to a personal relationship with Jesus and joined the Anabaptist fellowships that were springing up throughout much of Europe.

In addition, Anabaptists also played key roles in promoting the cause of social justice in their day. Many local groups within the movement were known for their economic sharing and their emphasis on treating people justly. Their leaders and followers addressed many of the economic and social concerns being raised by peasants who were revolting against the dictatorial nature of the feudal system.

Through the study of Scripture and an unwavering commitment to following Jesus in everyday life, Anabaptist Christians came to believe that it was wrong to participate in war. Like the early disciples, they refused to join the military even though Muslim Turks were attempting to invade Europe. Rather than fighting back against their enemies, Anabaptists chose to follow the example of Jesus, who "when he was abused, he did not return abuse; when he suffered, he did not threaten" (1 Pet 2:23).

If you would have asked them, I believe that Menno Simons and most early Anabaptist Christians would have joined the first disciples in saying, "Reconciling people to God and to each other is the center of our work!"

What does this mean for us today? Christians from an Anabaptist perspective believe that:

## 1. We are to help reconcile people to God

Just as God took the initiative in Jesus Christ to reconcile us to himself and to each other, so God is asking us to take the initiative to do our part in reconciling others to him. God has given us the ministry of reconciliation! Being reconciled to God leads to transformed living. Jesus changes the thinking, the friendships, and the behaviors of those who accept him. They become transformed spiritually, mentally, emotionally, physically, socially, and politically. This places them in stark contrast to the world.

## 2. We are to help reconcile people to each other

Forgiveness removes the walls of offense that exist not only between us and God, but also between us and others in the church. Eating the Lord's Supper together becomes a fellowship experience made possible by the forgiveness that we have received from God and each other. Christians are to be a blessing to people of all backgrounds and convictions. When we encounter individuals or groups in conflict with one another, we are to "think reconciliation" rather than judgment.

## 3. We are to be ambassadors of reconciliation in the world

While some Christians say that evangelism is at the center of our work and others place peacemaking there, it might be best to say that "reconciliation is the center of our work!" The purposes of God are "to reconcile to himself all things" through Christ (Col 1:20). It is due to their view of salvation as transformation that today's Anabaptist Christians refuse to be involved in war. Modern warfare trains soldiers to lie, to hate, and to destroy. Transformed people do not do such things. Reconciliation is hard work. It calls us to be willing to give our lives so that people in our world can be reconciled to God, to each other, and even to their enemies. There is no greater joy than to live a reconciled life and to bring others into a reconciled relationship with God and each other.

| MANY CHRISTIANS EMPHASIZE: | ANABAPTIST CHRISTIANS EMPHASIZE: |
|---|---|
| **1. Justification by faith**<br>Many Christians primarily emphasize the holiness of God and the need to be justified through faith in the sacrificial work of Christ. Conversion means being forgiven from sin and destined for heaven. | **1. Transformation of life**<br>Anabaptist Christians tend to emphasize the loving/nurturing nature of God. They desire to be transformed by the Spirit to become Christlike in attitude and action. Conversion means being reconciled to God and empowered to live like Jesus in daily life. |
| **2. Personal salvation**<br>Many Christians tend to think of reconciliation in personal terms. Peacemaking and social action are add-ons rather than essential to the gospel. | **2. Reconciled living**<br>Anabaptists tend to think of reconciliation in both personal and social terms. Evangelism and peacemaking come together in the term reconciliation. |
| **3. Military service**<br>Many Christians obey authority even if it requires actions contrary to the teachings of Jesus and conscience. Some believe in "redemptive violence" and the just war theory. When the government asks them to perform military service, they do so. | **3. Alternative service**<br>Anabaptists obey authority insofar as obedience to Christ will allow. They will refuse orders to participate in violence. Correcting injustices and being reconciled to enemies are important. Alternatives to military service that seek to resolve conflict are strongly encouraged. |

## 14

# The Discipline of Asking, "Where Is God at Work?"

*Ervin R. Stutzman*

> There has never been the slightest doubt in my mind that the God who started this great work in you would keep at it and bring it to a flourishing finish on the very day Christ Jesus appears (Phil 1:6 *The Message*).

> And we know that in all things God works for the good of those who love him, who have been called according to his purpose (Rom 8:28 TNIV).

One of the core tenets of the missional church is the settled conviction that God is at work to bless and redeem the world. A second is that God uses people to accomplish that purpose.

Despite our privileged calling to be God's witnesses and signs of the kingdom, we may be deemed faithful only to the extent that we align our work with God's work.

## Recognizing God's work requires discipline

How then are we to recognize God's work? And once we have seen it, how can we align ourselves with it? That is the focus of this chapter. The title implies that this may be hard work, requiring a certain measure of discipline. Thus, I shall set forth a brief theoretical foundation for noticing the work of God and then provide a variety of examples to illustrate it.

David B. Miller, a professor at Anabaptist Mennonite Biblical Seminary in Elkhart, Indiana, speaks of "tracking God" as one of the core tasks of the missional church. He employs the analogy of hunters, who often rely on clues to help them find wild game. A tuft of hair on a thorn bush, scratches on the side of a tree, a torn leaf—all point to the presence of animals passing through. So, too, God leaves subtle but visible clues.

To use another analogy, we are like detectives, looking for signs, evidence such as the "fingerprints and footsteps" of God. A ruler named Nicodemus once came to Jesus at night, speaking of the signs that pointed to God's enablement. Jesus told his that "the wind blows where it chooses, and you hear the sound of it, but you do not know where it comes from or where it goes. So it is with everyone who is born of the Spirit" (John 3:8).

It is not difficult to understand Jesus' analogy. However, it can be elusive to identify which effects are caused by God, and which are the result of some other cause, such as natural processes or merely human effort. The apostle Paul's confidence that God was at work among the church in Philippi and Rome arose from a deep familiarity with the Scriptures, which often ascribe specific work to God. So perhaps one of the first disciplines in seeing God at work is to familiarize ourselves with the biblical witness to God's work in the world and align our language to fit it. That is, to give God credit where credit is due. This is perhaps done most simply by speaking of God as the subject of an active verb.

## God as the subject of an active verb

Lois Barrett of Anabaptist Mennonite Biblical Seminary discovered that many Christians, including Mennonites, find it difficult to speak of God that way, at least as it relates to their personal lives. She says this proved to be true even when people were invited to respond to a direct question, such as "What has God been doing in your life?"

Consider the following responses from people who experience God as active in their daily lives:

- "Last week, God was with me during a very difficult transition at work."
- "When I was twenty years old, Jesus rescued me from a destructive lifestyle. I've been walking with him ever since."
- "I was at a loss for words, but the Holy Spirit gave me the words to say."
- "God surprised us by bringing a group of Hmong immigrants to our church who have helped us develop a new outreach."
- "The Spirit convicted me about the need for a Sabbath, so I took a day off just to relax."

Barrett says that in response to the question, "What has God been doing in your life?" we are more likely to say things like:

- "Our church started a new outreach to homeless people in the neighborhood."
- "I've been attending a Bible study."
- "We had a great worship service last Sunday."
- "I work as a volunteer for the Mennonite Central Committee sale. We set a new record last Saturday."

There is a significant difference between the two sets of responses. The former depicts God as the actor or initiator in a situation, whereas the latter puts humans in the driver's seat. I'm grateful to Lois for sensitizing me to the difference between these two ways of speaking. Ever since, I've been listening to testimonies at a deeper level all across the church. And I've been reading the Bible with new eyes for the "God sightings" throughout Scripture. Now, when I read verses like Philippians 1:6 or Romans 8:28, a new sense of God's action leaps off the page.

There may be a number of reasons why we as Christians are hesitant to speak of God at work. Perhaps we worry about presumptuousness, giving credit to God for the wrong things. Or perhaps the secularism of our culture has eroded our God consciousness to the point where it makes us hesitant to employ "God language." Or maybe we haven't cultivated the habit of seeing God at work or speaking of it. Whatever the reason for our hesitancy, I hope to address them in this article.

## Biblical writers understood and described God as active in the world

### God's work in creation

It is instructive that the writers and arrangers of Scripture put God as the subject of an active verb in the very first sentence of the Bible—"In the beginning, *God* created the heavens and the earth." That's one reason I value the term *creation care* as a way of speaking about environmental concerns; it emphasizes stewardship—cooperation with God by caring for the planet God created for human enjoyment.

Indeed, numerous psalms picture God as actively involved with the created order, including the animals. In a recent safari in Tanzania, our tour group paused to read much of Psalm 104, which names storks, donkeys, lions, and other wild animals. It declares, "All creatures look to you to give them food at the proper time. When you give it to them, they gather it up; when you open your hand, they are filled with good things . . . may the Lord rejoice in his works" (vv. 27-28, 31). Indeed, the psalms see God's work in the wider cosmos, "The heavens are telling the glory of God, and the firmament proclaims his handiwork" (Ps 19:1).

Many early Anabaptists viewed cultivation of the soil as a primary way to cooperate with God. It rings true with Psalm 104:14-15, "You cause the grass to grow for the cattle, and plants for people to use, to bring forth food from the earth, and wine to gladden the human heart, oil to make the face shine, and bread to strengthen the human heart." A missionary friend in Thailand quoted a farmer in their congregation as saying that the blessing and protection of their small farming operation can be attributed to God alone. They are utterly dependent on him, the Creator of the earth.

That's why I saw God at work behind the scenes at Four Seasons, a food distribution plant in Pennsylvania. First of all, the plant is owned by devout Christians who intend to align their work with God's. They realize that without God's creation of vegetation, there would be nothing for them to distribute. Further, Four Seasons reflects God's work by emphasizing and building on the organic nature of food. In fact, half their produce is certified as organic, a significant percentage increase over the past decade.

Because of their support of organic farmers, Four Seasons has become the distributor of choice in their Pennsylvania area. They also support other local farmers engaged in small-scale production. The closest grower raises produce just across the fence from the plant; he loads his wagon in the field and brings it across the parking lot to the warehouse.

There are indeed many faith-based organizations, such as Mennonite Economic Development Associates and Mennonite Central Committee, who work alongside farmers around the world, helping them feed the world more effectively by increasing their productivity and ability to work with the soil. These ventures cooperate with God's ongoing work in the world, creating abundance and feeding the poor.

## God's work through the Holy Spirit

In a different vein, there are many places in Scripture where we see God at work by the power of the Holy Spirit. Jesus often spoke of the work of the Spirit, as did many writers of Scripture. The story of the early church is particularly inspiring; various anecdotes show the Spirit of God at work. Acts 8:26-40 tells the story of God, via an angel, bringing the evangelist Philip into contact with an Ethiopian official. After Philip explains the way of salvation and baptizes him, he is swept away by the Spirit of the Lord (see vv. 26, 39). While I'm curious what this might have looked like had it been recorded by a video camera, I accept the testimony of the writer that God was the primary agent to bring about these events.

Chuck Neufeld, one of the most missional leaders I know, told the following story about a preaching assignment in an Ethiopian congregation named Berhane Wongel:

> I've got to tell you about what I'm claiming as the miraculous leading of the Spirit. Although I had originally planned to preach on a different passage, as Sunday approached I felt strongly directed to John 14:15-31. My sermon title was, "Because I live, you will live."
>
> The congregation had not been informed of my text or sermon title ahead of time. After the service, two women came running up to me. With great joy

and amazement, one of them shared how she had awakened in the middle of the night and had felt the Holy Spirit direct her to read John 14:15-31. She received that passage as a gift and shared it with the other woman present. Earlier that morning the two of them had claimed the passage as their theme passage for Berhane Wongel. They were totally amazed when they came to church only to hear me preach on their theme passage.

We were all amazed at such obvious and profound leading of the Spirit. I guess we shouldn't be that surprised—we were, after all, promised the Advocate, who would "teach and remind" us of all such things. Thanks be to God.[1]

Chuck does not hesitate to credit the Holy Spirit for "coincidences" like the one he described above, and neither should we. It is also true that some people experience such coincidences much more regularly than others. It seems that the Spirit works this way in people who consciously cultivate a God consciousness, an alert awareness of what God is saying and doing in a given situation.

## God's work through listening prayer

Again, *listening prayer* is a historic spiritual practice of silence and solitude that seeks to hear God's voice in the present. As Keith Yoder says, "In this kind of prayer one does not make requests or vocalize praise and thanksgiving. Rather one simply quiets the noise within and without and listens."[2]

Listening prayer may be one of the best disciplines to help us see where God is at work, or what God seeks to accomplish in and through our lives. Because Keith regularly writes a column entitled "Moments with Father," I asked him to tell me about his practice of listening for God. He noted that one "may begin by meditating on a particular Scripture passage and listening for additional thoughts and personal instruction, or we may ponder a question and wait with dependency and expectancy for God to direct our understanding."

Keith acknowledges that what he writes are "impressions received while listening to God in prayer." He tests these impressions with Scripture and the character of God's Son, by which God has already

---

1. Chuck Neufeld, "Berhane Wongel Ethiopian Evangelical Church Shines Brightly!" *Heart, Soul, Mind & Strength* (December 15, 2010): 1.

2. Keith E. Yoder, email message to author, March 5, 2015.

spoken. He finds the Holy Spirit drawing his attention to passages that have the concept, the wording, or both that come to him as he listens. The following sentences are drawn from one of his meditations. They are written as though God were speaking:

> Even as I wait upon you, I would have you wait upon me. You may wait for a person or event. Wait with me for the coming of the Lord Jesus to catch away his church as a bride. You may wait by a person, to stay as a presence, support or advocate. You may wait by a situation, taking a stand, keeping watch, seeking justice.
>
> You may wait upon a responsibility, guarding a stewardship to which you have been appointed . . . at a time . . . to a place . . . for a purpose. You may wait upon a person, attending to their interests and needs as a servant like a waiter or waitress. Often such waiting involves patient continuance. Often you wait, gathered together with others in a common purpose and hope.
>
> Waiting upon another, as I wait upon you, is to incline toward and accept others—to reach out to be near them, receive them and serve them. Waiting upon another is longing for their presence and strength—to know and be known by them. I long for you to wait upon me.
>
> In essence, waiting is attentive and engaged. Attentive—with one's eye upon others to know their interests, their needs, their nature. Engaged—ready to act on behalf of others, to move toward them. From waiting proceeds favor, mercy, strength and a godly heritage.[3]

Sarah Young illustrates the practice of listening prayer in a popular daily devotional book called *Jesus Calling: Enjoying Peace in His Presence*. Like Keith Yoder, she writes in the first person, as though God were speaking directly to the reader. She gives at least two supporting Scriptures for each day. This form of prayer can be a very helpful guide to seeing God at work in the world.

Waiting, attentiveness, and engagement are all spiritual disciplines that cultivate our ability to see and align ourselves with God's work in the world.

## God's work through reconciliation

Another way we see God's work in the world is through various forms of reconciliation. Indeed, as the apostle Paul says, "In Christ God was

---

3. Keith E. Yoder, "Waiting," *Come: Moments with the Father Devotional* (Leola, PA: Teaching the Word Ministries, 2012), 40–41.

reconciling the world to himself, not counting their trespasses against them, and entrusting the message of reconciliation to us. So we are ambassadors for Christ, since God is making his appeal through us; we entreat you on behalf of Christ, be reconciled to God" (2 Cor 5:19-20).

One of the primary ways we see God's reconciling work is when people surrender themselves to God through faith in Jesus Christ and experience God's peace in their hearts. We also see it in the various ways in which people are reconciled to each other through the work of God in and through us. These two forms of reconciliation may be seen as evangelism and peacemaking.

We can also see God at work in reconciling groups of people who were once alienated from each other. That's one of the reasons I often notice the work of God in the annual meetings of Christian Churches Together, an interdenominational group. In 2013, we met in Austin, Texas. One evening we worshiped at St. Mary's Roman Catholic Cathedral and then walked to the Central Presbyterian Church for a reception. The worship service and the two gathering places were chosen to celebrate a historic moment—the signing of a "common agreement on mutual recognition of baptism" between the Roman Catholic Church and four Reformed communions. I felt like an onlooker, since their agreement doesn't encompass the churches who celebrate believers baptism. Nevertheless, my heart beat with theirs as they shared how God had been at work among them to bring about this remarkable moment. For them it was akin to the way Anabaptists felt in Stuttgart, Germany, when the Lutherans officially asked forgiveness for the persecution of Anabaptists. I credit God for breaking down the figurative walls that had blocked the way to this aspect of Christian unity for nearly five hundred years.

Further, I see the work of God in knocking down the literal wall that once divided East and West Germany. Thousands of Christians prayed for this to happen over time. It seems that God honored their prayer, particularly in the way the wall came down without a single shot being fired. It seems to me that God is at work to some extent wherever alienated peoples, whether they acknowledge God or not, break down the barriers of enmity between them.

I observe this in my own congregation when we pack school kits for Mennonite Central Committee to distribute to children in other parts of the world. For the last couple of years, we have invited people from the Muslim community to join us in this work. This seems appropriate, given that many of these kits go to children who are Muslims. Although we have a different understanding of God, it seems that God is at work among us, enabling our cooperation as we seek to serve the poor together.

## God's work through life reviews

I will mention yet one final discipline as a way of seeing God's work—that of *life review* or hindsight. As we look back over our own lives, we do well to look for the fingerprints and footsteps of God in our lives. The same is true when we attend funerals or memorial ceremonies for Christians who have left a vibrant witness for God.

I have been particularly moved by men and women who reflected a calm demeanor as they faced their final days of life. In every case, their faith in God was a crucial part of their assurance. Recently, I met two people who came to faith in Christ because they observed the peace and assurance with which a Christian friend faced death. It prompts me to think that the close of one's life is perhaps one of the best times to look for indications of God at work.

In the short space of this chapter, it is not possible to trace out all the ways that God is at work in ourselves or others, but some clues are simply too obvious to miss. May God help us all to recognize at least those signs and give thanks to God.

15

# Cultivating a Spirituality That Sustains Missional Engagement

*Stanley W. Green*

## Introduction

If disaffection from religion is one defining aspect of our times, another equally undeniable feature of postmodernity is a burgeoning interest in spirituality. What exactly that means, however, is not always clear. There is a profusion of eclectic along with particular strains of spirituality. This surfeit of varieties of spiritualities leads to great confusion. Indeed, even a clear understanding of what *Christian* spirituality consists of is really elusive. Many helpful attempts have been made to clarify it. The nuances, however, are so broad-ranging that no clear consensus has emerged. Hardly surprising, even less effort has been devoted to elucidating a specifically *missional* Christian spirituality.

## What is Christian spirituality?

During the past dozen years, in a course focused on spirituality for mission at the Overseas Ministries Study Center in New Haven, Connecticut, I have been working with course participants who come from many places around the world to develop a clear formulation of a Christian spirituality that is missionally grounded. With thanks to faithful servants of God in Asia, Africa, Europe, and the Americas, I offer the following as one attempt at describing a peculiarly Christian spirituality:

> We grow in intimacy with God . . .
>     and in alignment with God's purposes for our lives . . .
> through a deepening relationship with Jesus Christ . . .
> while being transformed by the Holy Spirit . . .
> so that our lives reflect the example of Jesus.

While this description of a missional spirituality is a work in progress, I find it helpful for the following reasons. It is not static. It suggests movement and progress. It is dynamic, interactive, and highlights the centrality of relationship that is formed by the will of God as the guiding point of reference. In addition, it is trinitarian and assumes missional action that is informed by the example of Jesus.

Another recent description of a spirituality that is both Christian and resonant with missional promise is offered by Glen Scorgie when he writes: "Spirituality has always been characterized by three dynamics: a relational dynamic (Christ with us), a transformational dynamic (Christ in us), and a vocational dynamic (Christ through us). The Christian life has always involved connecting, becoming and doing. It is about living in relation to God, being transformed by the impulses of his divine life, and actively participating in God's purposes in the world."[1]

What I like about Scorgie's contribution is that it moves us in the direction of a much-needed holistic account of Christian spirituality. It describes a spirituality that engages the totality of our being and encompasses the comprehensive scope of our Christian journey. While Scorgie himself offers us a tripartite description of a Christian spirituality, he suggests that this is not an uncommon way of depicting spirituality and offers us three examples:

---

1. See http://glenscorgie.com/2008/10/16/toward-an-integrated-spirituality/ (accessed 10 November 2014); for more by Glenn Scorgie, see *A Little Guide to Christian Spirituality* (Grand Rapids, MI: Zondervan, 2007).

- Henri Nouwen references three movements that are critical to our spiritual journey: to our innermost self, to our fellow human beings, and to our God.[2]
- Richard Foster organizes his understanding of Christian spirituality also in three movements: inward in pursuit of transformation, upward in search of intimacy with God, and outward in search of ministry.[3]
- David Benner suggests that the spiritual journey involves relationship, transformation, and obedience.[4]

This tripartite framework, I believe, is also congruent with a distinctly Anabaptist missional spirituality described by the following rubrics: *relinquishment*, *embrace*, and *engagement*.

## A distinctly Anabaptist missional spirituality in three movements

### Relinquishment

Mennonites have long spoken of spirituality in terms of *Gelassenheit*—a yieldedness, or a letting go. This construal has to do with a radical openness and submission to God and a commitment to doing God's will. Christian spirituality is about letting go and holding on. We are invited to let go of our own willfulness, our selfish personal ambition, and our private schemes, and to hold on to God. Those are the two focal acts or practices in our quest to know God, to experience God.

This first movement in Christian spirituality, letting go or yieldedness, is also the most difficult. We all have a struggle with letting go of our ambitions. Too often *letting go* sounds like *resignation*, or a resort to apathy. If, however, we can understand this movement in terms of relinquishment rather than resignation, we can more closely approximate the spirit of Jesus' response to God. Relinquishment is not resignation. Yieldedness is not passive submission. Rather, it is a willful act of letting

2. Henri Nouwen, *Reaching Out* (New York: Doubleday, 1975).
3. Richard Foster, *Prayer* (San Francisco: Harper, 1992).
4. David Benner, *The Gift of Being Yourself* (Downers Grove, IL: InterVarsity Press, 2004).

go of our own personal ambition and surrendering everything antitheti-
cal to God's intent for our lives.

Jesus provides guidance in our journey of relinquishment when he
exclaims, "If any want to become my followers, let them deny themselves and take up their cross and follow me. For those who want to
save their life will lose it, and those who lose their life for my sake will
find it" (Matt 16:24-25). Furthermore, he says, "Believe me that I am
in the Father and the Father is in me; but if you do not, then believe
me because of the works themselves. Very truly, I tell you, the one who
believes in me will also do the works that I do, and will do greater
works than these, because I am going to the Father" (John 14:11-12).
In these words there is no sense of resignation on Jesus' part, no hint of
lazy submission, no trace of feeble-minded compliance, no question of
timid acquiescence.

Jesus is at home with his relinquishment. He yields his identity and
ambition to God. As he proclaimed on the cross, "Father, if you are willing, remove this cup from me; yet, not my will but yours be done" (Luke
22:42). All those who would follow Jesus and grow in his likeness must
be willing to take this first step of relinquishment, sometimes called
*conversion* or reorientation.

## Embrace

The second movement in our spiritual journey requires embrace of
God's purposes and destiny for our lives. The word *vocation* is derived
from the Latin word *vocare*, which means "to call." A vocation is a calling—which sets it apart from being merely a job. A calling is not associated with particular jobs or professions, but rather with a particular
relationship between the addressee and the one who calls. In his book
*Let Your Life Speak: Listening for the Voice of Vocation,* Parker Palmer
speaks of the importance of listening inwardly for the call of God. He
writes: "Vocation does not come from willfulness. It comes from listening. . . . Vocation does not mean a goal that I pursue. It means a calling that I hear. . . . It comes from a voice 'in here' calling me to be the
person I was born to be, to fulfill the original selfhood given me at birth
by God."[5]

---

5. Parker Palmer, *Let Your Life Speak* (San Francisco: Jossey-Bass, 1999), 4.

The biblical text suggests that the one who addresses us is the one who created us, the one in whose hands our destiny and every aspect of our lives are held. This destiny may be served in a variety of occupations or roles. God's call is focused specifically on the way that we are called to live or be in the world. Belonging to a particular profession or functioning out of a specific role may spring from this, but not necessarily. In a general sense, *every believer* is called—hence the Mennonite Church USA vision statement, "God calls us to be followers of Jesus . . ." As Anabaptists—and more latterly joined by our ecumenical companions on the missional journey—we affirm that God's call is addressed to *every* believer.

In Isaiah's encounter with God recorded in Isaiah 6 we learn that God has a claim on our lives. The narrative records that the Lord of hosts sat on a throne and his robe filled the whole temple—a temple that reverberated with the sound of the seraphs' acclamation: "Holy, holy, holy is the Lord of hosts; the *whole earth is full* of his glory" (Isa 6:3). That the divine judge filled *both* temple *and* earth gives us a glimpse of the universality of the God's lordship. The realm of God's rule extends not just to a small tribal corner in a closed society, but throughout the whole world where God is sovereign. The overwhelming presence of God establishes the universality of God's claim upon all humanity and over the prophet himself. He knows that he belongs to God, that he is answerable to God, and that God has a claim on his life. He understands in that moment that God is concerned with the whole earth, every nation, every family, and every individual person.

In the case of Samuel, prophetic action is grounded in *God's* voice and direction. We do not call ourselves. It is God who calls us and invites us to act on behalf of the healing and restoration of the world. In Isaiah's encounter we also learn that God's call involves holiness. In that encounter he is overwhelmed with the holiness of God. Within Christian traditions, the word *holy* was first used of God and meant to describe the status of being purposively separated, made distinct and special. Later, influenced by pietism and fundamentalism, it came to be associated with the notion of being untainted or undefiled. The short-form code for holiness in the church of my conversion was no smoking, no drinking, no gambling, and no dancing! The accent was placed on the negative, on being separate and detached—"in the world but not of the world."

Lamentably, for many in the Anabaptist stream this conviction led to an unhealthy disengagement, even isolation—so that for many Mennonite communities the more apt descriptor toward the end of the twentieth century became "of the world, but not in it." I find it extremely interesting that the passage in Isaiah suggests that holiness is not for the sake of purity or separation for its own sake. Holiness does not set us up to be judges of others who fall short—something that the Pharisees of Jesus' day reveled in. Neither does it give us permission to be puffed up with pride when we consider others' shortcomings. Holiness, Isaiah 6 suggests, is for the sake of engagement. The encounter makes it clear that the calling of God always proceeds from God's grace toward those who are undone by their wrong choices and faithlessness. The call, therefore, as an invitation to holiness, is not a call *out* of the world but *into* it. It is a call to bear witness in the world to God's purpose in Jesus Christ to restore all of creation to God's good purposes of healing and hope.

Importantly then, we need to remember that God's calling for our lives goes way beyond what we *do*. It is all about what *God* chooses to do, to which we bear witness. All people are called to be someone and to do certain things—it is part and parcel of human existence. Discovering and becoming who we are supposed to be and what we are meant to do in the world is a lifelong process of growth and change. In our culture's preoccupation with success and celebrity, it is easy to approach our calling in a way that is not much more than those two things—success and celebrity—covered by a thin veneer of spirituality. Parker Palmer, however, puts it this way:

> What God requires of those who call on God's name is responsive servanthood. God wishes to act in and through us. . . . We are not primarily responsible for shrewd analysis of problems, for strategic selection of means, for maximizing the chances of success. We are primarily responsible for turning to God, for attempting to know and do God's will. That well may lead us into actions which are not shrewd, strategic, or successful, as the life of Jesus

suggests. But as Jesus' life demonstrates, human action which is faithful to God's will have transforming effect.[6]

In other words, it is not about us, but about God and God's purposes. At the conclusion of Christopher Wright's magisterial book *The Mission of God*, he says, "I may wonder what kind of mission God has for *me*, when I should ask what kind of me God wants for *his* mission."[7]

## Engagement

If relinquishment and embrace are two important ways of being conformed to the image of God for our lives, then *Nachfolge*—following Christ, or engagement in God's mission as exemplified by Christ—is the third essential movement in an Anabaptist spirituality. Mennonites have consistently refused to separate spirituality from ethics, reflection from action, being from doing. It is indeed a telling indicator that our *Confession of Faith* places spirituality in the section on discipleship.

Christian spirituality is more than being open to *intimacy* with God. It is also doing the *will* of God. One of the early Anabaptist reformers, a mystic by the name of Hans Denck, put it this way, "To know God is to follow Christ daily in life." There is a transforming kind of spirituality being spoken of here that cares little about orthodox confessions, or the technical apparatus of churchly forms. The center to which contemplation and yieldedness draws us does not exist as something separate from our physical, emotional, intellectual, and social life. Christian spirituality can never be restricted to the individual quest, the private closet of prayer, the inner life alone. Jesus' life was animated by a spirituality of action.

Sadly, too many postmodern pursuers of spiritual fulfillment take their cues from popular culture. These seekers too often yearn for an experience of God in Christ without the costly discipleship that true spirituality requires. Turning the other cheek, going the second mile, loving our enemies, defending the cause of the marginalized, working for economic justice in the world, battling the scourge of global hunger are all evidence of our spiritual growth and formation.

---

6. Parker Palmer, *The Company of Strangers: Christians and the Renewal of America's Public Life* (New York: Crossroads Publishing Company, 1983), 139.
7. Christopher Wright, *The Mission of God: Unlocking the Bible's Grand Narrative*, 6th ed. (Downers Grove, IL: IVP Academic, 2006), 534.

## Conclusion

In light of these three characteristic movements that inhere in the spirituality described above, it seems clear that there is no distinction between an Anabaptist and a missional spirituality—nor should there be, if spirituality is about God's purposes for our lives and for the world.

It hardly does justice to an important Anabaptist conviction, even assumption, but limitations of space here require that I simply reiterate a common belief regarding the context of spiritual growth and formation. Anabaptists do not dismiss the need for solitude as essential to the process of spiritual development. Critical, however, to an Anabaptist understanding of our spiritual pilgrimage is the vital, even indispensable, role of community. Anabaptists assume the need for mutual accountability, encouragement, and guidance that community provides. Indeed, Anabaptists believe that God's voice is often heard, and importantly tested, in the context of community. It is through *relinquishment*, *embrace*, and *engagement*—in the context of the committed community—that we open ourselves to becoming what God intends us to be.

**16**

# Does Your Church "Smell" Like Mission? SR

*James R. Krabill*

West Africans are probably right. Mealtimes are not meant for talking, but for eating. If something needs to be said, it can wait until the meal is over. Had I followed such advice and talked less at the table, I would likely not have gotten myself in trouble. Let me explain.

It all began over lunch at an Indiana-Michigan Mennonite Conference ministers and elders' meeting when someone asked me to summarize what I was discovering in my many church visits about the status of missional engagement in the congregations of our area conference. That is when, instead of continuing to eat like I should have, I opened my mouth and commented, "It doesn't take long when I visit a church to determine how important mission is to the life of the congregation. Some churches just 'smell like missions,'" I said, "and some don't."

## So what does a mission-minded congregation "smell" like?

I should have anticipated the next question. "So what does a mission-focused congregation 'smell' like?" Unfortunately, I'm not sure I know. Have you ever tried to describe to someone what, say, pizza smells like?

Most of us would be hard-pressed to do that effectively. Yet none of us would have much difficulty in recognizing the particular odor of pizza when it hits our nose.

Perhaps we should start by stating the case negatively. What kind of congregation does not smell like mission? Some years ago, I was invited to a church to speak about Mennonite Mission Network's Bible teaching ministry with African-initiated churches in West Africa. Following the service, a high school senior approached me about short-term mission opportunities that would permit him to make use of the French language he had been studying in school. I suggested several possibilities and then added that he might want to consider a one-year exchange program in France available at that time with MCC.[1] He looked at me with a blank face and asked, "What's MCC?"

I wasn't sure how to respond. Upon further questioning, I discovered that the young fellow had been attending this congregation since seventh grade—a full six years. I have no way of knowing how regularly the chap attended or whether he listened carefully when he did. But I cite this case as one illustration where the congregational "odors of mission" might well have been a great deal stronger!

## Congregations generally fall into one of four categories

I find that the congregations I visit generally fall into one of four categories:

← INGROWN                                            OUTREACHING →

| 1 | 2 | 3 | 4 |
|---|---|---|---|
| little mission emphasis | occasional mission projects | regular missions program, but one among many | missions as key organizing factor |

---

1. MCC is the acronym for Mennonite Central Committee, which is a worldwide ministry of Anabaptist churches that shares God's love and compassion for all in the name of Christ by responding to basic human needs and working for peace and justice.

## 1. Little emphasis

First, there are those churches where mission emphasis is so minimal that to speak of local outreach or, even worse, of global ministries, feels like teaching people a foreign language. The mission visitor is viewed in such instances as an outside intruder, someone who temporarily hijacks the congregation from being about its ordinary preoccupations of introspection and maintenance. The smell of mission is indeed a rare and rather exotic experience in such settings.

## 2. Occasional projects

Then there are those churches that engage in sporadic mission projects, perhaps two or three a year, such as providing special music at a local rescue mission, baking pies for the relief sale, or inviting neighborhood children to vacation Bible school. Such projects are well-intentioned, but in the end short-lived. There is no continuity between flings, no sense of how these mini-excursions fit into the overall itinerary of where the congregation is going. This is mission by occasional whiffs.

## 3. Regular, but one among many

Third are those congregations for whom missions has become a regular, ongoing program of the church. The missions committee is the institutionalized form of that program. Missional activity is, in this instance, one of several or perhaps even many preoccupations of the congregation, existing independently but alongside the kids' club, the sewing circle, and the softball league. Each receives fair and equitable airtime Sunday morning, in the weekly bulletin, and during church business meetings.

It is particularly important in such settings not to miss the mission committee's periodic report, since this is one's principal source for knowing what the church is doing in the area of missions. The aroma of missions may be quite strong in such congregations, but there are so many competing and intermingling smells that the particular fragrance that missions has to offer is frequently diluted and perhaps even lost altogether in the collective scents being emitted.

## 4. Primary identity and central organizing factor

The fourth category is that of congregations who understand their participation in God's mission as core to their identity. For them, missional reflection and activity are *the* central organizing factors for all aspects of local body life. Certainly there are greeters, worship leaders, youth sponsors, and Christian educators within the congregation, but each from their position of responsibility sees it as his or her task to participate somehow in shaping missional identity within the faith community and extending Christ's love to people outside the community in the neighborhood and around the globe.

Congregations that smell this strongly of mission will give missional formation and motivation a high priority in the classroom, in Sunday school openings, in the church's worship patterns, in the narthex, in the library, in discussions about budget, and in the general atmosphere that characterizes the quality of human relationships and pervades every aspect of life within their faith community.

## Pick a number and explain why

I have found it an interesting exercise over the years to ask small groups or Sunday school classes in churches I have visited to situate their own congregation on the continuum from "ingrown" to "outreaching" by picking a number between one and four describing their congregation, where: (1) represents "little mission emphasis;" (2) "occasional mission projects;" (3) "regular missions program, but only one among many;" and (4) "mission is the key organizing factor" for the congregation.

Discussing, then, the small groups' findings with other members of their faith community has proven equally fruitful in generating a lively debate about missional awareness and involvement in the life of the congregation. Very few people, I find, choose to rate their congregations as either "ones" or "fours." Most select options in between. And most express dissatisfaction about being there.

A wide range of reasons are usually given to explain why a congregation might be stuck at a certain place. Do any of these sound familiar?

- *Overcommitment.* "Everyone is already too busy. There's no way we could do more."
- *Kinship.* "We can't seem to make new people really feel at home in our church family."
- *Leadership.* "It's not a high priority on our pastor's 'to-do' list."

- *Conflicts*. "We've got lots of problems in our congregation that need attention before we can even begin to think about reaching out to others."
- *Timidity*. "Most people in our church don't feel comfortable sharing their faith."
- *Finances*. "Within two years we will have paid off our debts on the new facility we've built. Then we're going to get serious about missions."
- *Worship*. "There's nothing about our Sunday morning service that would attract new people and keep them for long."
- *Security*. "I'm not sure we really want any new faces in church. Most of us like it cozy and comfortable the way it is."
- *Vision*. "We're great at supporting mission work overseas, but we have no vision for our own local community."
- *Ill-equipped*. "We really don't spend any time in our church helping members to understand the world in which they live and training them to build bridges from the gospel to people in the culture around them."
- *Dysfunction*. "We do have a missions committee, but it's not very active right now."
- *Fear*. "It's easy to just let a few people do missions for the rest of us. Most of us aren't ready to think of ourselves as 'missionaries'—at school, on the job, or in the neighborhood."
- *Discouragement*. "We've tried all the programs out there. Nothing seems to work for us."

## When all the programs fail, try . . . *IMAGINATION!*

Suppose we took a different approach to the problem. Rather than forever citing the litany of obstacles and excuses we feel and face in our congregations on this issue, what would happen if we spent more time imagining what kind of congregations we would like to become?

Life's most important changes happen when people begin to dream dreams, when they become inspired and motivated by new possibilities, by what gets them excited and gives them energy. The consequence of having no vision, the Scriptures tell us, causes people to "cast off restraint" (Prov 29:18) and leads them to anarchy rather than shared purpose.

Jesus demonstrated an enormous capacity to capture people's imaginations. For representing, as he did, God's comprehensive plan of salvation for the world, he spoke remarkably little about the programmatic specifics of that plan for personal and social change. Rather, through short stories and word pictures, he asked people to imagine a new life—one lived in close relationship with God and with others.

What if we were to follow Jesus' lead and begin imagining how that might look for our life together as God's people? Close your eyes for a moment. And give it a try!

- Imagine what your church would be like if its entire life and identity were consumed by finding ways to mirror God's love—as taught and modeled by Jesus—in your neighborhood or through your natural networks and relationships. Imagine how that might begin to alter your current congregational activities and priorities.

- Imagine your church, filled with God's Spirit, being of one mind and one body as it brings its life into line with God's great dream of restoring your neighborhood and setting things right with the world.

- Imagine your church—and every one of its members without exception—fully committed to seeing God's dream become a reality.

- Imagine your church having one central objective for every Sunday school session, small group gathering, and committee meeting it sponsored—to equip its members for living and sharing more effectively God's love in the world.

- Imagine your church joyfully recognizing and putting to full use the particular gifts and capacities God has given you. And imagine yourself desiring nothing more in life than to develop those gifts for the purpose of offering them back to God in passionate, lifelong witness and service to others.

- Imagine your church being so welcoming of sinners, so filled with compassion for the lost, the last, and the least, that word of your love and care spread across the street, throughout your neighborhood, and even around the world.

- Imagine your church designing and conducting worship experiences that celebrate what God is doing in your neighborhood and around the world, and that regularly invite each member to explore and expand their participation in these God-inspired initiatives.
- Imagine your church being committed to daily intercessory prayer for your neighbors, classmates, colleagues, and friends.
- Imagine your church being sought out by those experiencing injustice, because you have become known for insisting on fair and just relationships.
- Imagine your church seriously searching the Scriptures in a vibrant new way, recognizing them as a blueprint for creative engagement with the seductive forces and influences of the surrounding culture and society.
- Imagine your church being the best window your neighbors have into the life God intended. And imagine that what they saw pleased both them and God.
- Imagine your church so in touch with neighborhood ways of understanding and experiencing life that you begin to reach people's deepest hurts and needs.
- Imagine your church making headlines for its firm stand on loving enemies, offering healing to the broken, and extending open arms to people of diverse racial and cultural backgrounds. And imagine all of this happening to such an extent that you were required to risk your security as a community for what you believed and practiced.
- Imagine going to lunch with the person in your church you dislike the most. And over lunch God's reconciliation allows the two of you to become friends. And others in your church are inspired to follow your lead. And the reconciliation and wholeness your church experiences spill out the front doors, across the street, and into your entire neighborhood. And your church becomes known throughout your community as a place for restoration and wholeness.
- Imagine learning that other churches are experiencing new life in Christ just as you are. That a neighboring congregation shares its

experience with your church. And you find that both of you are catching the vision to extend your new-life experiences beyond your own neighborhoods. And a third church, then a fourth, links with you. And in collaboration with this community of churches and Mennonite Mission Network you begin calling out people from among you to share God's mission in neighborhoods both near and far. And together, you connect with other churches in still other places to support their sharing new life in their neighborhoods and beyond.

Now open your eyes. You're back in the real world. Back wishing, perhaps, you were "there," not "here." Back wondering what practical next steps your church could take toward becoming a more missional people—a people reconciled to God and, in turn, invited by God to demonstrate and proclaim that reconciliation to others (2 Cor 5:17-20).

## From the real world to the "dream world" . . . and back again

As you think back on the imagining exercise you've just completed, what words or phrases jump out at you? What ideas or concepts strike you as particularly important for understanding how the church might become more missional in its primary identity, purpose, and activity? Here are a few starter concepts that seem significant to me:

- God's great dream of "setting things right with the world"
- Mission as the heartbeat of congregational life
- Involvement of every member
- Shoulder-tapping
- Gift-affirming
- Member-equipping
- Bathed in prayer
- Rooted in Scripture
- Focused on Jesus
- Filled with the Spirit
- Holistic gospel—reconciliation, healing, and justice
- New life in Christ
- Racial and cultural diversity

- Passion for the lost, last, and least
- Relational in approach
- Reaching people's deepest hurts and needs
- In tune with the neighborhood
- In touch with larger social, cultural, and global trends
- Worship that celebrates God's dream becoming reality
- Prophetic witness
- Risk-taking
- Being, doing, and proclaiming held together
- Church as mirror of God's love
- Church as window into the life God desires for all
- Extending new-life experiences
- Sharing stories
- Catching vision
- Inviting participation
- Combining resources
- Networking
- Collaboration
- Beginning at home
- Spilling out the front door
- In neighborhoods near and far
- "Reaching from across the street, all through the marketplaces to around the world"

What an incredible agenda! Sounds a bit overwhelming, to put it mildly. There is good news, however. And that is that most congregations are already somewhere down the path on a journey toward missional faithfulness. Few, as we noted earlier, are actually starting from ground zero. Some of the above list—perhaps even much of it—is already deeply rooted in their consciousness and reflected at various points in their body life, congregational vision, and current activities.

If you are looking for a tidy checklist by which to assess, once and for all, the success of your congregation in becoming a bona fide, fully accredited, card-carrying missional church, you may be in for some disappointment and frustration. I can't provide you with such a list and neither can anyone else. On the other hand, I can't really describe for you what pizza smells like either. But, rest assured, if its odor drifted my way, I would know it in an instant. And so would you.

## A few thoughts to consider on the road to becoming a missional church

If you are fully satisfied with the level of mission focus and fervor present within your congregation, please let me know about it. I'd consider changing zip codes in order to experience it for myself. In the meantime, most of us are still somewhere on the way—seeking God's face, striving to align our spirit with God's Spirit and our best human efforts with God's divine activity. As we do so, here are a few points to consider along the way:

### 1. It's important to begin at . . . the beginning

I didn't invent the idea of "mission." Neither did you. Nor did the church. It was God who started it all. The God of the Bible is, above all, a missionary God. It was God, the Scriptures tell us, who took the initiative to pursue us, coming into our world, seeking, wooing, calling, restoring. It was God who sent Jesus, through whom all things in the universe are to be "summed up" and "brought together." There is only one mission, and it is God's. This means there are a number of things we will want to know more about:

- What is the nature of this divine mission effort? And what are its characteristics?
- How and where has God been at work throughout history, in our neighborhood, around the world?
- In what ways can we align ourselves with this mission initiative and participate in what God is already doing?

### 2. Smelly fishermen, ex-prostitutes, and tax collectors don't make much sense, but then . . . this whole thing wasn't our idea to begin with

Amazingly, and for some unexplainable reason, God has chosen the church—sinner folk who were and forever will be the undeserving recipients of God's grace and peace in their own broken lives—to be the primary instruments through whom that same grace and peace is extended to others. "By you all the families of the earth shall bless themselves," God told Abraham and Sarah. This is the principal reason why God's people were called out in the first place and for which the twenty-first-century body of Christ continues to exist—to participate in God's mission in the world. If this is true, then we will find ourselves constantly asking questions like these:

- Are we as God's people being faithful to our primary calling?
- In what activities are we engaged—as wholesome and well-intentioned as they might be—that actually distract us and dilute our focus?
- How much time do we spend in prayerful discernment as a faith community, seeking God's deepest desire for our life together, our neighborhood, and our world?

### 3. How you phrase the question makes all the difference

So which way is it? Does God's church need a mission? Or does God's mission need a church? Hmmm?!? The implications of how one answers this question can be enormous. Both statements no doubt contain elements of truth. Reflect on each for several minutes and see what a difference it begins to make.

- Who "owns" the mission in each formulation?
- What is God's role in each case? And what is the church's task?
- Which statement best describes your own view of mission and that of your congregation?

### 4. It may be more about redefining church than tweaking our idea of mission

Some people know how to say things to make you think. "The church that is not evangelizing . . . does not truly believe the gospel" (Wilbert Shenk).

Ouch! How about this one: "A church which is not an evangelizing church is either not yet or no longer the church, or only a dead church—itself in need of renewal by evangelization" (Karl Barth). Paul Dietterich has this to say: "The church is not an end in itself. Its only reason for being is to declare God's wonderful deeds." And Emil Brunner: "The church exists by mission, just as fire exists by burning."

- Do any—or all—of these statements strike you as true?
- How do the convictions expressed here resonate with what you receive as a regular diet in the life of your congregation?
- What difference would it make if the church took more of this to heart and actually ordered its life around such ideas?

## 5. Being more missional might actually mean doing fewer things

There is a Latin American proverb that says, "If you don't know where you're coming from, and you don't know where you're going, then any bus will do." Some congregations are clearly riding too many buses! What they need is not more *flurry*, but more *focus*. Becoming disciplined about being a missional church can provide just such a focus. Suddenly, instead of asking, "How many programs *can* we do?" the question becomes, "Which specific activity *must* we do in light of our congregational priority and commitment to being God's missional people in this time and place?"

- To what part of God's mission in your neighborhood or beyond is your congregation specifically called?
- What current congregational activities begin to pale in importance, or fade altogether, in light of these commitments?
- What discernment process do you have in place to continue testing and prioritizing new ministry opportunities that come your way?

## 6. Warning! The term *missionary* is currently under reconstruction!

Some congregations define the level of their mission-mindedness by the number of full-time mission workers they send forth from their ranks to ministry locations around the world. There is no doubt that missional congregations will be sending bodies. But more importantly, such congregations will begin to understand their entire body as being sent. "As the Father has sent me," Jesus tells his disciples, old and new, "so I send you" (John 20:21).

- Does every member of your congregation have a sense of being sent by God into the work world, the marketplace, the neighborhood in which they live?
- What difference would it make if they did?
- In what ways does your congregation inspire and equip its members for their daily mission assignments?

## 7. It'll require a stretch getting from "across the street to around the world"

Most congregations tend to focus either on local community involvement or on mission endeavors in some far-off, distant land. The first of these can lead to shortsightedness and provincialism; the second, to avoidance and denial of needs and opportunities God has placed in our own backyards. Healthy congregations, I believe, work at building mission awareness and involvement at multiple levels—in the neighborhood ("Jerusalem"), through participating in some kind of regional initiative ("Judea and Samaria"), and by connecting in one way or another with God's people in mission worldwide ("to the ends of the earth"). This follows the pattern Jesus outlined for his disciples at the end of his earthly ministry (Acts 1:8).

- Where is most of the energy for mission in your congregation: local, regional, or international?
- *Shortsightedness, provincialism, avoidance, denial*—do any of these terms describe your situation?
- What next steps would you need to take as a congregation to become more fully engaged in God's mission, "reaching from across the street to around the world?"

## 8. This is about much more than mission agencies and outreach committees

When I think back on the people who have shaped my views of mission over the years, I realize just what a diverse group of folks it is. My parents were clearly instrumental, but many others would have to be mentioned as well—a sixth-grade Sunday school teacher, a summer camp director, a youth minister intern, several close friends, my college campus pastor . . . and this is only a beginning. To inspire and train the whole church for participation in God's mission, it takes the *whole church*, friends and family, teachers and mentors, professors and preachers, churchwide institutions and their leaders.

- Who are the people in your life who have most encouraged your participation in God's mission?
- Whom have you, in turn, mentored along the way?
- In what ways could your congregation work at this more intentionally, rather than assuming it must just somehow be happening?

## 9. Guess what? We're not inventing the wheel!

It's not as if we have no clue about what a missional church might look like. For starters, there is Jesus, teaching, preaching, and healing his way through Galilee (Matt 9:35) and giving us the clearest picture ever of what it means to be about God's purposes in the world. The earliest disciples and faithful believers throughout church history embraced the challenge of continuing the work of Jesus in their own cultural settings and historical contexts. The stories of past witnesses are indeed plentiful. Yet the hard work of discerning how to be faithful in our own time and place still lies ahead.

- What do you think are the unique challenges the church will face in participating in God's mission in the twenty-first century?
- How much time does your congregation devote to studying and understanding North American culture in preparation for this formidable task?
- What lessons can we learn from God's people in Scripture and throughout history that might prove helpful to us in demonstrating and proclaiming the good news of Jesus today?

## 10. Some people outside North America know more about all this than we do

Much of the church's numerical growth in recent years has taken place in what we refer to as the Global South—Africa, Asia/Pacific, and Caribbean/Central and South America. The Ethiopian Meserete Kristos Church, for example, has welcomed 250,000 new members into the Mennonite family of faith since 1980. While there are, no doubt, many reasons for MKC's phenomenal growth, much can be contributed to a *clear vision* and a *focused plan*. The vision has been to place mission at the heart of the church's life. And the plan, to organize every part of the church—be it Bible schools, semi-missionaries, youth ministries, women's groups, or relief and development programs—around achieving the one common goal of "glorifying the Almighty God" and "serving the whole person" by "carrying out the Great Commission of Jesus Christ in homeland and abroad" and "providing both spiritual and physical assistance to the needy" (MKC brochure).

- In what ways does your congregation build awareness among its members of what God is doing through the church around the world?
- What do you believe are the key learnings we should be gleaning from missional communities of faith in other parts of the world?
- Would your congregation be ready to host an African, Asian, or Latin American missionary to assist you in reaching your neighborhood for Christ?

## And now, it's your turn!

If you had to define the term *missional church*, how would you do it? Here are a few examples to get you started:

A missional church is . . .

- *all* of God's people demonstrating and proclaiming
     *all* of God's gospel throughout
          *all* of God's world
- a church that understands its purpose in light of God's invitation to participate in aligning all human activity with the intentions of God
- ordinary people
     living extraordinary lives
          characterized by a hunger for spiritual growth
               seeking accountability to others in community
                    possessing a heart for the lost, last, and least
                         passionate about justice and righteousness

# My definition of a "missional church"

_____

_____

_____

_____

_____

_____

_____

_____

_____

_____

_____

_____

_____

_____

# 17

# Reading the Bible through a Missional Lens

*Michele Hershberger*

One day I asked students in my first-year Bible class to encapsulate the story of the Bible in three words. I received some creative, thoughtful—and true—sentences. Some of my favorites included "God is love," "Trust and obey," and "Jesus is Lord." But the three-word sentence I liked best was this: "God comes down."

God comes down. This is better than "God is love," because it is the active demonstration of that love. We "trust and obey" because of what God has done and is doing. And how do we obey and make Jesus Lord? By reaching out ourselves. I don't mean that we can be the incarnation in the same miraculous way Jesus was, but the Bible is full of stories where God's people helped connect others to God. God coming to us in human form to live among us and die for us—the missio Dei— and our continuation of that process is the biblical narrative in three words. Try to think of a Bible story that doesn't, in some way, show God reaching out to humankind. Granted, there are some stories that seem obscure, but even in these Scriptures, there is a subtle effort to reconcile a broken relationship, to heal the wounds of sin. God is working to bring shalom, and God does this in every biblical story by creating—or recreating—the People of God, a people out of all peoples. So if I can cheat on my own rules, I would summarize the whole biblical narrative in this way: God comes down to create out of all peoples a people whose purpose is to (wait for it) . . . do the same thing!

Being missional is not just *one* of the major themes of the Bible. It is *the* story. As Christopher J. Wright says, "It is not enough, however, just to say that mission has a solid biblical foundation, we also need to see that the Bible has its roots in mission. That is, the Bible is the product of God's engagement through God's people in God's world for God's ultimate purposes for the nations and the world . . . so from beginning to end, the Bible is 'mission,' by its very existence and by its comprehensive message. Mission then has to be a prime hermeneutical key for our own Bible reading and teaching."[1]

My reflections here will seek to show how the Bible has its roots in mission. I will illustrate the central tension between our missional calling and our call to be a particular people and explain why this lens "has to be a prime hermeneutical key."

## The story as seen through a missional lens

Several dominant threads weave through a missional reading of the Bible. First, this kind of reading notices that God is at work in every story trying to heal the broken relationships sin causes. And in every story, God does this through the creation of a people. This people group is unique in that it is voluntarily committed to God and each other through covenant, bonded together by the God's initiative of grace, open to everyone who is willing to follow Yahweh and be committed to helping God bring shalom. Some stories, especially in the Old Testament, seem void of shalom building, but the people of God could—and can—choose not to cooperate with God. Regardless of the messy stories, God is and remains missional. The Bible is the story of God reaching out over and over again.

Second, a missional lens highlights the incarnation as the most profound way that God came down. God moves into the neighborhood.

---

1. Christopher J. Wright, "Whose World? Whose Mission?" www.neac.info/talks/211145cw.pdf, as found in http://setsnservice.files.wordpress.com/2009/08/reading-the-bible-missionally-beta-version2.pdf.

The Word dwelt among us and we beheld his glory (John 1). We are missional primarily because God came down. Yet a true missional focus doesn't stop there. We still live in a sinful world. We still have to choose whether or not to become part of the People of God and work with Jesus to bring healing and invite others into God's People.

Third, a missional lens understands the church as a people out of all peoples. From Genesis 12:3b, where Abraham is chosen so that all the families of the earth may be blessed, through the book of Revelation, where people from every tribe worship the Lamb (Rev 5), the church is ethnically diverse and open to all those who will follow Jesus.

Fourth, those who read the Bible through the missional lens will see themselves also as sent, every day, in all of life. "As the Father has sent me, even so I send you" (John 20:21). The church is not a building, but a people who live differently. And we are missional in the same way God is missional. The method is integral to the message. We clearly offer a way to freedom from sin, the way of shalom, and we offer this shalom in a respectful, loving, shalom way.

## The missional lens of the Old Testament

After the first eleven chapters in Genesis where the author highlights the creation of the physical world, Genesis 12 opens a new "chapter" with the promise of another creation—the People of God. In a very real sense, the rest of the narrative is the story of God creating this people out of all peoples, a radical community that is so countercultural in its justice and love that through it, God brings this same shalom to the world.

God begins by choosing Abraham and Sarah. In this very action, God seems to both choose a peculiar people and also reach out to all peoples. Genesis 12:3 reads, "I will bless those who bless you, and the one who curses you I will curse; and in you all the families of the earth will be blessed." God's covenant people were singled out for blessing and also chosen to bless all others.

The people of God were not formally birthed, however, until the Red Sea event. It took three hundred years and four generations of "family preparation" and then the labor pains of slavery in Egypt to get them ready. But the Red Sea was so formative that they changed from being mere strangers to a people. This group was peculiar in that they trusted

Yahweh to do the impossible—free them from slavery—and they obeyed by doing something strange—putting the blood of an innocent lamb on their doors. They were inclusive—the first blush of a missional call—in that the offer to trust and obey came to all the slaves, an ethnically diverse group (Exod 12:38). God "came down" again to Moses on Mount Sinai and there God began the second delivery or salvation from slavery, a salvation from the bondage of sin.

God continues to come down in the form of judges and prophets. And the people struggled to decide whether or not they had been chosen as God's favorites or chosen for a mission. Why did they have God's covenantal blessings and obligations, they wondered? Was it because of their blood ties to Abraham? Because of certain rituals such as circumcision? And who could join God's people? Just anyone? What were the requirements for such inclusion?

Before the monarchy other people groups did join the Israelites—Kenites, Gibeonites, Ruth the Moabitess—and obeying Yahweh was the only criterion, although in many cases this meant significant worldview shifts and sacrificial actions such as circumcision. At other times, both pre- and post-monarchy, the people understood God's call as "kill all the Canaanites," a mandate that doesn't seem to square with Abraham's call to bless all families of the earth. Did the people misunderstand God's directives or was the threat of syncretism so strong that entire people groups had to be eliminated?

By the time of the monarchy, the missional identity was growing faint in light of a geographic and nation-state identity. Now God's people were defined primarily by their status as citizens living on the right landmass, while others were marginalized because they didn't have those things. God only lived in the land of Israel, and eventually, God was completely domesticated inside the temple. A fine example of this understanding of a geographical God comes through the story of Naaman the Syrian, who, after being healed of leprosy, wants to take back home some of the Israelite dirt he is standing on so that he can worship the Israelite God. The Lord was also a nation-state God, blessing the king and his citizens regardless of their wayward behavior. The prophets spoke against such false confidence, to no avail (Jer 7).

The people of Judah mistakenly thought they had a guarantee of God's blessings, as God's favorites. God saw their ill-directed confidence and handed them over to the Babylonians, who promptly led them into exile. Now left without temple, king, or land, Judah had to question what it meant to be God's chosen people, what it meant to live without any external guarantee of God's blessing. The exile was painful, but it was also a gift in that they could now reenvision themselves as chosen by God for mission.

But Judah did not take advantage of this second chance to be missional. Ezra, a scribe returning from exile in Babylonia, came back to Jerusalem and discovered that the 1 percent who had remained there had married foreign spouses. He pulled out his beard and tore his robes in repentance for a sinful people. He had concerns that these foreigners would dilute the faith and cause syncretism, a justifiable threat given earlier stories where idolatry brought ruin to the Israelites.

On the other hand, Ezra forgot the stories where God and God's people reached out to others, such as the rescue of an ethnically diverse group out of Egypt and other people groups joining in the wilderness and during the infiltration of Canaan. Through the prophets, God brought healing to foreigners, such as the widow of Zarephath and Naaman the Syrian. Should Ezra have given the foreign spouses an opportunity to become followers of Yahweh before dismissing them on the basis of their ethnicity? The rest of the narrative, particularly the story of Jesus, begs this question.

The story of Jonah can serve as a case study. Seen by many scholars as an allegorical sermon directed at the returnees from Babylon,[2] Jonah represents the majority of Jews who didn't want God to bless every family on earth through them. God sent Jonah to Nineveh to bring a message of judgment for their wickedness. As the capital of Assyria, Nineveh symbolized the worst type of enemy. Jonah instead fled to Tarshish via the sea in an attempt to escape his calling. The pagan sailors, at first so compassionate toward Jonah that they didn't want to throw him overboard despite their own peril, finally did hurl him over and Jonah was swallowed by a large fish. The fish, representing Babylon, held him for

2. Bernhard W. Anderson, Steven Bishop, and Judith H. Newman, *Understanding the Old Testament*, 5th ed. (Upper Saddle River, NJ: Pearson Education, 2007), 554.

three days and then hurled him out at Nineveh with a second chance for him to do his original mission.

Surprisingly, Nineveh repented, God granted them mercy—and Jonah was upset. Apparently, he did not believe Nineveh deserved this outlandish display of God's grace nor was he familiar with the theology of Micah 6:8, where God's people are called to "love kindness," or to rejoice when people get better than what they deserve. Like the returnees from Babylon, Jonah had a second chance to redefine his identity as one chosen for a mission, and like the returnees, he failed. At the story's end, Jonah was more upset about a bush than the potential death of a city, and God has a revealing rhetorical question: "And should I not be concerned about Nineveh, that great city, in which there are more than a hundred and twenty thousand persons who do not know their right hand from their left . . . ?" (Jon 4:11).

## The missional lens of the New Testament

But what if Jonah and Ezra were right? How did Jesus live with the tension of syncretism and inclusivity? In Jesus we see God's continued action to create a people chosen for mission. Jesus unsettled the worldview of the disciples many times. He ate with sinners and tax collectors (Matt 9:9-13). He intentionally walked through Samaria, a clear cultural miscue for a Torah-observant Jew wishing to avoid unclean Samaritans.[3] Then he added injury to insult by speaking to a Samaritan woman and, worse, asking her for a drink of water (John 4). In response, she became the first evangelist, running back to her village with news of the Messiah.

Jesus praised the faith of a Roman centurion and healed his slave (Luke 7:1-10). Further, Jesus cast his own identity in a missional lens. He visited the Nazareth synagogue as the Torah reader for the day (Luke 4:16-30) and surprised his hometown crowd first by claiming to be Messiah, but even more so by his clear statement against ethnocentrism (Luke 4:25-27). Jesus read from Isaiah 61, a messianic Scripture that also promises Jubilee. When Jesus declared himself as the fulfillment of this Scripture, the crowd spoke well of him (4:22). Even after remembering

---

3. Willard M. Swartley, *John,* Believers Church Bible Commentary (Harrisonburg, VA: Herald Press, 2013), 119 and 122–23.

his hometown status, they didn't harm him. But when Jesus threatened their identity as God's favorites by reminding them of God's providence for a Phoenician widow and Naaman the Syrian, they tried to throw him off a cliff. Jesus took the intended scope of Jubilee and applied it to people groups other than Jews. His fellow Jews were enraged.[4]

But Jesus' missional record is not without some stumbles, at least at first glance. Jesus told the Syro-Phoenician woman, "I was sent only to the lost sheep of Israel," and "It is not right to take the children's bread and toss it to the dogs" (Matt 15:24, 26 NIV). And while he S R did praise the woman and heal her daughter, the story still begs for an explanation. William Herzog II uses it as an example of an honor-shame riposte.[5] Nowhere in Scriptures is Jesus bested—except in this story. If this was an honor-shame challenge, then it affirms non-Jews and women in that a Canaanite woman did what no Jewish religious leader could do. Amy-Jill Levine suggests that Matthew used this story as part of an intentional literary pattern. In this most "Jewish" of all gospels, this story is a matched pair with Matthew 10:5-6, which also has Jesus saying, "go only to the lost sheep of Israel." These two Scriptures, found in the middle of the book, form a contrasting chiasm with the magi at the beginning of the book and Matthew 28:19-20 at the end. Both of these "bookend" Scriptures emphasize the inclusion of all people into God's people. Here Matthew creatively portrays the central tension of the unique calling of Israel and the specific call to be missional.[6]

Kenneth Bailey gives the clearest explanation of the story, calling the event a teaching moment for the disciples. Here Jesus compliments a Gentile woman by giving her a tough "exam" and she passes with flying colors, calling him Lord and the Son of David. And in this dialogue, not only is the woman affirmed and her daughter healed, but the ethnocentrism of the disciples is unmasked. Bailey says, "The disciples are watching and listening. Indeed, in all Israel they have seen neither such

---

4. Fred B. Craddock, *Interpretation, a Bible Commentary for Teaching and Preaching: Luke* (Louisville, KY: John Knox Press, 1990), 63.

5. William R. Hertzog II, *Jesus, Justice and the Reign of God: A Ministry of Liberation* (Louisville, KY: Westminster John Knox Press, 2000), 129–30.

6. Amy-Jill Levine, "'To All the Gentiles': A Jewish Perspective on the Great Commission," *Review and Expositor*, 103 (Winter 2006). Retrieved from http://www.rande .org/winter06.htm.

total confidence in the person of Jesus in spite of his hard words, nor such compassionate love for a sick child. Her response is a deadly blow to their carefully nurtured prejudices against women and Gentiles."[7]

But it is more likely, says Levine, that Paul strengthened the missional trajectory. He called for a radical union of two diverse groups—Jews and Gentiles. He heralded the ministry of reconciliation in 2 Corinthians 5:17, calling the Jewish and Gentile believers—together—a "new creation."[8] He reaffirmed this new creation in Galatians 3:27-29, writing "There is no longer Jew or Greek, there is no longer slave or free, there is no longer male and female, for all of you are one in Christ Jesus."[9]

## Called to be missional and particular

But the new creation Paul writes about is hard to live out. New people can feel like a threat, a threat to the very identity we have as a set-apart people. On one hand, we are called to be radically inclusive, calling all those we meet to join God's people. On the other hand, we are an exclusive people. We are called to be so different from the world—loving our enemies, sharing our possessions, forgiving the unforgivable—that we attract others to the kingdom. How do we resolve the tension between those two callings?

The Bible narrates the real threat of syncretism. Sometimes new persons influence God's people more than the other way around. And sometimes what looks like antimissional stories in the Bible are actually narratives struggling with this threat. While the threat of syncretism is never dissolved in the biblical narrative, nor in our lives today, the trajectory of the story points to a missional calling.

We see this most clearly in the early church as they reinterpreted what it means to follow Jesus at the Jerusalem conference and through the missionary acts of Paul. At the Jerusalem conference (Acts 15) the early church made a bold step toward a missional identity. Spurred by the conversion of a Roman centurion named Cornelius (Acts 10), where Peter

7. Kenneth E. Bailey, *Jesus through Middle Eastern Eyes: Cultural Studies in the Gospels* (Downers Grove, IL: IVP Academic, 2008), 224.
8. Ralph P. Martin, *2 Corinthians*, Word Biblical Commentary (Waco, TX: Word Books, 1986), 146.
9. Charles B. Cousar, *Galatians*, Interpretation, A Bible Commentary for Teaching and Preaching (Atlanta, GA: John Knox Press, 1982), 85–86.

realized that God has no favorites (Acts 10:34-35), the Jewish believers gathered to decide how to incorporate the new Gentile and Samaritan believers. One option, attractive for many, was to have Gentiles become Jewish in order to be followers of Jesus. This included a ritual bath, special diets, and, for men, circumcision. These acts essentially made Gentiles into Jews, nurturing the idea that being chosen meant being God's favorite. This practice had precedent in Old Testament stories where grown men were circumcised as part of joining the Israelites (Gen 17:23-27 and Gen 34).

Given this background and the importance of circumcision for the covenantal relationship itself (Gen 17:10-11), the decision to *not* require Gentile males to be circumcised is paradigmatic. This ground-breaking decision meant that Gentiles could become followers of Jesus as Gentiles, as equals. *Chosen* here meant chosen for a mission. One could argue that part of the conference's decision was also a compromise, as the new nonethnic believers were required to observe some Jewish dietary laws. But this small deviation doesn't derail the tremendous step toward a missional understanding over and against exclusivity that discourages true mission.

## Why the missional lens must be the primary hermeneutical key

It is not enough to see mission as a central theme in the Bible. When we fail to see the Bible as the story of mission, several negative consequences happen. First, we are tempted to see ourselves as God's favorites. The grandiose preexile confidence of Judah—when they thought they could do no wrong as long as they had the temple, a king in the line of David, and the beloved landmass of Israel—can be our fate as well if we lose our missional focus. One of the most beautiful benefits of being missional is that it keeps us humble.

Second, the missional lens can help us respond correctly to syncretism. We must pay attention to this tension for, when we avoid it, we intuitively shirk from being missional without understanding why. Sometimes people in the pews are told that they aren't living out their missional calling because they are lazy or not committed enough. I believe the problem is much deeper than that. We have a subconscious

fear of others; we are afraid they will change us. And there is some truth
to that fear as acknowledged in the biblical narrative.

X    New persons joining the church always bring new understandings to
the table and sometimes their beliefs and practices need to be challenged
and transformed. But it is easier to exclude them over cultural and ethnic differences than to address their behaviors and beliefs, given the high
value our society places on being nonjudgmental. The missional lens
comes to our rescue by reminding us that we are exclusive on only one
issue, following Jesus. Our mission, if we are reading our Bibles well, is
not about making people like us in our cultural, ethnic contexts. It is
about all of us, together, living out shalom as the People of God.

Part of fully embracing our missional calling is to live into the tension as the Bible itself does. This is the true gift of the missional lens.
Like the Bible, we can't choose either the option of rejecting all outside
influence because of the threat of syncretism or because we are God's
favorite, but we also can't uncritically accept the culture in which we
find ourselves. We live *in* this world, but we are not *of* this world (John
17:6). We must, like the Bible, find a middle road, seeking engagement
with the Other and offering our own truth to the Other. This we do
nonviolently, lovingly, speaking the truth in love (Eph 4:15).

Third, the missional lens as the primary hermeneutical key can
help save us from distorted theology, such as Christian Zionism and
American civil religion. Zionists read their Bibles with the lens of Jews
as God's favorites, and they emphasize the first part of Genesis 12:3, "I
will bless those who bless you and curse those who curse you," to the
exclusion of "and in you all the families of the world will be blessed."[10]
These Christians strive to influence U.S. foreign policy to give Israel
carte blanche in their efforts to secure former territory now belonging
to Palestinians. Other American Christians use a variation of "chosen as
God's favorites" and apply it to themselves, nurturing a nationalism that
borders on idolatry. "God bless the Jews" is replaced with "God bless
America," and we justify atrocities in the name of Jesus.

---

10. See Mennonite Central Committee Peace Office Newsletter, *Christian Zionism
and Peace in the Holy Land*, vol. 35, no. 3 (July–September 2005), especially
Alex Awad's description in his article, "Christian Zionism: Their Theology, Our
Nightmare."

The missional lens can also save us from self-centered theology. Without a true emphasis on mission, the cross can become all about saving and restoring—me. We see "accepting Jesus as our Savior" and baptism as the endgame, the final step we need to take, instead of the beginning of a wonderful journey of working with God to "bless every family on earth." A mission-centered salvation gives us the joy of colaboring with Christ, a calling that gives our lives purpose. We see God at work. We experience God through the presence and gift of the Other. Our missional calling saves us from our selfish tendencies and blesses both ourselves and others with hope.

The Bible is the story of God coming down. Inside this story is our own calling to join God in this ongoing endeavor, doing it in the same way Jesus did. We must choose to see ourselves not as God's favorites, but as chosen for a mission, wise to the threat of syncretism, but trusting Jesus to guide us as the new People of God. In this sense the biblical narrative continues, since the work of God creating a People of God is an ongoing one. May we join the story joyfully, living out our missional calling.

# 18

# A Discipling Model for Missional Engagement

*Marvin Lorenzana*

## Introduction

The gospel is the good news of God's redemptive initiative towards creation in Jesus the Messiah. It is an expansive, high-impact, dynamic, and transformative movement *of* people and *for* people. In a very real sense, the early church "sneezed" the gospel and the Roman Empire caught the Christ-flu! The viral, organic, and move-mental nature of the kingdom of God summarized in the gospel and taught by Jesus to his followers soon permeated a significant portion of one of the most powerful empires that the world had ever known.

The relational nature of the kingdom of God, accompanied with the simple and crystalline clarity of the gospel as proclaimed by Jesus and the early church, was so full of vitality that by the year AD 313 SR the empire had between twenty and twenty-five million followers of the new faith. In fact, the gospel grew at an outstanding 1,000 percent rate every decade for the first 250 years![1]

---

1. Alan Kreider, *Resident but Alien: How the Early Church Grew* [video recording] (Great Commission Distribution, 2009).

For the first disciples of Jesus, to love God, to love neighbor as one-self, and to make disciples by reproducing the life of Jesus in others were vital parts of their spiritual DNA. Being a Christian meant that they had to fully embody the gospel that they so passionately preached. As the apostle Paul would say to the Corinthian church, "being manifested that you are a letter of Christ, cared for by us, written not with ink but with the Spirit of the living God, not on tablets of stone but on tablets of human hearts" (2 Cor 3:3 NASB).

For the early disciples of Jesus, then, to follow their Lord meant to follow his footsteps in the three-directional spirituality modeled by him—*up* (loving God), *in* (loving the body of Christ/other disciples), and *out* (making new disciples).[2] In other words, to be part of the king-dom meant:

- nurturing an intimate, life-giving, all-transforming relationship with the Father;
- committing to a relationship with the body of Christ, the *ecclesia*; and
- making God's mission of reconciling all creation to God their own.[3]

## The contemporary church suffers from a severe case of missional amnesia

Today's church of Christ seems to be plagued with missional amne-sia. We have forgotten that the gospel, in order for it to be genuinely redemptive, needs to be modeled as faithful discipleship. Discipleship, however, is *not* just another program that we add to the mission state-ment of the church. Disciple-making is in fact . . . *the mission!* We need, therefore, to recover not only a language to communicate the gospel to the world, but also a way of embodying our faith in Jesus that brings back the move-mental DNA of the gospel as practiced and preached by the early church.

---

2. For more information on the concept of three-dimensional, three-directional spirituality, see Mike Breen, *Building a Discipling Culture* (Pawleys Island, SC: 3DM Printers, 2011).
3. See Col 1:20.

My argument in this essay is that the church that Jesus founded began as an unstoppable movement of people for people intended to be a permanent revolution with immense transformative power to change society at its core. This revolution possesses a DNA with all of the resources needed—the Holy Spirit, the intrinsic power of the good news, apostolic genius, etc.—for perpetual renewal season after season, year after year, century after century, by keeping God's mission at the core of its purpose on earth. The time has come for today's church to go back to the basics, back to embracing and fulfilling its primary mission—disciple-making!

In the first section of this essay, I will discuss briefly how the gospel was communicated in very simple terms throughout the Roman Empire by the first disciples of Jesus. Secondly, I will touch on the role that leaders in today's church must play in order to bring back the movemental DNA of the gospel in a postmodern environment. And finally, I will describe the Missional Discipleship Initiative (MDI) launched by Mennonite Mission Network—an initiative designed as one resource among many available to the church for reigniting missional conversations in local faith communities.

## Communicating the gospel in pre-Christendom

### The proclamation—"Jesus is Lord!"

The unique message of the gospel during the first years of the Jesus Movement was communicated in simple, forthright terms—"Jesus is Lord!" This declaration may have summarized the gist of what the gospel was all about for the early believers in Jesus. These three words constituted a simple enough statement for anyone to remember and to transfer to others, yet they were chock-full at the same time of enough dynamite from heaven to shake the foundations of the Roman Empire. The deep spiritual and political implication of this declaration was, of course, that if Jesus is indeed Lord, then Caesar is *not*, and the full, undivided allegiance of those living under that powerful proclamation belonged to Christ alone.

This subversive proclamation navigated easily throughout the empire from province to province, city to city, household to household, and, most importantly, from person to person. It was not only communicated by a simple, easy-to-say, easy-to-remember pronouncement; it was also fully embodied by those who in time would become martyrs for the cause of Christ. To die as a martyr made sense to those who truly believed that Jesus the Christ was Lord of all. After the fourth-century Diocletian's persecution, Athanasius wrote:

> Is martyrdom, then, a light proof of the weakness of death or is it a slight demonstration of the victory won over death by the Savior, when the young men and women that are in Christ are unafraid to die? For people are naturally afraid of death and of the dissolution of the body; but there is this most startling fact, that one who has put on the faith of the cross disregards even what is naturally fearful, and for Christ's sake is not afraid of death. . . . This is no small proof, but is rather an obvious guarantee of the power of the Savior.[4]

It is due in part to the functional transferability of the truth contained within the "Jesus is Lord!" declaration that it became viral in nature, eventually turning the entire empire upside down.[5] The problem with the way we communicate the gospel today is that, instead of talking about being a radical, hard-core, fully engaged, vibrant movement of people working for total societal transformation, we tend to communicate it as a domesticated civil religion[6] without any redemptive power whatsoever.

## Simplifying the *kerygma*

Another example of the simplicity of gospel communication in the early years was the *kerygma*.[7] The earliest recorded formula of the apostolic kerygma is probably found in 1 Corinthians 15:3-4, "For I handed on to you as of first importance what I in turn had received: that Christ died for our sins in accordance with the scriptures, and that he was buried, and that he was raised on the third day in accordance with the scriptures." Once again the message is simple—Jesus is indeed Lord of all because he died for our sins and was buried and powerfully raised from the dead by God on the third day! It is a simple message that was

---

4. Margaret R. Miles, *The Word Made Flesh* (Malden, MA: Blackwell Publishing, 2002), 20.
5. See Acts 17:6.
6. For more on the concept of the American church as civil religion, see Stanley Hauerwas, *After Christendom* (Nashville, TN: Abingdon Press, 1999).
7. From Greek, meaning *preaching* or *proclamation*.

communicated not only orally, but also by men and women living lives in a manner worthy of such a Lord and Savior. Hugh Thomson Kerr says it powerfully:

> Scholarship, as well as experience, attests the fact that the preaching of Christ, past, present, and to come, crucified, risen and ever living, reflects and repeats the true kerygma of the New Testament. There may be those who think this preaching is outmoded. There may be others who think it should be supplemented, but no one who seeks to be loyal to the primitive tradition can preach any other Gospel.[8]

This is a powerful statement indeed! There is no other gospel to be preached. I join with many others in the church today advocating for a massive move toward a more organic expression of the gospel and the vehicle that for centuries has safeguarded it—the church. The dividing line between being a vibrant *movement* of spiritual renewal and a dead *monument* of "that which used to be" is immense. One represents the church in its liquid form[9]—decentralized and organic, expanding pervasively from person to person without limits, and the other the church in its institutional form—structured and centralized, living and acting in support of its own selfish interests.

It is for this reason that I challenge current church leaders to explore  newer, fresher, and more effective ways of communicating the gospel in today's world. We are in desperate need of finding and implementing more creative, innovative, and real ways of inculcating the common believer—not just elite Christians and leaders—with God's kingdom DNA.[10]

This vital transmittal of DNA, however, does not happen by chance or osmosis. It requires a very intentional change in mindset, where leaders in the church go back to nurturing high-caliber discipleship relationships that will in turn produce a new breed of committed disciples urgently needed in today's world. In fact, the church in some places is

8. Hugh Thomson Kerr, *Preaching in the Early Church* (Pittsburgh, PA: Fleming H. Revell Company, 1943), 48.
9. I credit missiologist Alan Hirsch for this term, which is used in his seminal book on missional church, *The Forgotten Ways: Reactivating the Missional Church* (Grand Rapids, MI: Brazos Press, 2006).
10. That is, "love God, love neighbor, and make disciples." For more information on kingdom of God DNA, read Neil Cole, *Organic Church: Growing Faith Where Life Happens* (San Francisco: Jossey-Bass, 2005).

becoming once again what missiologist Alan Hirsh calls an "apostolic movement."[11] He writes:

> The name we give to this different paradigm of church is simply apostolic movement. It is not new—in fact, it is ancient—and it is the only way to describe the fluidity and dynamism of the spiritual phenomenon we see evidenced in the New Testament itself. In short, apostolic movement involves a radical community of disciples, centered on the lordship of Jesus, empowered by the Spirit, built squarely on a fivefold ministry, organized around mission where everyone (not just professionals) is considered an empowered agent, and tends to be decentralized in organizational structure.[12]

In an apostolic movement environment, the simpler, more organic and incarnational preaching of the gospel takes center stage once again.

## The issue of leadership

Today there is a serious shortage of effective leaders within the church of Jesus Christ. Church leaders are a vital piece in not only communicating the gospel in a way that makes sense, but even more importantly in embodying it before the world as living examples of its transformational power. If the gospel does not transforms their lives, why should it transform the lives of anyone else?

Furthermore, the kinds of leaders who are formed in the institutional church often become the bottleneck that blocks the flow of ordinary believers in exercising their ministry. This happens because professional leaders become the center of the church's action, relegating all others to become mere passive spectators. We need leaders who clearly understand that the real mission of the church has never been to plant churches, but—in the words of Jesus himself—to "make disciples."[13]

Even though the great commission is popularly known, with its explicit and unambiguous mandate, it is both fascinating and sad to see how the church over the centuries has tended to lose sight of its central disciple-making message. The contemporary church in the West will need to pay serious attention to its primary calling if it is to survive the

---

11. For more information about the concept of apostolic movement, refer to Alan Hirsh, Tim Catchin, and Mike Breen, *The Permanent Revolution: Apostolic Imagination and Practice for the 21st Century Church* (San Francisco: Jossey-Bass, 2012).

12. Ibid., xxxv.

13. See Matt 28:19-20.

present century. Either the church begins making disciples once again in S R
a relational-intentional way . . . or it dies!

For the church to recover the ability to communicate gospel as movement, it will need to take seriously the language of disciple-making and
missional church thinking and practice. If the gospel is to become once
again a potent societal force for change, the church will need to trade the
current institutional mindset for a missional one instead. As Neil Cole
rightly suggests, we leaders need to learn how to "Lower the bar of how
church is done and raise the bar of what it means to be a disciple in the
21st century."[14]

Mike Breen, a missional church theorist and practitioner who is also
the founder of 3DM Ministries,[15] talks about the importance of developing a discipleship language that can enable us to effectively make disciples in the local congregation. Words like *invitation* and *challenge* will
be central, he believes, in developing a discipleship culture. He writes:

> Invitation is about being invited into a relationship where you have access ✗
> to a person's life and all the vibrancy, safety, love and encouragement that
> reside there. To learn from the places you clearly see Jesus at work in people's
> lives, which you can see only by having access to them. But by accepting that
> invitation, you also accept the challenge that comes with it: The challenge to
> live into your identity as a son or daughter of the King.[16]

If Breen is correct and the quality and health of a local church are
directly related to the quality and health of the disciples that it forms
and sends forth in mission, then it is both necessary and urgent to find
and implement creative ways of bringing intentional discipleship of
mission-minded leaders back to how we do ministry.

In summary, for the church to become a true agent of societal change
and transformation, it must find a way to transmit the DNA of the
kingdom of God to every disciple of Christ. For this to happen, however, we need to develop new ways of communicating the gospel as
movement once again.

---

14. See Cole, *Organic Church*, 26.
15. For more information on Mike Breen and 3DM, go to: http://weare3dm.com/.
16. Breen, *Building a Discipling Culture*, 18.

## The Missional Discipleship Initiative (MDI) at Mennonite Mission Network

The church needs to go back to its roots where everything started and revisit the very reason for its existence—to make other disciples of Jesus!

For the past few years, a number of racial/ethnic and Anglo congregations have been implementing something that Mennonite Mission Network calls the Missional Discipleship and Leadership Mentoring Initiative (MDI). Churches interested in discipleship and leadership development issues are invited to explore implementation of MDI as part of a learning community, generally composed of three to five churches in a particular region of the country.

MDI offers participating churches vehicles and resources to put traction to the missional church conversation. The most important vehicles are missional discipleship groups (MDGs) and leadership development huddles:

- *Missional discipleship groups* are basic high-commitment, high-accountability groups composed of two or three people of the same gender who meet weekly for three primary reasons—to pray together, to read Scriptures communally, and to be accountable to one another on how each group member followed Christ faithfully during the previous week. What makes MDGs missional is their end goal to not just fellowship and seek mutual edification, but to multiply—making disciples who make other disciples who make still more disciples. MDGs provide a meaningful discipleship experience for anyone who is willing to participate in the local congregation.
- *Leadership development huddles* are fundamentally a leadership discipling tool. The huddles are composed of six to ten people, same or mixed gender, that meet on a regular basis to learn and practice missional church principles and to be accountable to one another. The goal here is to multiply missional leaders within the local setting.

Our hope with MDI is to offer congregations interested in missional discipleship formation vehicles and resources that can help them move forward in their missional journey.

## 19

# Worship Ideas for Missional Congregations

*Eleanor Kreider*

Through corporate worship God shapes question-posing individuals and intriguing communities. In worship God warms their hearts and sharpens their commitment. Their regular gathering to praise God—singing, learning, praying, and reconciling—gives impetus and strength to their witness, courage, and hope. And through them God draws others into the circle of faith as followers of Jesus, their Savior and Master.

## Common elements of missional worship

The Bible does not suggest a particular pattern for worship. But it indicates salient, common components for worship in missionally alert churches, no matter where they are located, geographically or chronologically. Each of these components plays its part in embedding a passion for God's mission in the hearts of the worshipers:

- *Saturating with Scripture*—the Bible permeates the church's worship
- *Telling God's big story*—the worship recounts "the historic signs" of God at work

- *Engaging with God*—the worshipers listen to God and speak and sing to God
- *Hearing God's call*—the worship calls all members to follow Jesus
- *Building up the body of Christ*—the worship is multivoiced
- *Proclaiming salvation to all*—the worship welcomes all, including people who are caught up in sin and fear
- *Inculturating the good news*—the worship partakes in and reflects the graced aspects of the local culture
- *Praising God*—doxological worship overflows into service to the world

These components of worship are essential. But two further components are particularly fruitful in nurturing and maturing the culture of a missional congregation—testimony and prayer.

## Key component 1: Testimony

### Testimony is bearing truthful witness

Testimony has to do with bearing witness, with truthful telling. This is an important way of responding to God within worship. As we worship together we listen and receive love and grace from God and then we respond with truthful witness from our own lives. We believe that the missional God is at work, relentlessly if often reticently, in the world and in our everyday lives. We are attentive to the particular, small "providential signs" that show God at work in little things, giving "distinctive guidance . . . to individuals for designated kingdom tasks."[1] Through these "signs" God calls us to collaborate with him. But we have to bring these signs into the light. We have to tell these stories.

In testimony we tell these stories. They help us see God at work. They also encourage and challenge us. As we listen to one another's experiences, God deepens our faith, builds our communal identity, and draws us into his mission.

What is testimony? Testimony is telling and listening to our congregation's fresh stories. What a familiar social interaction! We do this all

---

1. James Wm. McClendon Jr., *Doctrine: Systematic Theology*, vol. 2 (Nashville: Abingdon, 1994), 382, defines these as "instances of the distinctive guidance God gives to individual lives for designated Kingdom tasks."

the time with friends and family. But everyday storytelling can become a transformative, potent element when we allow it a place in our worship.

Some churches include "sharing joys and concerns" as part of their congregational prayer time. One Sunday members might hear reports of neighbors helping with storm damage to a roof, a surprise visit from a distant son to an elderly mother, a fruitful conversation in a coffee shop, a quote from the local paper about a river cleanup, and a request for more volunteers to help in a common project. These are everyday happenings, and some might feel they have no place in public worship. But I believe the stories, told well, can be evidences of God at work, bringing healing and hope.

## Why is testimony difficult?

The first challenge is to learn to see God at work in ordinary things. But we often hesitate to do this. Why do we find this difficult? Here are several reasons:

- Some people are not willing to ascribe any explanation to everyday happenings except "What a coincidence!" or "Of course, good people do good stuff." They cannot believe that God might be involved.
- Others are offended when people are too quick to explain every detail of their lives in terms of God's guidance. It seems prideful. The stories sound petty, presumptuous, or pious, as though the person is saying, "I know what God is up to, and I am an important player in God's work."
- At times people are hindered by testimony's apparent shallowness or even frivolousness in light of the tragedy and pain of the world. To these people, it seems right to take offense at expressions of praise in little things that are cut off from the serious realities of life. Their antidote is a kind of stoicism. It seems better to live morally, cultivating a spirituality of endurance and resistance rather than indulging in words that seem shallow and effusive. Doesn't humility require silence about things we don't understand?

- In addition to those reasons, many people find that the word *testimony* evokes events of a distant past involving predictable repeats of long outdated conversion or healing stories.

So it may not be easy to begin introducing testimony into our worship. But over time we can combine testimony with congregational prayer in a way that is rich and moving.

## Disciplines for truthful personal testimony

Testimony in worship requires discipline in an individual's preparation and in her willingness to receive the experience of others. Here are some personal disciplines that help prepare worshipers to give testimony in worship:

- *Noticing*—We notice. Every day we pay attention to things that happen in our daily lives. Every meeting, every difficulty, every moment, has potential meanings that we can see with the eyes of faith and hear with the ears of faith. We remember these moments and reflect upon them.
- *Listening*—We listen to Scripture. In our daily readings we perceive the sweep of God's story of creation and redemption, and learn to place ourselves with our stories into it. We think to ourselves, "It didn't just happen to Peter (or Mary Magdalene or Bartimaeus). It happened to *me*." In this way, we enter imaginatively into the stories of the Bible.
- *Praying*—We pray a *missional prayer*. Confident and expectant, we daily pray, "Lord, you will be at work today. Help us notice where you are working and show us how we can enter in." We pray *the Lord's Prayer*, asking for God's kingdom to come, for God's will to be done. Do we recognize the marks of God's will, God's reign in our world? Of course, we do! God's kingdom is coming where shalom blossoms, where reconciliation and wholeness appear. Where these things happen, God is at work, sometimes through miracle, and often through the hard work, wisdom, and fidelity of people of faith.
- *Preparing*—As we prepare for the Sunday service, we will ponder what we have experienced throughout the week and where

have we seen shalom blossom—where healing and transformation have taken place, where good relationships have flourished,
where people have had enough to eat, where enemies have been
forgiven, where children have been kept safe, where conversations
with seekers have been fruitful, where creation has been cared for,
and when we have heard the inner voice of God, the prompting
of the Spirit, giving us a surprising idea, a new thought, a rush of
compassionate feeling. When we have seen and heard things such
as these, we have worthy testimony to bring to the church. We
bring it for discernment, weighing its significance.

We tell our stories with humility. Always. We put them forward so
others can help determine their meaning. Are the stories occasions for
giving thanks? Do they provide impetus for action? Do they call for
silence and waiting?

## Disciplines for congregations

A church learns how to do testimony time well. It isn't automatic;
it is a fragile element, open both to beauty and to abuse. Testimony in
worship requires disciplines for the congregation as a whole. Here are
some ideas:

- *"ABC for sharing"*—one congregation invites testimonies that are
  audible, brief, and Christ-centered.
- *"No Godless testimonies"*—another congregation asks participants
  to mention the name of God at least once in a testimony.[2]
- *Discretion*—testimony givers who ask for prayer do so with con-
  fidentiality and care.
- *Remembering*—a notebook scribe keeps track of the testimonies and prayers, making it possible to follow them up in
  succeeding weeks.

We come to see that God's hand is in our lives! We notice the little
idea that springs to mind—make that phone call, send a gift check, apol-
ogize to a coworker. Maybe it came from the Spirit of God, motivating

---

2. Lillian Daniel, *Tell It Like It Is: Reclaiming the Practice of Testimony* (Herndon, VA:
   Alban Institute 2006).

us to do something necessary. When we tell and listen to testimonies we learn from others. When we hear of even small events of surprising courage or loving service, our hearts are stirred. We may want to feel and act in similar ways. Truthful testimony, whether of lament or joy, honors God and brings forth praise and thanksgiving. God is glorified. Praise overflows.

## How to include testimony in a worship service

The faith of individuals and of the church as a whole is built up through disciplined testimony. But where and when does a church make time and space for it?

- A church may include testimonies as part of the offering. As well as money, we present our faith stories of the week as thank offerings to God. We offer our whole selves, our resources, and our experiences in response to God's gracious provision.
- These offerings can merge into a more extended period of corporate prayers where we can present before God the particularities of our stories—the needs, thanks, vision, and hope not only of our local community but of the global church and the world.
- A church may begin in a structured way, with interviews or stories carefully presented. As time goes on, this can develop more freely with more spontaneous anecdotes and responses. A common part of each contribution should be words to the effect: "God was in this."
- Once introduced, testimony time must be continued as a regular part of worship. People anticipate bringing their stories each week. They are disappointed if they find no opportunity to say what they want to offer.

As people listen to testimonies, they learn to see their own lives with the eyes of faith. They might think, "Oh, something like that happened to me this week, too. I wonder if God was trying to get my attention." They receive encouragement to be more alert to both the mundane and the surprising. They expect to see God's hand at work.

Conscious that guests or unexpected visitors may be present, we must be prepared for their responses. Some people may be put off by this robust inclusion of everyday life. They may not return. Others may be intrigued and even drawn by the honesty and vulnerability of testimony and prayer. Testimony and prayer build up the faith of the congregation, but they also make their mark upon guests and observers.

Through testimony we see the church in action. Testimony demonstrates and deepens the unity, holiness, and witness of the church. More than at any other point in worship, testimony reveals God's formation of a distinctive, missional community.

## Key component 2: Prayer

### Prayer—becoming collaborators with God

Missional prayer is not an individual worship leader's hobbyhorse. It is not a private enthusiasm. Missional prayer is the concerted offering of the entire church. Though individuals may have special sensitivities to certain areas of God's mission, all of us need to see the wider horizon of God's mission. According to 1 Timothy 2:2-4, Christians pray for kings and authorities not only so that believers may have safe, comfortable lives; it is so that God's plan may be fulfilled that "everyone may be saved and come to the knowledge of the truth."

Prayer is our language of communication with God, our way to enter into God's heart. What is God's part in our praying? God wants relationship with us, so when we pray, God is delighted. God honors our praying. God hears our anguished or feeble cries. And New Testament writers attest that God prays with us. According to Paul, the Spirit prays in and for us when we don't know how to pray (Rom 8:26). According to Hebrews, Jesus, in God's presence, "lives to make intercession" for us (Heb 7:25).

What is our part in our praying? We long for relationship with God  and for his leading and comforting. We hold God to his promises. And we bring our petitions to God, asking, seeking, and knocking (Luke 11:9). As he strengthens us and gives us courage, God draws us into his mission, into his project of making all things new, of reconciling all things in Christ. Both as pray-ers and workers, we become collaborators with God, God's coworkers.

## Disciplines for congregational prayer

Corporate prayer, like testimony, is a practice that needs to be learned. To collaborate well with God, as prayers, Christians must learn to pray together. Corporate prayer requires disciplined persistence. Here are some disciplines for congregational prayer:

- The prayers will address the named concerns from testimony time.
- The prayers embrace the worldwide church, well beyond local concerns.
- Leaders of the prayers may use a simple sequence of content: personal, local community, congregation, global church, powers and authorities, justice and reconciliation.
- The prayers will reflect Jesus' own prayer for the unity of his followers, for a significant reason, as he put it, "so the world may know" (John 17:23). Church unity is a missional concern.
- All, including guests, may participate in testimony and prayer.
- Participants may adopt varied physical posture and gestures as they pray—kneeling, standing, raising hands, responding vocally.
- A prayer notebook may keep track of thanks and petitions. This encourages both persistence in prayer and gratitude in remembering.

## Combating the powers and wrestling with God

Prayer brings lament and grief before God. It expresses our terror at the violence and oppression set loose in our world. It confesses our temptation to lose hope in the face of ruthless evil. But it also strengthens the backbones of believers as God leads them in the struggle against evil. Listen to the testimony of an early Christian concerning prayers of the church: "Prayer washes away sins, repels temptations, extinguishes persecutions, consoles the discouraged, delights the generous, accompanies travelers, calms waves, paralyzes robbers, supports the poor, rules the rich, lifts up the fallen, upholds those who are falling, maintains those who are standing. Prayer is a wall of faith, our arms and weapons that protect us on every side against our enemy."[3]

---

3. Tertullian, *On Prayer*, 29.

Tertullian and his fellow Christians prayed standing, combating the powers and wrestling with God. He likened prayer to doing battle with God—"massing our forces to surround God." Those North African Christians fulfilled Jesus' admonition to "pray like this"—they were persistent in prayer, and did "not lose heart."

## Prayer matters!

Like the early Christians, we can take heart in John's vision from Revelation 8:3-5. Our prayers, raised like incense to the presence of God, set loose seismic events on earth. The prayers of the saints unleash unknowable power. Our prayers may free God in mysterious ways to act in new ways. These are imponderables, but Scripture affirms that history is shaped by prayer. Events in our world are set in motion by transactions in "the heavenlies." We cannot explain this. But we do know that we are called to faithful and persistent prayer for the coming of God's reign here "on earth as in heaven."

## The Lord's Prayer—a model for missional praying

After all, the Lord's Prayer is our best teacher and guide for missional praying. Jesus, in Luke 11:1-2, presents it to his disciples, saying, "Pray like this!" Usually we recite the Lord's Prayer as a text to repeat without deviation. This is a valuable way to pray. It is not "vain repetition." However, we may take the Lord's Prayer not only as a prayer text but as an agenda for our praying. At the heart of his prayer Jesus placed "Your kingdom come, your will be done on earth as it is in heaven" (Matt 6:10). Let this be our main theme—to pray in the reign of God, to pray in the will of God for shalom and healing, everywhere, in the lives of all people, in the here and now. This is not abstract. The Bible and the experience of the church over the centuries and around the world make the direction of God's mission clear. It is the direction of forgiveness, food, healing, protection from evil, and the salvation of all people. The Lord's Prayer with its central focus on God's will and reign—this is what Jesus' life, ministry, death, and resurrection were all about. Praying this prayer every time we meet attunes us to Jesus' mission, and forms us to be participants with him. We pray into God's passion—the reconciliation of all things in heaven and on earth in Christ (Col 1:20).

## Testimony and prayer—missional practices of Jesus' disciples

We enter into the heart of God when we hone our capacities to see God at work in the particular stories of our own lives and when we learn to pray—apparently impossible—prayers in light of the pain and struggle of our world. That's what prayer is—aligning ourselves with God's mission, with God's desires for the shalom of all people and all of his creation. When Jesus teaches us to persevere in prayer, it is not to twist God's arm into doing something God would rather not do. Instead, persistent prayer aligns us with the things the loving God is already doing.

Worship is the arena in which God shapes worshipers into faithful and attractive followers of Jesus. Through the testimonies and prayers that have been at the heart of their worship, they have been changed. Their lives are open to God who makes them Christlike. People observe this and ask whether they can visit a Christian worship service to see what it is that makes these Christians so attractive. In worship, the guests will watch and listen. They may be curious, repelled, or puzzled. They monitor the worship for integrity of speech. They see, to their astonishment, that prayer is the powerhouse of the Christian community. And they want to have a part in it. They may be drawn to God through the testimony and prayer. God shapes the church and draws seekers to faith through worship. That's what God is doing, and God calls us to join in.

**20**

# Worldly Sermons

## Experiencing God's Word beyond the Church

*Isaac S. Villegas*

Where do sermons happen? What is preaching supposed to sound like? Who is authorized to proclaim God's Word?

### Sermons in Luke's gospel—different forms in different places

In the first several chapters of Luke's gospel we find multiple contexts for sermons and we discover that these sermons take on different forms from one another.

- There's Gabriel, God's messenger, an angel, a preacher from heaven who speaks the good news to Mary—that she will bear a child and that this child will be the Son of God.[1]
- There's Mary, who sings her sermon—"God has brought down the powerful from their thrones, and lifted up the lowly; God has filled the hungry with good things, and sent the rich away empty."[2]

---

1. Luke 1:30-35.
2. Luke 1:52-53.

- There's Zechariah, the priest, who preaches with a prophecy—
  "By the tender mercy of our God, the dawn from on high will
  break upon us, to give light to those who sit in darkness and in
  the shadow of death, to guide our feet into the way of peace."[3]
- There's John, the baptizer from the wilderness, who proclaims the
  good news from Isaiah, a word of repentance—"Prepare the way
  of the Lord, make his paths straight."[4]
- And there's Jesus, who shows up for worship at the synagogue in
  Nazareth and preaches the gospel of Isaiah—"The Spirit of the
  Lord is upon me, because he has anointed me to bring good news
  to the poor."[5]

Preaching in Luke takes all kinds of forms in all sorts of places—
from speaking reflections on a passage from the Scriptures to singing
of God's promises; from sitting while speaking in a house of worship
to standing by a river while prophesying the advent of deliverance.
And, for the bystanders in those stories, they never know ahead of time
when they might hear a sermon. There's no way to know when they
might get caught up in a movement of the Spirit. From Luke's gospel we
learn that we never know when and where the word of the Lord might
happen, when and where we might stumble into the proclamation of
God's Word.

## "Worldly sermons"—those happening beyond church walls and liturgies

Where do sermons happen? What is preaching supposed to sound like?
Who is allowed to proclaim God's Word? According to Luke's gospel,
a sermon can happen just about anywhere. In this chapter, I invite you
to wonder with me about the possibility of what I'm calling "worldly
sermons"—that is, sermons that happen outside of our worship services,
outside the wall of our churches, beyond the design of the Christian
preacher, beyond the reach of our liturgies and practices.

---

3. Luke 1:78-79.
4. Luke 3:4.
5. Luke 4:18.

Dietrich Bonhoeffer and Karl Barth are my guides in this exploration. In one of his letters from prison, the German theologian Dietrich Bonhoeffer asked a question that is as much for our cultural moment as it was for his. "What does a church, a congregation, a sermon, a liturgy, a Christian life, mean in a religionless world?" he wrote in 1944. "[H]ow do we go about being 'religionless-worldly' Christians, how can we be *ek-klesia*, those who are called out, without understanding ourselves religiously as privileged, but instead seeing ourselves as belonging wholly to the world?"[6]

With the stories I'll share in this chapter, I focus on one part of Bonhoeffer's question, the part about sermons. He calls us to leave behind the comforts of our privileged Christian milieu and instead immerse ourselves in the world, in the lives of our neighbors, near and far. He invites us to become an *ekklesia* (Greek for "called out") people, to live into our identity as people who are always called out from what we know and to venture into the unfamiliar.

The three stories I share below echo Bonhoeffer's call. I start with a story that is thoroughly churchy, although the location of the worship service may be unfamiliar. The story in the middle is not quite church and not quite worldly, but somewhere in the middle of the two, a blurry environment. And I end with a story that is unambiguously outside the domain of churchly worship—*extra muros ecclesiae*, "outside the walls of the church"—as the Swiss theologian Karl Barth would put it.[7]

Yet, in all three, I found myself caught up in sermonic events, moments when sermons happened around me and to me, although they didn't look or sound like anything we usually experience in our Sunday worship services. With the last story I get to the question at the heart of my exploration here, a question rooted in Bonhoeffer's question. Can there be "worldly sermons"—that is, proclamations of God's Word that have no explicit or formal connection to our faith or church life?

---

6. Dietrich Bonhoeffer, letter to Eberhard Bethge (April 30, 1944), in *Dietrich Bonhoeffer Works, Vol. 8: Letters and Papers from Prison*, ed. John W. de Gruchy (Minneapolis: Fortress Press, 2010), 364.

7. Karl Barth, "The Light of Life," in *Church Dogmatics* IV.3.1, trans. G. W. Bromiley (Edinburgh: T & T Clark, 1962), 37–157. My quotations here and below come from pp. 110–35.

In the second volume of Luke's story, the book of Acts, preaching events become all the more surprising as they increasingly take place in prisons, culminating in chapter 28 when Paul speaks the gospel while under arrest. That's how the book ends. Luke tells a story in Acts of incarcerated proclamations. Because Bonhoeffer asks his question about worldly sermons while writing from captivity, and because Luke turns our attention to the carceral setting as the site of God's Word, I'll follow their lead and tell you these prison stories.

We can't talk about the Christian story without talking about incarceration and wondering again and again about Jesus' first sermon where he promised the liberation of the imprisoned, proclaiming "release to the captives." Hopefully, at the very least, something in these stories will draw you into the lives of your neighbors who live in prison—an invitation, as Bonhoeffer would put it, to learn how to belong wholly to them and their world.

## First story—Word made music

I stood outside the fence, waiting for Dave to unlock the gate. He is a prison chaplain and he organizes an evening service for the men to whom he ministers. Dave welcomed me to the chapel, and so did all the men gathered for worship. As we began the service, we were informed that a beloved member of the community, of the church in prison—a man who had been in the hospital due to illness—had just died. The tone of the evening shifted. The men took turns sharing about their friend, what they learned from him and how much they would miss him.

Toward the end of the service, Dave invited the choir to the front and asked them to lead us in a song to close our time together. The men assembled as requested, dressed in their prison attire—white shirts, green pants, black boots. "One of these mornings you will look for me and I'll be gone," they sang, "I'm going to a place where I'll have nothing, nothing to do but just walk around, walk around heaven all day."

While the rest of the choir intoned those words in the background, another member stepped forward and sang of the people with whom all of us will be reunited in heaven—mothers and fathers, grandparents and grandchildren, sisters and brothers, all our loved ones who have been taken from us, including our friends—and he named the friend who had died that week. "I'm going to a place," the lead vocalist continued, "a place where there will be no more prison clothes, where there will be no more state boots, where there will be no more count time." Worshippers shouted their amens and stomped their feet and called out to Jesus, "Yes, Lord! Yes, Lord! Yes, Lord!" The song was good news—the music of the gospel.

I was there to preach, but I became part of someone else's sermon—a sermon sung, the *Word* of God as the *music* of God, preaching as a communal proclamation drawing together all the people gathered for worship, a song as a collection of our longings for God's redemption. As I joined my voice to theirs, their hope became my hope, their gospel became my gospel. Our bodies sounded out a sermon, as we became the body of Christ in prison—not only the Word made flesh, but the Word made music.

## Second story—Does God hear sermons?

Last year my friend Lauren and I taught a class for people who are incarcerated. Every Monday a correctional officer would escort us through gate after gate, door after door, as we passed through chain-link fences and spirals of razor wire, down an elevator without any buttons, through cold corridors, deep into the catacombs of North Carolina's maximum security prison. There, buried underground, was a classroom.

When we arrived, our students would welcome us with smiles, shaking our hands. Every week we would discuss the assigned readings—a book or an article, and sometimes an essay one of them had written.

For one discussion we read Will Campbell's autobiography, *Brother to a Dragonfly*. Lauren started our class by telling us about Campbell's life and ministry, about who he was and what he did. At the end of her brief lecture, she picked up her Bible and said that she was going to read a passage that was central to Campbell's ministry. She stood up, opened her Bible, and found the place where Jesus' first sermon is written. She read from Luke 4, where Jesus takes the scroll of the prophet Isaiah and declares the good news that the oppressed will go free and the prisoners will be released.

Then Lauren closed her Bible and sat down, and there was silence. I glanced around the room, looking at the faces of the men, their eyes crying out for those words to be true, for the gospel to be true—for the doors of their cells to open so they could be free, just like Lauren and me—and all of us could walk out of there after class together.

For all of us gathered in that room, the words from Scripture kindled our hope in the promises of God, promises of a reality that none of us could inaugurate. We couldn't make the words of Jesus come true. They were words that could only be announced, declared, proclaimed, preached—words that invited us to hope for another world breaking into this one, soon, though perhaps not soon enough.

After class, Lauren and I made our way back through the labyrinth of hallways and elevators—a return to daylight, trees, and grass. As I drove home, I wondered what would happen with the good news Lauren had spoken into that prison, into our lives. All of us had heard the good news. But had God heard it? Had God heard the longing of the men gathered in that room, as they clung onto the promises of Scripture and yearned for God to remember those promises? Had God heard Lauren's words—which were in fact *God's* words—and would the promises of Jesus be fulfilled, as prophesied by Isaiah? Would those thick walls submit to the Word of God—now reverberating through the cinder block rooms and concrete halls—and begin to crumble?

## Third story—#blacklivesmatter

The night after the news that the police officer who had choked Eric Garner to death would *not* go to trial, I walked with my neighbor Cullen toward the drums and shouting we had heard coming from downtown Durham. A crowd had gathered in a main street, blocking traffic. Cullen and I passed around the line of police in riot gear and made our way into the throng of protestors, chanting in unison phrases like, "We can't breathe," and "Hands up, don't shoot," and "Shut it down."

As the gathered community proclaimed each phrase, repeated over and over again before moving to the next, my mind jumped back to a page in my Bible that I had been reading earlier in the day. It was one of the Scriptures assigned by the lectionary for that week—the third chapter of Matthew's gospel where John the Baptist emerged from the wilderness to announce the advent of the Messiah and God's salvific liberation. "Repent," John roared, "for the kingdom of heaven has come near."

There, in the streets, with the protesters, as my mind drifted back to the text from Matthew, I heard in the chants around me the shouting of John the Baptist—all those voices crying out for justice, for the redemption of a society that hasn't found a way out of the wilderness of racism. Then, as I stood in the crowd, I noticed others around me pointing up at the building towering over us. I could see in the narrow slits of windows, far above us, shadows of heads and shoulders and arms—signs of life peeking out from the massive and ominous concrete block, our city jail.

With her arms stretching toward the prisoners looking down at us, a woman beside me started a new chant, calling out, "Brick by brick, wall by wall, we're gonna free us, free us, free us all." Soon others joined their voices to hers. "Brick by brick, wall by wall . . ." Then, with my eyes locked on the shadows in the windows, I chanted, too, "Brick by brick, wall by wall, we're gonna free us, free us, free us all." We were voices crying out in the wilderness, chanting our prayer, words that echoed with Isaiah's prophecy, with Jesus' words, the Word of God, "to proclaim release to the captives . . . to let the oppressed go free."

## God's Word calls from the world around us

It is always important for us to discern what to preach in our congregations and how to preach it. That's how I spend a lot of my time. But we should also think about how to decenter ourselves from the task of preaching and put ourselves in the position of receiving the good news, of welcoming the gospel in unfamiliar settings and from unexpected tongues. We need to dislocate ourselves and our congregations as the exclusive site of God's Word, and reposition our lives in order to see and hear God *extra muros ecclesiae*, as Barth puts it.[8]

Barth argued that the church doesn't have a copyright on God's Word. God isn't a possession. Instead, God is free to speak and act however and whenever God sees fits, with or without Christians, with or without the church. The world "is not wholly destitute of the Word which the community [of Christ] has been set among it to proclaim,"

---

8. Ibid.

Barth declared. "The community is not Atlas bearing the burden of the whole world on its shoulders."

The world belongs to God, not the church. As God sustains the world, God provides other words, other speakers, other holy places in which the Word echoes, independent of our Christian proclamation and embodiment. These are God's words "from a different source and in another tongue," "true words of a very different origin and character."

Those of us inside the church need to cultivate a disposition of gratitude, Barth counsels. We need to "be grateful to receive [the Word] also from without, in very different human words, in secular parables." Because God speaks and acts beyond the reach of the church, Barth warns against a sectarianism that shuts itself off from God's Word made strange in worldly sermons. "Christianity," says Barth, "must avoid any pride or sloth in face of them. It must be ready to hear them, and it must do so."

The world echoes with God's Word. It is a beckoning Word, drawing us into the world around us, into the lives of our neighbors, people and places from whom we can hear worldly sermons. God is there, speaking good news, singing the gospel, prophesying mercy and grace, and protesting against the violence of a chokehold and all the other ways our society suffocates the life of God's children.

You never know when you might find yourself caught up in a worldly sermon—Christ's life *extra muros ecclesiae*—outside the church.

**21**

# A Congregational Example of Missional Bible Study SR

*Lois Y. Barrett*

## Asking the right questions

Missional Bible study represents a method of Scripture study that I have been using for a number of years in a variety of church groups: workshops, seminary classes, and my own small group in my congregation in Wichita, Kansas. (A copy of the Bible study method is at the end of this chapter.) After an initial round of reporting on what was noticed when the Scripture passage was read aloud, the missional Bible study questions focus on three areas:

- The context—Where are we?
- The gospel—What is God doing?
- The church—How is God calling and sending God's people to participate in God's mission in the world and to be a sign of God's future?

Each of these three sets of questions is divided into two parts:

- A consideration of these issues in the biblical text itself, and
- A consideration of these issues in the group's—or congregation's—own situation.

In these missional Bible studies at Mennonite Church of the Servant, my congregation in Wichita, we have applied these questions to New and Old Testament passages, to narratives, to epistles, to psalms. Although context may be easier to discern in narrative passages, even the most theological passages have a narrative behind the text, for which groups have usually had little difficulty discovering at least some aspects.

## Assumptions and applications of missional Bible study

What are the interpretive and theological assumptions behind the missional Bible study, and how can we apply this methodology to a contextual reading of Matthew 13:24-58?

### The reign of God

The reign of God is a key theme of missional theology. The reign, or kingdom, of God—in Matthew, "kingdom of heaven"—is present, explicitly and implicitly, throughout the Bible. Many helpful surveys of the reign of God in the Bible have been written, so I will sketch only the outline of the topic. In one of the earliest parts of the Bible, Exodus 15, the song of Miriam ends with the enthronement of God: "the Lord will reign forever and ever" (Exod 15:18). Even when Israel demands a human king, God is seen as the true king. The Psalms extol "my God and King" (Ps 145:1). Prophets tell of the messenger "who announces peace, who brings good news, who announces salvation, who says to Zion, 'Your God reigns'" (Isa 52:7).

The reign of God is the center of Jesus' proclamation (Mark 1:15) and of his parables. In the Lukan version of the Last Supper, Jesus confers on his disciples "a kingdom, so that you may eat and drink at my table in my kingdom, and you will sit on thrones judging the twelve tribes of Israel" (Luke 22:29-30). According to the apostle Paul, God has "transferred us into the kingdom of his beloved Son" (Col 1:13).

First Peter 2:9 refers to the church as "a chosen race, a royal priesthood, a holy nation, God's own people." The Bible ends with praise "to the one seated on the throne and to the Lamb" (Rev 5:13). Thus, God is the ultimate ruler over all human rulers, the one to whom God's people are called to give their ultimate allegiance.

This kingdom, or reign, language is only a part of the political language of the Old and New testaments. The word *ekklesia,* usually translated "church" in English, is not only any assembly, but the political gathering of citizens of a city for decision making, a town meeting. The gospel, *euangelion,* the announcement of good news, can be more specifically the announcement of a royal arrival to the city. Thus, the gospel is public, not only private.

The reign of God is not only about my individual destiny or behavior, but also about the establishment of an alternative community, a new *polis*, with its own characteristic behaviors and practices, its own culture—in the sense of "the way we do things here." The alternative *polis* is the preview of God's future when God's reign will be fully realized. The new community is called to live now according to the pattern of the age to come. As we will see in Matthew 13, this requires a new perspective that is not flummoxed by small size or the presence of evil.

Likewise, the covenant language of the Bible is used not only in marriages and adoptions, but also in international treaties. *Tsedeq* and *diakaios* are usually translated "righteousness" or "justice". One is righteous, or just, when one is living within the provisions of a covenant. These are words connected with salvation. This salvation includes new creation, not only of the individual, but of a new community that extends beyond old ethnic and national boundaries, and restoration of the entire cosmos, according to Romans 8:18-21. Therefore we read the biblical text with God's universal and ultimate rule in mind.

## God's activity in the world today

The rule of God in the world implies God's activity in the world today. I have discovered that many North American Christians are not sure whether God is active in the present—perhaps in the heart of the individual, but in the world? As I have participated in research in congregations of several denominations across North America, I have been amazed at how many people respond to the interview question, "How do you see God at work in this congregation?" with a list of projects and activities they are doing.

One can do hour-long interviews with twenty-four members of a congregation—pillars of the church and marginal members alike—and never hear God used as the subject of an active verb. In other cases, people's understanding of what God might do is extremely circumscribed. When people offer prayer concerns in Sunday morning worship and in small groups, it sometimes appears that people think that God's activity is limited to healing the sick, or at least comforting them.

If to be missional means to participate in what God is doing in the world, one must believe that God is doing something and that it is possible for Christians to discern this. This Bible study method requires people to look for where God is at work in their lives, in their congregation, and in the world.

## Context and theology

This method of Bible study recognizes that all texts have contexts. There is no gospel without a context. In fact, a primary theme of the Pauline epistles is the spread of the gospel from a Jewish Palestinian context to Greco-Roman contexts. This, again, is a topic much explored. But there are some differences this recognition of context makes in our biblical interpretation.

Contextuality leads to multiple "right" interpretations. While we may come to some agreement on the context of a particular biblical text, each group interpreting that text is coming from a different context. We do not want to simply read ourselves into the text, or go around finding proof texts for what we already believe. But our particular situations as congregations or small groups will affect the ways in which it is possible for us to identify with the contexts already present within the text. This does not mean there cannot be misinterpretations. Certainly there can, but we can allow for multiple good interpretations or even missing pieces.

As I have practiced this method of Bible study over the years, I have learned to be silent when the group did not come up with an interpretation that I had thought was particularly insightful. I know that, when I have come back to the same text again and again, I have seen new things that I missed before. So I need to trust that others will do the same and not try to impose all of my wonderful ideas on them this time around.

## "This is that . . ."

This way of studying the Bible presupposes that God not only acts, but is continuing to act now in the same way as in the past. We can trust that God continues to speak and act in ways that are congruent with how God has spoken and acted in the past. God's people are called to discern how the experiences of the people of God in the present are connected with the experiences of the people of God in history, particularly as we know it through the Bible.

James McClendon called this principle "this is that." He wrote:

> Scripture in this vision effects a link between the church of the apostles and our own. So the vision can be expressed as a hermeneutical principle: *shared awareness of the present Christian community as the primitive community and the eschatological community.* In a motto, *the church now is the primitive church and the church on judgment day*; the obedience and liberty of the followers of Jesus of Nazareth is our liberty, our obedience, till time's end [emphasis in the original].

> A prime case is Acts 2, where Simon Peter, preaching on the day of Pentecost, refers to a passage in the prophet Joel:

> > In the last days—the Lord declares—
> > I will pour out my Spirit on all humanity.
> > Your sons and daughters shall prophesy,
> > your young people shall see visions,
> > your old people dream dreams (2:17 NJB).

> Peter applies this passage to events occurring as he speaks, saying, "this is that which was spoken by the prophet Joel" (2:16 KJV); that is, the events of Pentecost are the events of the prophetic message. And this is the familiar biblical pattern: This is that.

> This is not merely a reading strategy by which the church can understand Scripture; it is a way—for us, it is the way—of Christian existence itself.[1]

---

1. James Wm. McClendon Jr., *Ethics: Systematic Theology,* vol. 1, rev. ed. (Nashville: Abingdon, 2002), 30–33.

We find a similar understanding in Deuteronomy 26:6ff. In the recital of God's amazing deeds, the Israelites are to begin, "A wandering Aramean was my ancestor." But quickly the recital goes into the first person, "When the Egyptians treated *us* harshly and afflicted *us*, by imposing hard labor on *us, we* cried to the Lord, the God of *our* ancestors; the Lord heard *our* voice and saw *our* affliction, *our* toil, and *our* oppression. The Lord brought *us* out of Egypt . . ." Within the Bible itself, we see that the biblical story is not just something to learn about, but a narrative in which the church is called to participate. *This* event is related to *that* past event. John Addison Dally says it this way:

> [These texts] reveal a deep pattern in the Bible of God's sending the offer of life under God's reign and the various human responses that sending elicits. The shape of that offer is a rehearsal of what God has done in the past in order to delineate the shape of what God is doing now, in the listeners' hearing, followed by an invitation to receive or participate in that action. It requires a community of faith convinced of its agency, one willing to use that agency to discern God's action in its midst and to respond to it. Such a reading of the Bible reopens the story of salvation instead of treating it as a finished outline about which listeners can only be informed and persuaded.[2]

Thus this form of missional Bible study asks similar questions of the biblical contexts and the readers' contexts. It assumes continuity between how God has acted in the past and how God acts now; it assumes continuity between how God's faithful people acted then and how they are to behave now.

## "Then is now"

Not only is the present-day church in continuity with the past story of God's relationship with God's people, the church now is connected with God's future. The church is called to be a sign and foretaste of the age to come. The church is called to act now according to the pattern of God's future, to be a preview of what God intends—not only to proclaim the gospel, but to be a sign of the reign of God. McClendon notes: "Authentic Christian faith is prophetic faith; it sees the present in correct perspective only when it construes the present by means of the prefiguring past (God's past) while at the same time construing it by

---

2. John Addison Dally, *Choosing the Kingdom: Missional Preaching for the Household of God* (Herndon, VA: Alban Institute, 2008), 102–103.

means of the prophetic future (God's future). 'This is that' declares the present relevance of what God has previously done, while 'then is now' does not abolish the future but declares the present relevance of what God will assuredly do."[3]

N. T. Wright also advocates this understanding of the present people of God shaped by the future.

> We read [Scripture] as the narrative in which we ourselves are now called to take part. We read it to discover "the story so far" and also "how it's supposed to end." To put it another way, we live somewhere between the end of Acts and the closing scene of Revelation. If we want to understand Scripture and to find it doing its proper work in and through us, we must learn to read and understand it in the light of that overall story.

> As we do this—as groups, churches, and individuals—we must allow the power of God's promised future to have its way with us. . . .

> The Bible as a whole thus does what it does best when read from the perspective of new creation. And it is designed not only to tell us about that work of new creation, as though from a detached perspective, not only to provide us with true information about God's fresh, resurrection life, but also to foster that work of new creation in the churches, groups, and individuals who read it, who define themselves in terms of the Jesus they meet in it, who allow it to shape their lives. The Bible is thus the story of creation and new creation, and it is itself, through the continuing work of the Spirit who inspired it, an instrument of new creation in human lives and communities. . . .

> Thus, just as the proclamation of Jesus as Lord results in men, women and children coming to trust and obey him in the power of the Spirit and to find their lives transformed by his saving lordship, so the telling of the story of creation and new creation, of covenant and new covenant, doesn't just inform the hearers about this narrative. It invites them into it, enfolds them within it, assures them of their membership in it, and equips them for their tasks in pursuit of its goal.[4]

The church is called to participate in this story by being the preview of the age to come, the foretaste of the heavenly banquet. Does the church always live up to this calling? Is it always a good preview of the age to come?

---

3. James Wm. McClendon Jr., *Doctrine: Systematic Theology*, vol. 2 (Nashville: Abingdon, 1994), 69.
4. N. T. Wright, *Surprised by Hope: Thinking Heaven, the Resurrection, and the Mission of the Church* (New York: HarperCollins, 2008), 281–283.

Certainly, congregations are sometimes like the ten-dollar television set that my husband and I owned early in our marriage. It got so you could get either the sound or the picture, but not both at once, unless you stood there holding the dial between channels. Now, that fall, Tom and I wanted to watch the World Series. Well, we had our choice; we could listen to it or we could watch it. That TV was not a perfect representation of the baseball game, but it was the best we had.

Sometimes the church is the best the world has to see what the reign of God is like. A part of the church's participation in God's mission in the world is its calling to give the world a glimpse of the reign of God by looking at the church. In its life together, the church is a witness to God's saving action and ultimate rule before the watching world—to use John Howard Yoder's phrase.[5]

## Interpreting Matthew 13

With these things in mind, let us look at the parables of Matthew 13:24-58 from the context of my own congregation, Mennonite Church of the Servant in Wichita, Kansas. It is a small, high-accountability congregation that includes among its practices the annual sharing of spiritual pilgrimages in small groups before the covenanting service during Holy Week. It is economically diverse, somewhat racially diverse, with a wide range of educational backgrounds. It includes a mother whose children may be taken away, as well as those who are active in peace movements and immigration support networks. If we read Matthew 13 with these folks, this is what we might hear.

### What is the context of the biblical passage?

- Evil is present among the good. What are we supposed to do about it? Do we sort it out? Will God sort it out? The people to whom Jesus was speaking were probably wondering, "Will there be justice in the end?"
- They are concerned about being small. Maybe they are wondering if they will grow.

5. John Howard Yoder, *Body Politics: Five Practices of the Christian Community Before the Watching World* (Nashville: Abingdon, 1992).

- Perhaps some people listening to Jesus wondered, "How much can I risk on the reign of God? Is it worth everything I have?"
- Verse 52 seems to imply that the context is the training of scribes for the kingdom of heaven.

## What in these contexts are like our context?

- They would ask—and answer—questions like, "Where are we feeling dispossessed? Oppressed? Treated unjustly? Where are we feeling small, vulnerable? Where are we hesitant to risk? What is our training for the reign of God?"

## In the biblical text, where is God at work?

- They would note the actions of God or God's agents—angels—or the Son of Man in the text. The Son of Man is sowing good seed. Angels "will collect out of his kingdom all causes of sin and all evildoers, and they will throw them into the furnace of fire, where there will be weeping and gnashing of teeth."
- In the parable about the catch of fish: The angels will come out and separate the evil from the righteous and throw them into the furnace of fire, where there will be weeping and gnashing of teeth.
- What does the text tell us about God's future? It appears that God is sorting people out; God is setting things right and bringing justice.

## In our context, where do we see or sense God at work in the same way?

- Some of the people in my congregation would be uncomfortable in these texts with God's judgment. How could a loving God bring about "weeping and gnashing of teeth"? On the other hand, some would say justice needs to happen. But they might ask, "Do we need to wait until the end, or can we hurry it up?" Someone else might ask, "How is God's judgment good news? Do we really want to live in a world where there are no consequences for doing evil, even in the end?"

**In the biblical text, how are God's people called and sent to participate with God in what God is doing?**

- Someone notes that, in the parable, the weeding and the sorting are not our job! The disciples have to live with enemies, the actions of the devil. What people do in the text is to watch a mustard seed grow into "the greatest of shrubs," watch yeast rise and leaven three measures of flour, go in joy and sell all that one has and buy that field, or sell everything for the pearl of great value.

**In the biblical text, how are God's people called to be a sign of God's future?**

- We are called to leave the rooting out of evil up to God and not to use violence to get rid of evil; evil doesn't destroy evil. We are called to risk everything for the sake of God's reign. Maybe this is the training for the kingdom of heaven.

**In our context, how is God calling and sending the church? How does this text call and send the church to be a sign of the reign of God? When others are watching the church, what do they see that would give them a hint of what God is doing in the world, or what God intends for the future? How can this text help the church align all that we do, say, and are with God's future?**

- Responses might include: "This text helps me keep on working for justice without having to 'win' every time. This text helps me to value faithfulness over effectiveness." Some might wonder: "How *do* we train people for the reign of God? Should our congregation be more intentional about this?"

**What practices does this Scripture lead us to?**

- Some would say, "Quit worrying about being small; God is going to use us anyhow. We are called to risk everything and trust in God's justice, in spite of the way things look now. In spite of our initial worries about God's judgment, this is a hopeful text."

In every context in which the church finds itself, it is called to study the Scripture with these questions in mind.

## Missional Bible Study
A method of Scripture study for the church

### Read the Bible passage.
*Questions:*

- When the passage was being read, what word or phrase popped out for you?
- While the reader kept on reading, where did your mind stop to wonder?

### The context—Where are we?
*Sample questions:*

- Biblical context:
  - » What is the context of the biblical passage? Geographical? Political? Social?
  - » What is the nature of the people, powers, and systems in this context?
  - » Where are people trapped by sin and evil?
- Our context:
  - » What is *our* context? Where are we? What is our world like?
  - » Is there anything in our context that is like the context of the biblical passage?

### The gospel—What is God doing?
*Sample questions:*

- Biblical text:
  - » In the biblical text, where is God at work?
  - » What is God's good news?
  - » What does the text tell us about God's future?
  - » How is God calling people to change or to enter the reign— the kingdom—of God?
  - » How does this text point us to Jesus?
- Our context:
  - » In our context, where do we see or sense God at work?
  - » What is God's good news for us?

» How is God calling us to change?

» How is God challenging us to enter the reign—the king-dom—of God?

## The church—How is God calling and sending us to participate in God's mission in the world?

*Sample questions:*

- Biblical text:
  - » In the biblical text, how are God's people called and sent to participate with God in what God is doing?
  - » How are God's people called to be a sign of God's future?
- Our context:
  - » In our context, how is God calling and sending the church to participate in what God is doing in the world?
  - » How does this text call the church to discern its missional vocation?
  - » How does this text call and send the church, in all of its life together, to be a sign of the reign—the kingdom—of God? How can everything we do be more in sync with God's mission in the world?
  - » When others are watching the church, what do they see that would give them a hint of what God is doing in the world, or what God intends for the future? How can this text help the church align all that we do, say, and are with God's future?
  - » Through this text, what can we learn about how God is not only calling and sending us, but also empowering us, giving us what we need to work with God?

22

# Best Practices for Planting Missional Peace Churches

*Mauricio Chenlo*

We will focus in this chapter on three important aspects of planting missional peace churches. These are: *systems of call, sustainability,* and *multiplication.*

## Systems of call

### Entrepreneurial leadership

At the heart of any form of church planting are leaders who have been called to partner with God to create something out of nothing. This is a trait common to church planters. It is foundational for any sort of faith adventure of attempting to gather together a group of followers of Jesus.

Before calling his apostles, Jesus spent significant time shaping his own call and messianic identity. He was even tested by Satan in his call to be God's chosen messenger to bring in God's kingdom.

Jesus' followers who are called to start a new church are by nature of their call entrepreneurial persons. The dictionary defines *entrepreneurial* as "a person who organizes and manages any enterprise, especially a business, usually with considerable initiative and risk." Two key words need to be highlighted in this definition—*initiative* and *risk*.

In the last eight years in my role as a denominational minister for church planting I have met a significant number of leaders who have taken risky initiatives. These were often regular folks without much knowledge of the risks they were about to face:

- a journalist in Colorado Springs responds to the growing numbers of Latino immigrants and decides to start a Spanish-speaking congregation in partnership with an Anglo Mennonite church;
- a couple of professionals become involved with immigrant clients through their medical and nutritionist practices and host a home Bible study group in rural Minnesota;
- a group of young artists work together to launch an art school for children and are encouraged by the children's parents to start a gathering for worship.

Significant risk factors and a great degree of creative collaborative thinking and practice were key ingredients to these experiences. It is always easier to begin a new project with the structures and security systems in place. There is not much risk in a job that comes with the security of a monthly check and paid benefits.

Missional peace church planters are entrepreneurial by nature of their call. The history of Anabaptism spreading around the globe is filled with examples of farmers, carpenters, businesspeople, and men and women in many other types of vocations and professions who responded to the call to start something "out of the blue," wherever God had placed them. In today's context, the work of the kingdom will greatly benefit from leaders who take risks and venture into new forms of being church.

## Assessing the called

Most church planting coaches and experienced leaders on the field strongly recommend assessing those leaders who feel called to plant a church. In the business world this is known as quality control. Initiating a new church is a serious endeavor. Groups wanting to experiment with church planting need to be prepared to lay solid groundwork for this endeavor. That doesn't mean that one needs to get picky and filter leaders by their academic or professional background, but it is important to be sure that entrepreneurial church planters have a significant percentage of success in what they are doing. On the Mennonite Church USA website we suggest several types of assessment depending on the type of call and circumstances.[1]

What does it take to be an effective church planter? Dr. Charles Ridley conducted a study of church planters in the United States and Canada. Based upon his research and subsequent field-testing, he developed a list of thirteen characteristics that define effective church planters. For over a decade, these have been used to select church planters. The top three characteristics are:

- visioning capacity
- intrinsic motivation
- ability to create ownership of ministry

We believe that these features are key to anyone trying to start something new. No matter what church model the leader is going to pursue—a missional radical community, a conventional program church, a house church, and so forth—assessing the skills of potential church planters will definitely add value to those involved.

## Partnering with local congregations and conferences

A partnership is an arrangement in which parties agree to cooperate in the advancement of their mutual interests. There are strategic and spiritual reasons why church planters partner with existing churches and church planting networks. Partnering increases the possibilities of success for those who really want to become a presence of Christ in a new environment. Partnering is intrinsic to God's trinitarian nature and the church as a diverse body of believers.

You will be surprised by how many local churches, nonprofits, and urban agents will welcome your vision and desire to be a kingdom presence. It is important to have clarity of who your potential partners might be. This is why articulating your vision and sense of call are so

---

1. http://www.mennoniteusa.org/what-we-do/holistic-witness/church-planting/assessment-tools/.

important in communicating with your potential partners. Clarity in advance prevents unnecessary miscommunications and potential areas of conflict and disagreement.

## Sustainability

### Coaching

Statistics show that church planters have a much higher success rate when they are involved in intentional strategic relationships that help them in the development of a church plant. Coaches are a significant asset for those interested in pursuing a church plant.

Church planting coaching evolves around gospel, personal, and spiritual conversations. Coaching church planters is not something merely centered on strategies and tactics. Church planters benefit from coaching greatly when they are facing discouragement, lack of motivation, conflict, and many of the typical challenges facing someone planting seeds of the kingdom.

Coaching relationships should happen naturally. Ideally church planters will know specific leaders with whom they feel an affinity and who can serve as models for their ministry. If not, missional leaders from the larger system—conferences and national—will provide names of potential coaches willing to walk with new church planters.[2]

### Long-term planning and development

Most church planters I know generally resist the idea of long-term planning. This is due mainly to the nature of the work, as even Paul recommended, "Do not worry about anything" (Phil 4:6). We live in a high-pace world and many balls need to be juggled simultaneously. I really enjoy traveling to my native country, Argentina, where I am refreshed in conversations with church leaders by a sense of total dependence on the Lord. But we live in America, where management is one of the leading brands of the culture. Church planters cannot escape this reality. They also have a busy life with family, work, and leisure time, and they need to take care of spiritual and physical wellness.

---

2. For additional resources on coaching, visit the Mennonite Church USA website under "church planting" at: http://www.mennoniteusa.org/what-we-do/holistic-witness/church-planting/.

Efficient church planters normally set goals and use calendars to improve their work. I have used the Wheel of Life, an efficient tool to discern proper use of time for different roles and responsibilities, with several leaders I coach. Most of them were not familiar with this tool and have resisted the idea of thinking carefully about their different responsibilities. But after getting used to it many have expressed appreciation for using it consistently. There are several versions of the Wheel of Life; search for it online and you can pick your favorite version.

Church planters also spend significant time developing their donor base. They normally begin with their inner circle—family, friends, colleagues, etc. It all depends on the model one is using. If your project is quite informal and bivocational, you probably don't want to stress the development factor. Another consideration is your life circumstances—marital status, age, financial obligations, etc. Even if you are not thinking of receiving any financial support from your base group, it is always wise to learn some of the basics of financial development. It will help you in different areas like organizing special events and supplying new disciples with spiritual resources.

## Bonding with a local network of missional peace churches

In the last few years we have seen a significant number of church planting networks emerging around different visions, values, and practices. One way to get to know some of them is by attending the annual church planting conference called Exponential.[3] Though quite white/Anglo in composition and singularly evangelical in perspective, we have found it useful to connect with people who in key areas share a similar theology to Anabaptists.

You could also visit the sites of several networks and find out more about their values, practices, and vision. At Mennonite Church USA we are working to create a church multiplication network that will include active participation from conferences already involved in church planting work or wanting to become more intentional about developing missional agenda.

Little has been written about church planting networks that hold the vision of peace and justice as central values of their practices. One

---

3. See http://www.exponential.org/.

such group is ANEC—Atlantic Northeast Conferences—of Mennonite
Church USA, which has gathered on a regular basis to share about its
church planting work.[4] We have worked with ANEC to help organize
three church-planting retreats on the East Coast with encouraging
results. As of today, most conferences participating in ANEC are organizing their own agenda to follow up with their own church planting
projects. If you are interested in learning more about ANEC and any of
its participating conferences, contact us or one or another of the conferences that best fits your interests and views.

## Accountability structures

Another important practice for the call to initiate a new missional
faith community is to have a set of relationships with people who might
function as listeners, supporters, and accountability stakeholders in the
work you are doing. Within Mennonite Church USA conference systems, there are groups that require church planting committees or support groups that play this role.

In choosing accountability structures, leaders will want to be sure
that members of the group selected will bring input and gifting that
particularly sheds light on blind spots. Accountable leaders are much
aware of their blind spots. For example, if you know that one of your
weaknesses is paying attention to details, you will probably benefit from
someone in your support group who will fulfill that role. Finances and
down-to-earth economics is one of the areas in which many church
planters don't do well. Having someone to fill that gap will be a much-
appreciated function.

Your support group is not the only circle from which you will benefit. Relating to your regional conference will be another important circle
of relationships. Most conference systems have something in place to
connect church planters to existing clusters of churches that meet peri-
odically for fellowship, mutual support, shared-event coordination, mission festivals, financial matters, and other issues.

For assistance in this area, visit your regional conference website and
find out if they have a church planting or missional communities' commission. Learn how you can connect with this commission and develop

---

4. For more on this network of conferences, see chapter 33 by Gay Brunt Miller.

an accountability group. If you have your own accountability system already in place, seek advice from your conference on how to include them in your circle.

## Multiplication

### Reproduce through discovery and sending new leaders

Most church planters share a natural passion for reproduction. Reproduction is part of their DNA. That said, it is not always evident that planters develop "discovery" and "sending" systems. There seems to be a trend to just move based on the agenda of accomplishing those goals that relate to the immediate needs of group development. Planters spend so much energy in getting their group started that little time and energy are left for thinking about how the new church plant might serve their context in reproducing leadership systems.

I believe that discovery is inherent to every planter. But discovery systems are not always a conscious practice in the ministry of planters. For example, churches wanting to plant new churches normally have solid ministries among youth and young adults. Calls are birthed and tested in the context of serving within the varieties of ministries displayed by the church. Yet in today's religious context, most young adults seem to be skeptical of institutions in general and the church in particular. That is why it is important to work side by side with young adults who are transforming the culture of calling.

I have met several young adults in the last few years who have an entrepreneurial spirit but who will not function in the typical traditional systems and language of call currently in place in our churches. Many in this younger crowd are attracted to explore the social and cultural issues challenging our world today—environment and natural resources, growing local gardens, food sustainability issues, exploring diverse religious paths, resistance to violent means to solve social conflict, nurturing local communities, fair trade; the list could go on.

Our discovery and sending initiatives need to be quite flexible and creative in dealing with this diversity of interests. Most young adults resist the idea of being straitjacketed or being "pushed" or "labeled." Nurturing entrepreneurial social and spiritual leaders is one of the biggest challenges we face today as established church institutions.

## Networking new projects with established churches

Not all churches are missional and even fewer are interested in church planting. But the missional movement in America has produced a significant number of independent churches and networks of churches that are driven by planting new churches. Among Mennonites, few established congregations have included planting new churches in their bylaws and vision. Anabaptist entrepreneurial planters will struggle to find established Mennonite churches wanting to support them.

In many ways, planters attracted to the Anabaptist vision and church development will need to work side by side with pastors and leaders of established churches to spark a vision for expanding the presence of Mennonite churches. It is what Alan Hirsch has called "the forgotten ways." Most of our churches and leadership have forgotten what brought them to life. Many have thought for decades—if not centuries—that the mission field is out there in some Third World land and all we need to do is to recount moving stories to constituents about how thousands of converts are being produced in those "poor" nations.

The landscape has changed, however, and younger generations of millennials no longer believe in the colonial pattern of mission work. They are locally focused and want to see transformation happening right here in the homeland. Missional leadership and established churches will be revitalized and find themselves greatly enhanced by connecting with the passions and visions of younger generations. As a result of these encounters, new opportunities to serve God's kingdom purposes will most assuredly multiply.

**23**

# Shared Theological and Missiological Commitments for Church Planting in Mennonite Church USA

The following shared commitments grew out of conversations about church planting at the fall 2013 meeting of the Constituency Leaders Council of Mennonite Church USA. During the following year, conference ministers, church planters, and coaches as well as mission agency and denominational staff participated in the drafting and editing of these commitments.

## 1. God is a sending God.

### God loves the world and sent his son into the world not to condemn the world but to save the world

In church circles, we tend to forget that the object of God's love and redemptive purpose is not the church but the world. God seeks to save the world from sin, injustice, and evil. God sent Jesus into the world to free the world from darkness and to offer abundant life.

### Jesus invites people to new life and draws them together to become kingdom communities which he sends into the world

The resurrected Jesus sends his friends into a broken, hurting world to continue his work. Jesus calls and transforms people and knits them together as sisters and brothers who love each other and live in communities of grace, peace, and joy. These communities are witnesses to God's new order where Jesus is Lord, in the midst of the crumbling old order of sin, injustice, and domination. Jesus' followers carry on this task with a deep sense of humility, remembering that the church is a community of sinners being redeemed by God's grace.

### We trust the Holy Spirit to form, guide, and sustain these missional communities

As the risen Christ sends his disciples he breathes the Holy Spirit upon them. Missional communities are not formed by human intentions and effort alone. Instead, missional communities are yielded to the empowering and transforming work of God's Spirit that instructs, guides, and sustains them.

## 2. Visible kingdom communities are God's primary strategy for bringing healing and hope to every person and to the world.

### Kingdom communities are God's primary strategy for reconciling a broken world

Christians join God's mission in many ways—through marriage counseling, good preaching, letter writing campaigns, and acts of compassion, just to mention a few. But God's primary strategy for impacting our world is by birthing and nurturing kingdom communities. Like yeast in the dough, these communities permeate and transform the world around them. It is through the church that God wants to make known God's plan of reconciliation to the people and systems of the world (Eph 1:10; 3:10).

### Kingdom communities live incarnationally

In Jesus, the Word became flesh and dwelt among us. Likewise, Jesus-centered communities will enter deeply into relationships with their neighbors. Churches that are planted need not only to proclaim the good news, but to be good news. New churches will incarnate the reign of God through practices of mutual aid, love of enemies, and servant leadership. This will take new churches to places where sin, hatred, poverty, alienation, and oppression await redemption.

## Kingdom communities engage their context with the good news of Jesus Christ

Social, cultural, and geographical contexts are diverse by definition. Church planters will be students of the culture and will "learn the language" of their particular context. New church communities will look and act different in different contexts. As apostles to the world, we engage our current changing contexts with Jesus' whole gospel in creative and relevant ways.

When entering a new context, church planters will pay attention to what God has already been doing in that place. This includes approaching existing Christian communities with an open and charitable spirit, a desire to be in relationship, and a willingness to cooperate in God's kingdom work.

## Kingdom communities bear witness to the transforming power of Jesus' life, death, and resurrection

Jesus empowers sinners to become children of God, members of a new spiritual and social order. Through word and deed, members of his body communicate God's new possibilities with power and conviction. In and through Christian community, we and our neighbors encounter the living Christ who loves, forgives, and continually transforms us.

## Kingdom communities make disciples and continue the work of Jesus in their setting

Jesus-centered communities shape and form people to be more like Jesus. When they abide in Christ, they carry on the sin-forgiving, bread-breaking, enemy-loving work of Jesus, their Savior and Master. They invite those around them to join them in following Jesus in a community of faith. New church communities seek the welfare of the city where they are planted and seek to bless the community around them.

## 3. The church equips God's people for planting kingdom communities. This involves:

### Calling out church planters and testing this call

Church planters sense a call to join with God's Spirit in forming new worshiping communities. This call is tested and confirmed by their faith community and supporting or sponsoring congregations. Leaders who are called to initiate new faith communities are willing to take risks and make significant sacrifices to pursue this calling.

### Practicing spiritual disciplines and continued theological reflection

Church planters are committed to grow in their faith through regular Bible study, prayer, spiritual accountability, and other disciplines. Church planting can be carried out effectively by those who have various levels of theological training. Ongoing study and training broadens one's understanding of God's reconciling mission in the world, strengthens one's skills, and deepens one's reliance on the transforming work of the Holy Spirit.

### Forming teams

Church planters are encouraged to form a team of coworkers. An effective team brings together many gifts and is able to connect with a range of people. Enduring, vibrant congregations that reflect the Spirit of Christ are often led by a team of people who share leadership roles, rather than by one charismatic and powerful leader. Care must be given to nurture this team as a discerning spiritual community and to work well with conflicts that naturally arise.

### Entering partnerships and accountability

New church plants find their place in the broader body of Christ for mutual support and accountability. These communities and their leaders intentionally nurture relationships with local congregations, area conferences, mission agencies, and denominational staff. Strategic partnerships enhance possibilities of success and provide opportunity for mutual blessing in pursuing God's kingdom vision.

# PART 4

# Stories and Testimonies

24

# The Role of Theological Education in Developing Missional Consciousness

*David B. Miller with Sara Wenger Shenk*

> One of the most important theological developments in the last century has been the articulation and application of the doctrine of the missio Dei. As a Trinitarian doctrine, missio Dei resulted in discussions about "mission" moving from the periphery to the center of theological debate. As such, we have seen the rise of the categories of "missional theology" as well as "missional church." What has lacked, however, is commensurate work in applying the doctrine of the missio Dei to the field of theological education. (J. R. Rozko[1])

## The cultural and institutional challenges we are facing

The first decade of the twenty-first century has been anything but a time of stability and security for churches and seminaries in North

---

1. In "Implications of the Missio Dei for Theological Education," American Society of Missiology paper presented at the society's 2012 annual gathering.

America. The much-discussed cultural shift in the West toward post-Christendom, while superficially belied in national surveys of belief (two 2012 polls placed self-described Christians in the United States between 73 percent[2] and 77 percent[3] of the nation's population; 67.3 percent[4] of respondents to a 2011 survey of Canadians self-described as Christians) is evidenced in the decline of most denominational traditions in North America.[5] A closer look at all three of these surveys revealed even sharper declines in active affiliation with and participation in churches. The fastest growing "faith" in both nations was the "nones."[6]

At the same time, theological schools in North America were facing the concrete effects of the upheaval caused by the precipitous downturn in financial markets and increase in unemployment that simultaneously shrank endowments and reduced charitable gifts. These challenges placed upward pressure on tuition expenses, while making potential students more reticent to leave jobs and assume debt for an education that may not result in secure employment. The result has been a net decline in total attendance—both head count and full-time equivalent—across all member institutions of the Association of Theological Schools (ATS).[7]

The realities, trends, and challenges facing both Mennonite Church USA and Mennonite Church Canada are similar. These statistics and developments trouble administrators and board members whom we have entrusted as the stewards of denominational organizations and agencies. However, while the moment certainly calls for strong, courageous, and wise administration, the urgent questions facing the church

---

2. For 2012, Gallop reported 77 percent of U.S. residents identify as Christian: http://www.gallup.com/poll/159548/identify-christian.aspx.

3. The Pew Forum: http://www.pewforum.org/2012/10/09/nones-on-the-rise/.

4. http://www.canada.com/life/Christians+still+robust+even+more+Canadians+claim+religious+affiliation+national+survey+finds/8354132/story.html?__federated=1.

5. Even the Southern Baptist Convention, which had long experienced slow growth while mainline denominations declined precipitously, has experienced seven consecutive years of membership decline: http://www.christianpost.com/news/southern-baptist-report-shows-decline-in-membership-attendance-for-7th-year-in-a-row-120576/.

6. In the above polls, "nones" are comprised of self-described atheists, agnostics, and those who simply respond with "none" as the best description of their faith.

7. Research findings of the Auburn Center for the Study of Theological Education reported in InTrust (Spring 2013), http://www.intrust.org/Portals/39/docs/IT-413wheeler.pdf.

and seminaries are not simply matters of administrative adjustment. If we approach these challenges as primarily threats to institutional survival we will reveal ourselves as those still bound to the thought patterns and practices of Christendom, which conceived of the church in primarily institutional terms.

## The need to recenter our theology and practice on God's mission in the world

For over twenty-five years mission thinkers and writers[8] have been challenging us to understand the significance of these trends and to repent of the habits and practices that replaced the movement and mission of God with an institution that sought to manage the world. They have called us to recenter our theology, our practices of faith formation and instruction, our affection, our discernment, and our actions on the missio Dei—the mission of God in the world.

Mission originates in and belongs to God, not the church. Keeping this clear has been a persistent challenge for the church of all denominational traditions. The church has been more threatened by its (our) own internal "will to power"—too easily mistaking our plans and purpose for God's—than it has been by any external resistance.

God's mission is a passionate one—"I have heard their cry . . ." (Exod 3:7); "For God so loved . . ." (John 3:16); "If you had only recognized . . . the things that make for peace!" (Luke 19:42). And God's mission is the means by which that passion may become incarnate—"The Spirit of the Lord is upon me . . . to bring good news to the poor" (Luke 4:18); "Christ Jesus, who, though he was in the form of God, did not regard equality with God as something to be exploited . . ." (Phil 2:5-6).

When the mission belongs to God, the church exists as a servant to that mission. The church does not have an end in itself, but is both called and sent by God. It is not an institution dispensing salvation in the form of "life insurance," but is a foretaste of the world that is coming. The pattern of this calling and sending is seen in the life and

---

8. See: Lesslie Newbigin, *The Gospel in a Pluralist Society* (Grand Rapids, MI: Eerdmans, 1989); Wilbert R. Shenk, ed., *The Transfiguration of Mission: Biblical, Theological and Historical Foundations* (Scottdale, PA: Herald Press, 1993); Darrell L. Guder and Lois Barrett, *Missional Church: A Vision for the Sending of the Church in North America* (Grand Rapids, MI: Eerdmans, 1998); and others.

teaching of Jesus. It is repeated in the giving of the Holy Spirit and the sending of the early church. "Jesus said to them again, 'Peace be with you. As the Father has sent me, so I send you.' When he had said this, he breathed on them and said to them, 'Receive the Holy Spirit'" (John 20:21-22).

None of this begins with questions of organization, structure, membership guidelines, or institution. However, the questions of how power is used, what ends are sought, what sacrifice might be required, and what means are acceptable are central and defining. Long-formed habits of organization and institution, coupled with relative power, privilege, and social respect, have over time distanced us from the priorities and means of the reign of God.

This is neither surprising nor the result of some devious plot. It is the nature of structures. It was the reason that the commandments concerning Jubilee were given (Lev 25), in recognition that over time power and control would become concentrated in ways that tend to work against justice and mercy. It was the reason that Israel was commanded again and again to look toward the "widow, the orphan, and the alien" to know if justice and mercy were being realized.

An extended period of Christian privilege is now being shaken in our culture. We can either learn from this moment to reengage the prophetic imagination of the biblical text or we can resist with strategies designed to "take back our culture for God," seeking a short-term victory with means incompatible with the way of the Lamb (see Rev 5).

In such a moment as this, we may consider how the practice of administration—that good gift of God's Spirit—has too often been disconnected from the life of Jesus and patterned more after the prevailing political or business systems of our given moment in history. We do well to consider how our congregations and educational institutions—like all institutions—have been tempted to become servants of the church as organization, rather than the church as missional movement. But now, with the institutions themselves at risk, perhaps both academy and congregation can return to their first call—to be witnesses.

## The seminary's role in developing missional consciousness

Here the seminary has gifts of deep memory, with historical understanding to reclaim the wisdom of an earlier moment and to seek patterns for embodying this wisdom in a present moment. Our task becomes that of training scribes for the kingdom of heaven "like the master of a household who brings out of his treasure what is new and what is old" (Matt 13:52). Deeply immersed in "the strange new world within the Bible,"[9] we learn the insistent cadences of prophetic speech that turns over tables in the pursuit of justice and the calm of love that casts out fear.

For several years, Anabaptist Mennonite Biblical Seminary has focused the goals of our master of divinity program around three pedagogies: of knowing, being, and doing. This triune focus reflects an understanding that true knowledge is not merely a matter of the intellect—that which we apprehend from our neck up. Our minds are one of the means by which we are formed to love God, but so also are our being and doing. This threefold pedagogy reminds us that learning is not just the acquiring of information, but that information is to be disciplined in truth-telling and engaged toward reconciliation and liberation. We do not truly know or understand until our knowing begins to accomplish the work of our own transformation. So our study includes the examination of our own motives and yearning. In the process we pray and study, we investigate and confess, as acts of knowing that shape being.

Similarly, knowing and being are not ends that exist for themselves, but are released, disciplined, and tested in acts of ministry and service. The classroom where students are prepared for missional leadership includes the campus and the city, the meetinghouse and the county jail, the hospital and the community organizing meeting, the homeless shelter and the mediation center. We act and then we reflect. We are loaned the eyes and experience of persons of varying cultures and colors, knowing that our seeing is too partial to be very helpful or trustworthy if we have not also been challenged to look through the eyes of another.

---

9. Karl Barth, "The Strange New World within the Bible," in *The Word of God and the Word of Man*, Douglas Horton, trans. (Gloucester: Peter Smith, 1978), 33–35.

We act and we ask—where was God beckoning? Why would Jesus weep over this city? Are the institutions of this city—from banks to schools, police to newspapers, city government to church agencies—serving the common good or are they self-seeking fallen powers? Does the life within and between the congregations of this city reflect the redeeming power that breaks down walls of hostility so that reconciled and reconciling communities may make known the manifold wisdom of God (Eph 3:10 NIV)?

Each of these locations—meetinghouse, jail, hospital, mediation center—becomes a classroom in which we learn, and a laboratory in which we experiment with embodiment of the reign of God. Our faculty includes not only the doctors of theology and Bible, pastoral care, and preaching, but also the survivors of abuse, the undocumented, the dying, the incarcerated, the business owner and the line worker, the pastor of a persecuted church in the Middle East and a Muslim imam in our own community. Through these we begin to see more deeply in reverent awe and wonder the God who is uniting all things by proclaiming peace to those who are near and those who are far off.

Some days are mundane. Some days all seems wearisome. Some days, however, the Word becomes flesh and dwells among us. On those days we rejoice to be a missional seminary moving within the missio Dei, on behalf of the church.

25

# Gifts That Anabaptists Offer in Interfaith Encounters

*David W. Shenk*

> "This tells all about it!" Muse sang and danced, holding up a worn seventy-year-old booklet. It was the gospel of Matthew in Zanaki, her mother tongue. Muse was bent with arthritis, yet there she was—bearing witness to Jesus in the Bumangi church where I had grown up.

## Confronting white ants at Bumangi

My parents were pioneer Anabaptist missionaries. The Zanaki people among whom they served had never before heard the gospel. They had no schools. Modern medicine was unknown. Eighty percent of the children died by the time they were two. My parents walked from hamlet to hamlet introducing people to Jesus, in whom God offers salvation.

Jona and Leah joined them. Jona was probably the only Zanaki Christian in the world at that time. My mother began a little medical clinic. Together my parents taught literacy under a tree. As a small fellowship of believers developed, they constructed a grass thatched church where believers gathered, especially on Sundays. At the front of the church was a neatly written Bible verse: "For God so loved the world, that he gave his only begotten Son that whosoever believes in him shall not perish but have everlasting life."

The chief assigned Bumangi Hill to my parents. That hill was covered with white ant mounds. White ants destroy houses. The tribal elders suspected that the gospel would be bad for the Zanaki people. So they entrusted the final decision to the spirits of the ancestors. If the white ants destroyed the houses my father built, the elders would know that the ancestors had determined that the gospel was not good. However, if father destroyed the white ant hills and succeeded in building permanent houses, then the ancestors had determined that the gospel was good. Father with his team of workmen destroyed every white ant hill! The first Zanaki believers referred to the white ants as a parable. The gospel rooted out evil while bringing life-giving transformation.

Our family thrived at Bumangi. Mother occasionally exclaimed, "Our family is so blest to live among these wonderful people!" Because my parents loved the people, they yearned for them to know of Jesus.

## Jesus coming down at Bumangi

"Do you know about God?" my parents asked their Zanaki acquaintances.

"Yes!" they said. "God is the Creator. His name is Murungu. But he went on a journey and will never return. So we do not know much about God. That is why we venerate the gods of nature and the ancestors."

So my father translated the gospel of Matthew into Zanaki. This was the first book ever written in Zanaki. The translators used the Zanaki name for God—Murungu. Imagine the surprise of newly literate people reading that Jesus is Murungu who has come to live among us.

Recently Grace and I took our three oldest grandchildren to Tanzania. We wanted them to get in touch with the missionary journey of their great-grandparents. On our Sunday at Bumangi the church was packed with some seven hundred people. Children of one particular couple—Nyakitumu and Wakuru—traveled many miles to meet the great-grandchildren of those who had brought the gospel to their people. Nyakitumu and Wakuru had been the first couple married in the

Bumangi church. Their children shared accounts of conflict between their parents and the ancestral powers. Noteworthy was female genital mutilation. That practice bound girls in puberty to the authority of the ancestral spirits. When Wakuru met Jesus, she knew that Jesus' intention was to free her from this practice and the ancestral powers, so she boldly rejected this practice.

Wakuru's father had arranged for her to marry an old polygamous man. She also dissented from that arrangement. The battle raged for months. Never before had a teenaged girl been empowered to break free from tribal custom and the authority of the ancestors. The whole society was shaken by her bold insistence that Jesus was her ultimate authority. During the many weeks when Wakuru was chained alone in her parents' hut, she would calm her spirit, singing, "There's not a friend like the lowly Jesus."

Then several years later one of the first Christian young men in the society sought her hand in marriage. Again there was a colossal struggle. Nyakitumu was of the blacksmith clan and Wakuru of the basket-weaving clan. Tribal custom meant it was impossible for them to marry across clans. Their Christian wedding was an unimaginable break with social taboos. The tribal elders cursed them so they would never have children. But God blessed this family with thirteen children. And in time they became the pastor couple who replaced my parents.

The children of Nyakitumu and Wakuru said, "Jesus is God reaching down to lift us up into abundant life. Our mother on her own would never have been able to escape from the powers that controlled our tribe. But when Jesus reached down our mother clung onto his hand."

Some years later after my parents had taken their journey to heaven, Nyakitumu wrote me a long letter describing the fiftieth wedding anniversary he had celebrated with Wakuru. Polygamous societies in this part of the world never have wedding anniversaries. This was the first such event in the history of the Zanaki people. They killed a bull and hundreds joined in the feasting. Choirs sang and danced. Children and grandchildren came from across Tanzania. Government officials gave speeches. Bishops and many pastors were present. Wakuru spoke of her husband, saying, "He never beat me. He just loved me!"

## The gospel to the nations

As the little church at Bumangi developed, the believers had a passion to share the gospel with other language groups. So our congregation sent a young couple to another clan. This was the sermon text at their commissioning: "And this gospel of the kingdom will be preached in the whole world as a testimony to all nations, and then the end will come!" (Matt 24:14). As a child, I was tremendously gripped by the amazement of it all, that the preaching of the gospel to the nations was preparing the world for the coming of Jesus.

I serve quite extensively within the world of religious pluralism. However, in my reflections here I will focus primarily on Anabaptists sharing the gift of the gospel within African traditional religion—a local tribal faith—and within the world of Islam—a universal missionary faith. Nyakitumu and Wakuru are accounts of Jesus meeting the adherents of traditional African tribal society. I will now share from the world of Islam.

## Signs of the gospel in Islam

I asked an Anabaptist pastor in Indonesia why he had become a Christian. He responded, "I was the imam in the local mosque. An acquaintance gave me the New Testament. In John 14:6, Jesus says, 'I am the way, and the truth, and the life. No one comes to the Father except through me.'" I was astonished.

The pastor continued. "Muslims repeat the compulsory Fatiha prayer seventeen times daily. In the heart of that prayer is the plea to God, 'Show us the straight path.' I was surprised that Jesus declares that he is the answer to the prayer that I prayed seventeen times every day. So I believed in Jesus. From that moment I knew I was in the straight path; after that I ceased praying the Fatiha and instead I pray thanking God that Jesus is the Straight Way. It is surprising to me that the Fatiha—the opening verse of the Qur'an—prepared me to believe in Jesus."

Ahmed Ali Haile, a Somali believer in Jesus, has a similar story. "Islam prepared me for the gospel," he says. "In the evenings the kindly imam would call us little boys around him and teach Islam. Quoting from the Qur'an, the imam told us that the Torah, Psalms, and Gospel are also God's word. So I determined to find those Scriptures sometime.

And that happened when I was fifteen years old and ill in a hospital. There, the first Christian I ever met gave me the Bible. In the reading of the Bible faith in Jesus was born in my soul."

Ahmed appeared at the door of a Christian living in his town and told him of his decision to believe in and follow Jesus. His friend counseled, "This could mean death. It might mean being put out of your home. You might lose friends and be denied employment or scholarships." Ahmed responded firmly, "I have decided to believe in Jesus Christ." He knelt in prayer, confessing his sins and committing his life to Jesus Christ.

Ahmed exclaimed, "That day I had come home. Although Islam was a sign pointing me to the gospel, it is the church that became my true home. The church is like a Somali nomadic hut. At the center is a pole. That pole is the cross. Christ crucified and risen is at the center of the gospel and the center of the church. The curved sticks that form the wall and roof of the hut are the believers. We are each tied together at the top, tied to Christ who is the center. The woven matting over the hut is the grace of Christ who covers us with his righteousness. None of those central dimensions of the gospel are found in Islam. So why would I return to the mosque when I have entered the church whose center is Jesus Christ?"

The parents of Ahmed were devout Muslims and hospitable. His father always supported Ahmed in his decision for Christ. Although his parents never confessed Christ in baptism, Ahmed believed they were examples of the persons of peace whom Jesus commended (Matt 10:11-12).

Ahmed's conversion was a tremendous turning for him. Ahmed called his conversion a paradigm revolution. Shortly after his commitment to Christ, he participated in a youth Bible study of Philippians 2:1-11. In this passage Christ comes down all the way to the cross. This astonished Ahmed. In Islam God is never affected by what we do. God never comes down to save us. But here he met the God who suffers with us and because of us. That was the moment of clarity for Ahmed. He knew there could be no reconciliation between Islam and the gospel. While he always appreciated signs of the gospel within Islam—such as the affirmation of biblical Scriptures—he also knew that Islam in its essence is not the gospel.

That discovery formed Ahmed's later ministry as an apostle of peace among Somali Muslims. His peacemaking commitments were centered in Jesus crucified and risen, for he believed that only in the cross is the essence of our broken relationship with God and one another restored.

In time cancer entangled Ahmed. I was with him a few weeks before his death. We ate a roast that evening, prepared by their daughter. We had prayer and embraced as we declared, "We shall not say goodbye, for Christians never say goodbye—see you later!"

## Ten gifts in a world of many religions

In the accounts I have described, there are several gifts that characterize global Anabaptists as they bear witness in a world of many religions. Here is a summary:

1. Discern that religions do not save and in fact often detract from the gospel. It is Jesus who saves, not the religions.
2. Empowered by the Holy Spirit, go and bear witness among the religions that Jesus Christ is Savior and Lord, giving special attention to those where the gospel is not yet known.
3. Recognize the church as the community of the redeemed from every tribe and nation whom Christ is forming as kingdom people.
4. Build upon the reality that the Holy Spirit has planted signs of the gospel within all religions and ideologies. These signs are a preparation for the gospel.
5. Give thanks for all expressions of shalom both within the church and beyond it.
6. Be a people of the Scripture who make the Bible accessible to as many people as possible.
7. Be aware of and confront diabolical powers that oppose the gospel.
8. Participate in the transformational power of the gospel.

9. Understand that the gospel is distinctive. No philosophy or religion has ever imagined the good news of the gospel—God so loved the world that he sent his Son!

10. Live as a participant of God's kingdom and in the expectancy that Jesus is coming again to fulfill that kingdom.

## Great commission Anabaptists in Singapore

An Anabaptist, Ton Kok Beng, pastors the Singapore Mennonite Churches. In his youth he was a devout Taoist. He is also the president and one of the founders of Bethany International University (BIU), which relates closely to the Mennonite Church. This university trains missionaries from around the world as ambassadors of Christ among the religions.

Several years ago I gave the commencement address at BIU. Then the rector and president gave the commissioning. This was the mandate given to each graduate: "Go into all the world and preach the gospel to all creation. Whoever believes and is baptized will be saved, but whoever does not believe will be condemned. And these signs will accompany those who believe: in my name they will cast out demons; they will speak in new tongues; they will pick up snakes with their hands; and when they drink deadly poison, it will not hurt them at all; they will place their hands on sick people, and they will get well" (Mark 16:15-18).

Amazingly, the court records of the sixteenth-century Anabaptist martyrs reveal that their favorite preaching text was the very same text proclaimed in the commissioning at the Singapore missions training center. That commencement event revealed that the sixteenth-century Anabaptists have reappeared . . . in Singapore! And they are in fact found in vibrant faith communities around the world.

# 26

# What Anabaptists Bring to the Interchurch Table

*Jamie Ross and André Gingerich Stoner* SR

## "We don't want to hoard these possibilities"

The topic at the 2007 meeting of Christian Churches Together in the USA (CCT) was evangelism. Each year, bishops, presidents, heads of communion, and ecumenical officers gather for three full days of prayer, relationship building, and conversation around important topics of faith and discipleship. Mennonite Church USA delegates voted in 2007 to become full participating members of CCT.

I, André, have had the honor of witnessing a tremendous growth of respect and trust among participants in this circle over the years. At my first meeting, I found myself sitting on the airport shuttle between a Catholic bishop and the presiding bishop of a large Pentecostal denomination. They were chatting, catching up on news, and swapping stories like old friends. Ten years earlier, they were at best strangers to each other, but CCT has created and deepened the bonds of friendship and unity across the body of Christ.

CCT is organized according to faith families: Roman Catholic, Orthodox, historic Protestant, evangelical/Pentecostal, and historic African American churches. Presentations are often structured according to these families. Mennonites, however, don't quite fit into these neat categories. We are as historic as any of the Protestant churches, yet we share practices of believers baptism, a high regard for Scripture, and much more with evangelicals and Pentecostals. Further, our perspective as critics of mainstream American culture sometimes leaves me in these meetings identifying most closely with the perspective of the African American churches—churches that have profound experiences of living at the edge of American privilege and power.

Listening carefully during the various presentations on evangelism, I recognized some as quite familiar, while others were novel to me. I was challenged, instructed, sometimes surprised, and encouraged. During this time together, we all noticed a remarkable convergence around the importance of integrating the witness of word and deed. Repeatedly we heard how service, social justice, and evangelism are all integrated in the witness and mission of the church.

But things that were unsaid left me troubled. This conversation on evangelism was happening, after all, during the middle of the Iraq War when many Christians were wearing American military uniforms and waging battle in predominantly Muslim countries. This reality was not addressed.

Finally, during a plenary discussion, I stood and affirmed much of what I had heard in the conversation about evangelism, then shared the following:

> When Mennonites meet someone and try to share the love of Jesus with them, an important starting point for us is the commitment that we will not kill them. Having this reputation has opened all kinds of doors and opportunities for Mennonite Christians. For example, the city of Qom in Iran is the global center of Shiite scholarship. In a city of one million Muslims, there are, as I understand it, exactly two Christians: a Mennonite couple who are studying and learning about Islam, and who are often invited to share personally and extensively about their Christian faith. This opportunity is given to them because the Muslims there know that Mennonites are deeply committed to Jesus, the Prince of Peace.

I paused a moment before continuing with a smile: "We don't want to hoard these possibilities. We want all of you to get in on these kinds of opportunities to share God's love!"

## Gifts to give and receive

Anabaptists and Mennonites have a number of rich gifts to share with the broader body of Christ, including the centrality of peacemaking, discipleship, and our belief that God's primary instrument in the world is the church. We don't own any of these perspectives, but this combination of gifts is rather unique and is of benefit to the broader body of Christ.

One of the treasures of Mennonite life and practice is the commitment to following Jesus in daily life. The life and teachings of Jesus are not just a comma in the creed between the virgin birth and Jesus' crucifixion, but should be our daily bread. Jesus is not just someone to believe in. Jesus is to be obeyed and followed. The way to get to know Jesus is not only by studying or worshiping him, but also by following him each day. This is the Jesus who heals the sick, befriends the outcast, shares bread with the stranger, gives his cloak to the poor, forgives those who betray and abandon him, and loves even his enemies. Using stories and images, Jesus helped his followers imagine the world as God intended it and empowered them to begin to live into that new reality.

Anabaptists and their Mennonite descendants have long held the conviction that God's primary strategy for God's reign to break into this world is through the church. The church, in this understanding, is an alternative community that embodies kingdom values. It is not a chaplain to the state, blessing the current order, but a community that in its life and witness points to the new order God intends for the world. The church is not merely an association of people interested in spiritual things, but a community that embodies an alternative economics and politics. Many Christian traditions still believe that the most important way to influence the world is to pull the levers of power in Washington, D.C., or state capitals. Mennonites are inspired by Jesus' image of leaven in the dough. Like yeast, the church is called to enter deeply into its context and transform the whole by first and foremost being the church of Jesus Christ.

But not only do Mennonites have gifts to offer, we also have important gifts to receive from the broader body of Christ. When we cling to our unique treasures, faith can become distorted and we sometimes lose perspective. While Mennonites have emphasized following Jesus and discipleship, we have important things to learn about abiding in Jesus and grace. While we have highlighted peacemaking, we are often uncomfortable inviting others to give their allegiance to Jesus. While we emphasize the life and teachings of the person of Jesus, some of us are hesitant to claim the presence and power of the Spirit with us. While we pride ourselves in eschewing violence, in our American context many of us have made our peace with injustice. Pentecostals, evangelicals, Catholics, African American churches, and Christians in the Global South all have much to teach us.

## Finding our place at the interchurch table

For centuries Mennonites lived in relatively isolated communities, both geographically and culturally. Perhaps in part because of the emotional legacy of the trauma of persecution, we remained largely separate from other Christian traditions.

During the last half of the twentieth century, however, through our service, relief, mission, and peacemaking efforts, we emerged from our cocoon and began to engage in interchurch encounters and collaboration. Often our academics and theologians were key links to the broader Christian world, presenting and interpreting Mennonite life and practice.

The shift that has taken place in just the past twenty years in our relationships with other Christians is mind-boggling. Christian traditions and denominations that had at one time participated in persecution of Anabaptists or condemned them as heretics are now seeking relationship with us. Churches we viewed with skepticism and mistrust have become important partners. Mennonites have had formal dialogues with Reformed, Catholic, and Lutheran bodies at national and global levels, resulting in moving words and deeds of repentance, forgiveness, and reconciliation. In a highly symbolic step, Mennonite Church USA joined Christian Churches Together in 2007, thus formally taking our place at the table with other parts of the broader body of Christ.

## New possibilities

In December 2013, Bill Hybels, pastor of Willow Creek Community Church, preached a sermon on Jesus' way of peace, drawing heavily on a chapter from a Herald Press book by John Paul Lederach. Lederach, the son and grandson of Mennonite ministers, is known widely as a teacher and skilled practitioner of international peacemaking. Seven months later, a new edition of the book, now entitled *Reconcile*, was released with a foreword by Lynne and Bill Hybels. At the Willow Creek Association's Global Leadership Summit, Hybels promoted the book to the 190,000 people in three hundred cities around the globe who were tuned in for the plenary session. Soon after, the book began to climb the ranks of the Amazon.com bestseller lists.

Peacemaking is just one of the treasures Mennonites have stewarded as we tried to stay faithful to Jesus. But this newfound interest in peacemaking is not an Anabaptist or Mennonite thing. It is a Jesus thing. Jesus blessed peacemakers, taught love of enemies, and lived it even to the cross. As the cozy alliance between American culture and Christianity is coming undone, many Christians are reading the Bible and seeing Jesus with new eyes.

Today, we as Mennonites are finding ourselves welcomed as full-fledged, respected members at the interchurch table. This is not the time to hide or hoard our gifts. It is time to share them graciously and generously. And many of us are discovering that our brothers and sisters at the table have rich gifts to share with us as well. Together we are recognizing that none of us own these treasures. They are all gifts from God and intended to be enjoyed and shared with abandon as we extend the table and keep welcoming others to the banquet.

# 27

# Cross-Cultural Education as Missional Discipleship

*Linford Stutzman*

## Introduction

"What is grace?" he asked.

Surprised, I stole a quick glance at the inquirer to see if he was just trying to be funny. The man, an orthodox Jewish resident of one of the large Jewish settlements near Bethlehem in Palestine, was facilitating a group discussion with our thirty Eastern Mennonite University students who were in the Middle East on a semester of cross-cultural study.

The EMU students, along with about twenty yeshiva students, young Israeli soldiers, and soon-to-become soldiers, had just watched a provocative film together. The film had depicted a tense situation at a checkpoint in the West Bank—or Palestine, depending on who you are talking to—manned by young Israeli soldiers who were tensely facing an unruly and potentially dangerous crowd comprised of a number of young, impatient Palestinian males. At the center of the drama was a soldier struggling with the choice between acting with compassion—allowing an ambulance transporting a Palestinian mother with her dying daughter through the checkpoint—and obeying orders to not allow anyone through because of a suicide bomber alert. In the end the

263

young Israeli soldier chooses to disobey orders and act with compassion. He gets killed by the suicide bomber. The film ends.

The discussion that followed between the young Israelis, all of whom are in the army or soon will be, and the Mennonite students, none of whom have been or ever will serve in the military, is heated and passionate, a clash between naivety and cynicism, between "realism" and "idealism." The Mennonite students are shocked at how easily their commitments to pacifism are dismissed, how efficiently their theories are dismantled. They gradually become silent as they listen to the Israelis point out to the EMU students that their pacifist assumptions have been developed in a region of the world protected by the most powerful military might on the planet.

One EMU student timidly attempts to shift the basis of her pacifist convictions to Jesus' teaching and actions by suggesting, "I just think that grace might begin to change the dynamics here."

"What is grace, and how would that help Israel's security?" the facilitator of the discussion asks. He is not trying to be funny. The question is genuine.

All eyes are now on the student facing a group of intelligent, opinionated, passionate, and motivated young Jewish peers who had never heard of grace. The silence is followed by a halting, self-conscious attempt by a young Christian trying to explain, for the first time in her life, a concept that had seemed so clear thirty seconds earlier. In that moment, I recognized once again that cross-cultural education provides the ideal conditions for missional discipleship.

## The missional discipleship nature of cross-cultural education

From the call of Abraham and Sarah to Paul's missionary travel in the Roman Empire, the biblical story chronicles the fact that believing God's promises enough to respond to God's call to "leave" is always a cross-cultural educational experience.[1] Those who leave home because they believe God's promises must learn how to live in an unfamiliar and

---

1. This is clear all the way from Abraham's call to Jesus' promise to his first-century followers concerning the rewards and challenges of leaving behind all that is considered necessary for stability, security, and control (Mark 10:29-30).

unpredictable world over which they have little control of anything but their own responses. And where this learning occurs, the reality of God's call and promises are demonstrated, often publically.

Learning to live by faith in God is inseparable from mission in the biblical story. It becomes clear, reading the biblical story carefully, and examining the maps of biblical travel, that the wilderness and the sea, two places where nonnatives feel the most vulnerable, incompetent, and insecure, are the ideal contexts not only for learning to live by faith in God but for demonstrating and explaining this faith to others while feeling that way.

Like the faith-learner-witnesses in the Bible, cross-cultural education is inherently missional *if* the student who participates is shaped by faith, or is open to being shaped by faith. To live by faith in God among strangers, sometimes enemies, in the cross-cultural wilderness or sea, in conditions where one is not in control, where the future is uncertain and the present unstable, where one is not self-sufficient but must rely on the goodness of strangers and God in order to thrive or even exist, to live by faith in God under these conditions is where missional discipleship can occur as in the biblical narrative.

In short, learning from strangers in unfamiliar surroundings is essentially missional in the travel narratives of Scripture. This is precisely why cross-cultural education is an ideal context for missional discipleship.

The only story of Jesus' boyhood in the Gospels is Luke's account of the adolescent Jesus traveling with his family to Jerusalem. Jesus is left behind when the group of Nazareth travelers return home. When Mary and Joseph return to Jerusalem to look for Jesus, they find him in the temple surrounded by teachers of the Law.

Having imagined this event since childhood, based on the nineteenth-century painting *Jesus in the Temple* by Heinrich Hofmann that hung in my parents' home, I was surprised when I reread the passage closely some years ago. There, we are told that Jesus was "*listening to the teachers and asking them questions*"! (Luke 2:41-52, my emphasis). I am certain that, even as a twelve-year-old, Jesus' questions to the learned teachers of the Law were a witness to the kingdom of God. At a very young age, away from his parents and his village faith community,

learned how to communicate the good news of the kingdom by asking questions.

This is an essential missional skill that can be learned by students
today studying in places like Jerusalem, Marrakesh, and Mexico City. I
have observed several ways this happens in cross-cultural study programs:

- Cross-cultural students are invited and welcomed by strangers
  from other cultures, religions, behaviors, and opinions. Under
  these conditions of both cultural contrasts and warm welcome,
  relationships are built from the beginning on mutual appreciation, positive curiosity, and openness.
- The hosts benefit. They are remunerated for teaching, or for supplying food, shelter, and other services. This is a form of "blessing" for hosts, especially in economically disadvantaged areas of
  the world.
- Because the students come as learners, rather than teachers, the
  hosts are open to honest engagement of questions and other
  points of view, such as demonstrated in the story of the settle-
  ment visit above.
- Learning from strangers cross-culturally forces students to grap-
  ple with questions they otherwise might not consider, such as,
  "What is grace?" These questions often have to do with basic
  assumptions about Jesus and the kingdom of God. Christian students thinking out loud in a group of Jews or Muslims can be
  somewhat embarrassing for both students and leaders (as it could
  have been for Jesus). However, it is also a nonthreatening and
  effective way for the student and others to consider Jesus and his
  message. It is a form of witness.

## Conclusions
I have led cross-cultural programs for EMU in the Middle East for over
twelve years. Here are a few of my observations:

- Christian cross-cultural study programs led by faculty who can
  demonstrate the way of Jesus and mentor students is the most
  effective for missional discipleship learning. Less effective are

cross-cultural study programs that send students off on their own rather than having faculty take students to learn from others. It should be added that cross-cultural study programs that offer the same safe learning environment of the home campus by using the home university's faculty to do the teaching on the cross-cultural study program, or that design the curriculum to match classes on the home campus, generally fail to maximize the missional discipleship learning potential.

- Christian cross-cultural study programs should arrange for students to learn from and develop positive relationships with everyone in the region, even on both sides of a conflict, both with people whose cause they are predisposed to support and those they have judged as the perpetrators of injustice and are predisposed to condemn. Cross-cultural study in areas of conflict is especially suited not only for *learning* to "love your enemies" but also to practice it.

- Students should have the opportunity to develop positive relationships with those they regard as enemies, not their own personal enemies, but those they consider enemies of the oppressed. "These are the tax collectors of today," I tell the students. "You have the unique opportunity to actually be like Jesus by accepting their hospitality and blessing them."

- Students need to struggle with faith issues—or what they believe to be the foundations of their lives—for these may not derive from Jesus' teaching, but rather from cultural assumptions about what will earn them status and recognition and make their lives comfortable and secure. Students must be taken far outside their smug zones and made to struggle.

- Jesus did all of the above with his disciples and we should be following his example in the way we design and implement cross-cultural experiences.

Today's young adults will rise to the challenge. They will go more readily to places that promise a certain level of risk, discomfort, extreme challenge, and even suffering than to places that promise enjoyment, comfort, and fun. These latter things are what the world offers. But Jesus offers the opposite, inviting us to his abundant life experienced only by letting go of precisely everything that gives us security, stability, predictability, and control in life.

Cross-cultural education is an opportunity to follow Jesus like the disciples did, to learn from both mistakes and successes, and, in the process, to give a powerful witness in word and deed to the reality and relevance of the good news of the kingdom of God in a world of broken promises.

# 28

# Applying Academic Research to Congregational Realities

*Jim S. Amstutz*

In 2004 I began a doctorate of ministry program in missional leadership at Fuller Theological Seminary. Each year of the program focused on an area of study germane to creating and engaging the missional journey— leadership, ecclesiology, and community—with the fourth year devoted to writing a comprehensive research project. Now, a decade later, it is fair to ask how this course of study shaped congregational life.

## Awareness

*New York Times* columnist David Brooks says that the highest form of wisdom is "awareness of the landscape of reality."[1] The seminal body of work by missiologist Lesslie Newbigin and the subsequent North American interpretation and application of that work led to the for-

---

1. David Brooks, "Baseball, Soccer and Life," *Intelligencer Journal/New Era* (Lancaster, PA) (July 15, 2014): A9.

mation of the Gospel and Our Culture Network. This formative work invites congregations of all denominations to become keenly aware of the changing cultural and theological landscape. Terms like *postmodern* and *post-Christian* take on new meaning when we embrace these foundational understandings. Greater awareness in turn leads to reshaping how we lead, preach, dwell with Scripture, and position ourselves as people of faith for missional transformation.

Building on this awareness, Patrick Keifert invites pastors and congregations to rethink how they utilize demographic data in the locality where they serve. Instead of marketing the church and its programs to the consumers in our community, we should learn to "narrate the numbers." He writes: "The numbers gathered in demographic surveys become part of (1) the biblical narrative, (2) the narrative of the local church, (3) the local church's role as public moral companion within civil society, and (4) the narratives of real, specific persons and households within the service area of the local church."[2]

Awareness is a spiritual practice that leads us deeper into the mission of God by connecting what we read in Scripture with what we experience and witness in our local community and beyond. An example of this was the Listening Ministry Team formed at Akron Mennonite Church—where I was pastoring—around Luke 10:1-12. We spent a year and half reading this passage daily as individuals and weekly out loud when we gathered on Sunday mornings during discipleship hour. Then we brought stories into the circle about people we met at work, in our neighborhoods, at the local elementary school. We began embracing the sending of the seventy as our missional mandate. Connections formed and meaningful relationships led to gifts being tested in a host of ministry opportunities. "Maybe my church can help" was the bridge from awareness to action.

## Interpretive leadership

These encounters required me as a pastoral leader to provide interpretive leadership. Drawing upon the rich tradition of a shared Christian praxis—action-reflection-new action—we were able to articulate the

---

2. Patrick Keifert, *We Are Here Now: A New Missional Era* (Eagle, ID: Allelon Publishing, 2006), 79.

understanding that God was *already* at work in our local community and that what we were learning *locally* had striking parallels to what we had earlier learned in *national* and *international* contexts of cross-cultural engagements.

Our congregation had benefited greatly over the years from the institutional connections we shared with Mennonite Central Committee, Ten Thousand Villages, and Mennonite Disaster Service. It had always made sense to us to send our youth group to the SWAP program in Appalachia to repair broken-down porches. It was, however, a much harder sell to repair a porch on Franklin Street in the nearby city of Ephrata. Tracking and interpreting this resistance and disconnect was the basis of my doctoral thesis.[3]

## Local theology

As a mostly white, middle-class, suburban congregation we continue to seek ways to broaden our understanding of diversity and community. Another bridge under construction in our efforts to incarnate a local missional theology is that of the increasing poverty culture in our community. Using the parameters of the school district where our church is located, we learned about the number of students receiving free and reduced-cost lunches at the elementary school less than a mile from our church and the growing number of people experiencing homelessness, hunger, and unemployment. This awareness, coupled with the lack of affordable housing in the vicinity, led another ministry team to form around a collaborative, faith-based transitional housing ministry.

My personal involvement in these efforts began informing my preaching. We took the opportunity to learn more from experienced missional theologians and practitioners in our annual mission festival and adult summer Bible school. We needed to understand the *why* behind the *what* for these efforts to make sense and be sustainable. We joined in the ecumenical effort to prepare and serve weekly community meals, sponsor an Iraqi refugee family, and equip church members as tutors, budget coaches, and mentors for people experiencing homelessness.

---

3. *The Porch Project: One Congregation's Journey toward Missional Transformation* [unpublished DMin final project], 2008, bound copy. Available on Theological Research Exchange Network, www.tren.com.

These were not flashy, high-profile projects. But this too is part of the missional discovery of finding God in the everyday. As Alan Roxburgh writes: "The primary way to know what God is up to in our world when the boundary markers seem to have been erased is by entering into the ordinary, everyday life of the neighborhoods and communities where we live."[4]

We learned that God doesn't always bless our good intentions. Sometimes our efforts to help can actually harm. We had previously participated in numerous "fix it and forget it" short-term projects, but when the mess is in our own community, the chronic problems are harder to ignore. We learned that you can never force someone to make good decisions and that too often "pray-and-pay" isn't enough. Walking alongside people whose network of support is fractured and frayed helps us realize that we may not consider ourselves rich in material things, but we do possess a wealth of relationships. The missional invitation is to broaden that network to include people who need a trusted friend.

## Deep change

An unexpected outcome of bringing academic research on missional transformation to the congregational level is a long-term pastorate. A Presbyterian pastor in my doctoral cohort at Fuller became a trusted friend and ministry colleague. We've been at our respective churches for over thirteen years and agree that our studies in missional leadership contributed to staying with our current congregations.

Robert Quinn argues that if we want the organizations we serve to change, we ourselves need to be willing to change:

- Deep change at the collective level requires deep change at the personal level.
- Organizational change cannot occur unless we accept the pain of personal change.[5]

---

4. Alan J. Roxburgh, *Missional: Joining God in the Neighborhood* (Grand Rapids, MI: Allelon/Baker, 2011), 133.
5. Robert E. Quinn, *Deep Change: Discovering the Leader Within* (San Francisco, CA: Jossey-Bass, 1996), 193.

Readings and research in leadership, ecclesiology, and community engagement profoundly deepened the well of my ministry at Akron Mennonite Church. I have had the opportunity to provide some missional coaching to other pastors and congregations, which in turn has provided new insights and learnings for our congregation. The missional journey is essentially about adapting, two-way learning, listening and cocreating, loving and creating space for those on the margins.

When our youth group was preparing a service trip to Chicago one summer, I provided some orientation over a series of Sunday mornings. Our group was split into two teams, one working with children in a parks and recreation program and the second teaching vacation Bible school to children in a homeless shelter. I believe that the preparation for that trip was as important as the experience itself. Some of those students are now in college and still talk about how formative that Chicago trip was for them. When we position our youth and adults for these experiences, being intentional about *how* we go is vital. The local, long-term partners who welcomed us affirmed this preparation and guided us in a daily rhythm of framing each encounter and reflecting as a group afterwards. It was transformative.

## Gratitude

When a group of us were invited by James Krabill in 2007 to share our stories and learnings as Mennonite pastors who had done doctoral work in missional church studies, we all said yes.[6] What I experienced in that gathering at Associated Mennonite Biblical Seminaries[7] was a renewed collective energy and commitment to serve the church at the congregational level. The missional framework we now embrace as a denomination was stewarded to us largely through the scholarship of Wilbert Shenk and Lois Barrett. They were two of the Anabaptist voices from the beginning around the Gospel and Our Culture table in North America. Their writings and scholarship added much to the rich mix of missional material available to all of us.

---

6. Walter Sawatsky, ed., "Pastors Discovering Missional Church Praxis," *Mission Focus: Annual Review* 15 (Elkhart, IN: Associated Mennonite Biblical Seminary, 2007), 150–54.

7. Now Anabaptist Mennonite Biblical Seminary.

I am also indebted to my professors at Fuller, Alan Roxburgh and Mark Lau Branson, for pushing us as pastors out of our church offices and into our neighborhoods and beyond to see and hear what God was up to. Now Mennonite Mission Network is providing resources and expertise to help us all live into the missional calling of God. For that I am deeply grateful.

PART 5

# Missional Journeys: Congregations and Conferences

# 29

# Growing Anabaptist Faith Communities in Dover, Strasburg, and New Philadelphia, Ohio

*Chet Miller-Eshleman and Mattie Marie Mast*

## Introduction

Meandering through New England on vacation recently, I (Chet) was surprised by how many church buildings no longer function as gathering places for once vibrant faith communities. Many of these have grayed and declined. Many have closed their doors. Church buildings now serve a panoply of functions—homes and farmers' markets, tree nurseries, souvenir and T-shirt shops, museums, and bars. Yet even as North American churches decline, a surprising number of new faith communities are being planted and watered by pioneers who, despite challenges, see great opportunity. We would like to take you to east-central Ohio where a small, yet growing network of Anabaptist churches has taken root.

Thirty minutes east of the largest Amish community in North America lie three closely situated rural towns near the banks of the Tuscarawas

River. These are Dover (pop. 12,800), Strasburg (pop. 2,617), and New Philadelphia (pop. 17,300). Despite several Mennonite congregations in the larger region, there has been little organized Anabaptist presence in these three communities.

A number of people began asking: Is there need for another faith witness in this context? Just what do Anabaptists have to offer here? Eventually, in the fall of 2007, God's Spirit began to orchestrate an encouraging response to these questions and the LifeBridge network of churches was born.

## Three LifeBridge communities have emerged

LifeBridge wants to be known for genuinely living faith in community, daily walking the talk, being culturally relevant, and understanding and eagerly living out the teachings of Jesus. We find that people are not asking, "What would Jesus do?" but rather, "What is Jesus doing?" And they want to be a part of that transformation and healing.

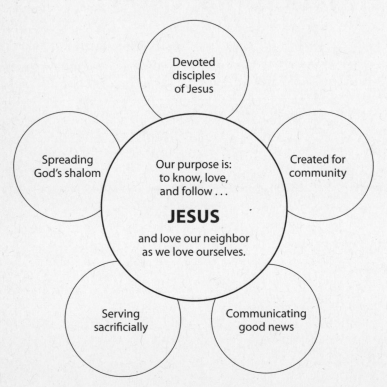

The flower or windmill image (see figure) reflects the core beliefs of LifeBridge Community Churches. The shared vision is "to grow a network of Jesus-centered families of faith that penetrate and transform the neighborhoods where we live and work" (from website: lifebridgedover .org). But beyond this common focus, each of the communities is developing their own presence and ministries in the contexts where God has planted them.

## LifeBridge Community Church in Dover

LifeBridge Dover first began in the fall of 2007 in Chet and Holly Miller-Eshleman's living room with their three children. Chet walked Dover's sidewalks, connecting with people, listening to their needs, hopes, dreams—and plenty of criticisms of "the church" as they had experienced it. By January 2008 a small group held its first public worship at the Comfort Inn, then in an abandoned retail store.

At year's end, members of the emerging church dug deep into their pockets, and with partner support from area Mennonite churches, a historic red brick building was purchased on Dover's square. Each Saturday morning volunteers from LifeBridge sweated shoulder-to-shoulder alongside others from Walnut Creek, Martin's Creek, and Berlin Mennonite churches, remodeling this historic building to be more meeting-place friendly.

Today the building provides space for a baby room that donates cribs, car seats, and clothing to low-income expectant mothers. There is a library with Internet access where neighborhood children find a quiet space for homework and tutoring. Generous volunteers remodeled the kitchen and fellowship hall for weekly Sunday noon "communion" meals. During the week both LifeBridge and the community take advantage of counseling and informal mediation, youth groups, Spanish and English classes, food distribution, and Jesus-centered LifeGroups. A homeschool co-op bustles about the building with high-energy teachers and kids, studying the classics, drama, and the arts and promoting Christ-centered spiritual growth.

An early morning men's group meets nearby at the local coffee shop. Many youth attend Wednesday evening activities, finding healing and a safe place to share. The children's ministry is robust, providing concrete ideas for parents to integrate quality time and worship at home and ways to be a family of faith. One of the church families donated land for a community garden that LifeBridge and neighbors share. Grass-fed beef graze for those who contribute financially and help to water them.

LifeBridge Dover enjoys a relationship with a sister church in the country of Colombia, where Chet and Holly served for four years with Mennonite Central Committee. The churches regularly exchange visits and are mutually encouraged and challenged as they enter each other's reality.

On Sundays about 140 attendees fill the sanctuary at LifeBridge Dover. To continue growing and reaching people and become a more effective planting church, building expansion is envisioned for next spring. While the current aging building has its headaches and limitations, members feel called to remain there and be a vibrant missional faith community—a true life-bridge—in downtown Dover.

## LifeBridge Community (North) Church in Strasburg

In August 2011 the leadership team of LifeBridge Dover invited Jason and Heather Rissler and family to be church planters in Strasburg, ten miles north of Dover. The Risslers bought a house in Strasburg to "incarnate" themselves in the fabric of the community. After years of living in inner-city Harrisburg, Pennsylvania, they loved the open field behind their house and Ohio's wide open spaces. They quickly realized, however, that the local culture seemed like a "tribe" and that making friends with groups and families would require time.

The Risslers began meeting in their home for Bible studies, barbecues, and birthday celebrations. The Rissler children attended the local public school as well as Cub Scouts. These involvements became organic ways of making friends. However, the process was not unlike going to another culture—after the honeymoon stage came moments of loneliness and strangeness. God's invitation during this process was to come humbly before the Lord. Indeed, God was at work in Strasburg in ways no one could have imagined and, today, surprises are still unfolding.

In their quest to connect with the community the Risslers began meeting other Christian families who had a heart for Strasburg. It seemed serendipitous! Most of these families were attending churches at some distance from the town, yet felt a call to live the good news of reconciliation in Strasburg. By divine appointment they began finding each other. Some were meeting for Bible studies in their homes with extended family members, neighbors, and friends. One group met in a local coffee shop and one family initiated a unique social service ministry. Imagine—total strangers, meeting each other and discovering that they shared the same passion! What joy, knowing that God was on the move in Strasburg, too.

A few people began meeting for a Monday morning prayer walk in Strasburg. To get further acquainted, to hear each other, and to listen to God, they also started meeting the last Sunday afternoon of each month. More recently, they are planning a monthly celebration that connects all the smaller groups and have begun reading a book together, *The Externally Focused Church* by Rick Rusaw and Eric Swanson,[1] to receive further guidance.

The local historic churches have also joined in this God-movement. Combined Lenten services bless the community. Out of this has developed a monthly prayer time for all members of local churches—a remarkable achievement given the wide variety of Christian traditions represented. Each summer Christian music groups are invited to perform in the local park. Indeed, this linking of arms and energies in the name of Christ to be salt and light in the small rural town of Strasburg is nothing short of a move of God, facilitated—we must add—by the key role Pastor Jason has played in networking and bringing diverse groups together.

How does all this fit into growing a LifeBridge community in Strasburg? There are still more questions than answers. But the Risslers are certain that God is leading. As the worshiping community outgrew the Risslers' living room they began looking for a larger rented space. The local Methodist church responded by offering LifeBridge a place to meet on Saturday evenings. The evening gathering has grown in size and consists of children's classes, a twenty-minute teaching session, small group sharing, prayer, and snacks.

---

1. Rick Rusaw and Eric Swanson, *The Externally Focused Church* (Loveland, CO: Group Publishing, 2004).

## LifeBridge Community, New Philadelphia

Presently, Pastor Chet and LifeBridge Dover leadership, in partnership with the East Ohio Church Planting Team, are laying the groundwork for an Anabaptist church plant in the neighboring city of New Philadelphia, three miles east of Dover. Nathan and Michele Nordine of LifeBridge Dover recently sensed God's leading to move to New Philadelphia and purchase a home. They lead a Sunday evening small group in an outdoor park pavilion where they reflect on the "red-letter words" of Jesus (Jesus' actual words in the New Testament). Together with others they are asking themselves, "Is God guiding us to plant an Anabaptist faith community here? If so, how soon? And are *we* to lead it?" It is an exciting time of discernment and building relationships in New Philadelphia, as we sense that God is about to move in a new way in this bustling county seat city.

## Four reflections, learnings, and challenges

### 1. The need for both vision and flexibility

Planting and growing Anabaptist communities that in God's timing reproduce and plant others continues to be our compass, providing direction, guidance, and motivation. However, what works in one place may not be the road map for another. The Spirit blows in different ways. We are learning to release and bless one another and collaborate where we can.

### 2. The need for self-care

"Planting a church, by its very nature, is all consuming," writes Pete Scazzero in *The Emotionally Healthy Church Planter*.[2] How are we to balance family and growing and planting a church? How are we to nurture the inner life with God in order to avoid burnout? How are we to become aware of our own shadows, our own self-will, and our "monsters" within? Who is our pastor, our spiritual director, our circle of friends?

---

2. Pete Scazzero, *The Emotionally Healthy Church Planter* (USA: Exponential Resources 2012), 8; ebook available at https://www.exponential.org/resource-ebooks/the-emotionally-healthy-church-planter/.

### 3. The need for strong financial partnerships

Fully salaried, bivocational, tentmaker-planters—there are clearly different ways of financing church plants, but robust financial partnerships are critical. Neighboring Mennonite churches have given support in prayer, finances, and short-term personnel to the church plants in Dover and Strasburg. Pastor Chet received a full salary in the beginning from neighboring churches; LifeBridge Dover eventually assumed this cost as membership grew. Pastor Jason began with full salary and may soon become bivocational. The New Philadelphia leader will likely be bivocational to ensure sufficient funds for existing plants that need financial support to prosper. If various existing churches each give a little as a form of partnership in local mission, church planters experience the affirmation of strong support and are freed for their mission and mandate.

### 4. The need to rediscover evangelism in bold, culturally relevant ways

The early church and our sixteenth-century Anabaptist forefathers and foremothers were known for their bold, Spirit-filled, compassionate evangelism. Their hearts burned for their neighbors who did not enjoy friendship with Christ and a vibrant faith family. Church planting that takes root and prospers in today's tough soils must include a fresh, robust witness that can, and must, take many creative forms. This is no small challenge, as Mennonites have long placed evangelism, especially as winsome verbal witness, on the back burner. This needs to change. One of the greatest joys in church planting is rediscovering that not only youth but adults, including the elderly, can share Jesus in a natural way that deeply satisfies and invites others into new life in Jesus where God's kingdom is ever breaking in and shining forth.

30

# The Journey Mennonite Church Story, 1930–2015

*Howard Wagler*

## God has always been and still is a missionary God

God is at work wherever his people gather and call on his name. The story of the beginning of a small mission church in Hutchinson, Kansas, has become the story of God leading in such a way that today the church is located and reaching out into multiple communities. God has always been and still is a missionary, sending God. From his call to Abram in Genesis 12:3, "In you all the families of the earth shall be blessed . . . ," to Jesus' call to his followers in John 20:21, "As the Father has sent me, so I send you," God continues to challenge us today.

At Journey Mennonite Church, we have seen our mission statement as a call from God that does not change:

> We welcome everyone to
> > Worship fully,
> > > Connect with others,
> > > > Grow in Christ, and
> > > > > Serve with passion.

Using this statement as the background, God has ignited in our hearts a vision for the next three years to be "Sent—becoming missionaries where we live, work, and play."

## There will be no preaching and hearing without those sent

I have been personally impacted by a passage from Romans 10:13-15:

> For, "Everyone who calls on the name of the Lord shall be saved." But how are they to call on one in whom they have not believed? And how are they to believe in one of whom they have never heard? And how are they to hear without someone to proclaim him? And how are they to proclaim him unless they are sent? As it is written, "How beautiful are the feet of those who bring good news!"

There will be no call, no belief, no hearing, and no preaching, unless there are *those sent to share the good news.* All Christ-followers are sent to announce this good news and this begins by building a relationship with one person at a time—learning to know a person well enough to earn the right to share the good news of Jesus' love, forgiveness, grace, joy, and peace.

## The origins and early impact of the ministry

JMC began during the Depression years of the 1930s when a cry went out from the southeast side of Hutchinson, Kansas, that folks were in need of food and clothing—two of the basics of life.

That call ignited the hearts of two groups of Christ-followers— Yoder Mennonite Church, ten miles southeast of Hutchinson, and West Liberty Mennonite Church, fifteen miles to the north. These faithful Christ-followers brought not only food and clothing to Hutchinson; they brought the love and compassion of Jesus as well. The love these folks had for the people in the community caused them to leave the comfort of their own faith communities and serve on the southeast side of the city.

Out of this initiative, the Hutchinson Mission was born in 1937. Summer vacation Bible school soon took place with one hundred to two hundred kids flooding in. Due to this growth, the group constructed a building in the early 1940s and in 1943 voted to become Pershing Street Mennonite Church.

There was something compelling about this group of people. The congregation was progressive for Mennonites at the time—possessing an organ for congregational singing, allowing women the choice on wearing the head covering, ministering to divorced couples, and allowing men to wear shirts with ties. Recently, when the early pastor's wife, Zella King, was asked what it was that kept the Pershing Street Mission going after the Depression era had ended, her answer was very clear: "It was a place where people felt welcome when they didn't feel welcome in other places." Whenever and wherever God's people love and live like this, people are drawn to them because God is at the center.

## Pershing Street expands to a developing neighborhood in South Hutchinson

Due to the lack of space for the growing body of believers, the pioneering folks at Pershing Street sensed God's call to a missional future in South Hutchinson, where a new community was being developed at that time. The first stage of the building took place at the church's present location with the first public service held on Good Friday of 1972. The congregation took on a new name, South Hutchinson Mennonite Church (SHMC). For twenty years, from the early 1970s to the 1990s, folks at SHMC welcomed, shared Jesus, baptized, and loved the people God sent their way.

Space needs emerged again in 1993–95 and congregational leaders began praying to discern how we might consider multiple worship experiences. Out of this a second worship experience was offered, followed in 2000 by yet a third worship experience. These initiatives presented opportunities to broaden the congregation's worship styles while holding tradition as a high value. The importance of decisions made and owned by individuals in the congregation was also evident at this time. The style of leadership empowering the congregation to "lead from the bottom up" has served the community of faith well, with mutual respect and accountability held high.

Some members had concerns at this time that people attending different services would soon not know other members of the congregation and that this might result in a church split. Congregational leaders began asking the question, Is it God's desire that we all know everyone, or is it more important that everyone is known well in a small setting? The result of these discussions led the congregation to add more small groups and Sunday school classes where everyone could experience intimate fellowship, personal growth, and pastoral care. During these years a number of associate pastor transitions happened as growth took place.

## Moving toward multisite locations

In 2004, SHMC was once again experiencing space needs and began to ask God what the next step should be. We engaged a process of studying multisite churches—communities of faith in multiple locations that share one mission and vision, one leadership team, and one budget. Because we had many people driving a distance from outside communities it seemed right to consider multiple locations rather than adding more buildings at the current location.

We prayed, thinking God was leading us to the north side of Hutchinson. But in 2006, God took us by surprise in a different direction—to a community southeast of the city where the facilities of the Yoder Mennonite Church were offered to us as a generous gift. After a lengthy discernment process with prayer and seeking God's leading while developing relationships with people in that community, we began using the existing Yoder Mennonite Church facility for worship in the fall of 2008. In so doing, the Journey@Yoder mission center was born.

Three years later, in 2011, the JMC leadership team began praying once again about where God might want us to take another missional step. We thought as before that God was leading us to the north side of Hutchinson, but for a second time God had other plans. During this season of sensing God's leading, we received an email from a young pastor serving in a location some distance away, asking if SHMC would be open to conversations about a new mission center in the area around McPherson, Kansas.

After an extended discernment time of prayer, listening to God, and meeting with persons from the McPherson and Moundridge communities, we invited a pastor in August 2012 to work in the McPherson/ Moundridge area. Six months later, on January 27, 2013, the Journey@ McPherson Mission Center was launched at McPherson Middle School, a temporary facility.

God has worked in incredible ways with a mission initiative that began on the south side of Hutchinson by persons from McPherson County and Yoder, Kansas, now returning to minister again in those very communities. This is the amazing work of the Holy Spirit!

## Consolidating our efforts under a new name— Journey Mennonite Church

With new initiatives developing in multiple locations, it became necessary for us to look for a common name. After meeting with focus groups and with prayer and discernment, our congregation voted in early 2012 to change our name to Journey Mennonite Church. That name, then, became official in January 2013. Today JMC staff consists of:

- Lead pastor: Howard Wagler (1992–current)
- Campus pastor: Eric Miller—Journey at South Hutchinson, J@SH (2007–current)
- Campus pastoral team: Dale Kauffman, Philip Kauffman, Mark Horst, David Horst, and Judy Miller—Journey at Yoder, J@Y (2014–current)
- Campus pastor: Jim Ostlund—Journey at McPherson, J@Mc (2012–current)
- Student and family pastor: Jesse Blasdel (2006–current)
- Children and family pastor: Sheri Saner (2005–current)
- Support staff: two full-time and one part-time persons

We continue to sense God's leading in 2014 and beyond. We believe it will be important for JMC to create partnerships in the communities where our campuses are located. We are in conversation with the city council, school and business groups, and others. JMC's goal would be to have a 24/7 impact in our communities by having our facilities used equally during the week and on weekends.

Currently, JMC is taking steps to improve the mission centers in all three locations. In McPherson, a former grocery store downtown is being renovated with plans for occupancy by midsummer 2015. The Yoder campus is undergoing several upgrades to the spaces used by youth and children. The South Hutchinson campus is planning construction in the next two years for additional multiuse space as well as a joint venture with the city of South Hutchinson for a wellness center.

As God leads us into new initiatives, congregational discernment is most important. This happens as elders, pastoral staff, and focus groups pray, listen, and discern together before launching any new missional endeavors. This process cannot be rushed and must be held loosely as we allow the Holy Spirit to lead into vision for each new year.

Following this process on an annual basis, new teaching series are planned to help JMC stay anchored in God's incarnational, missional calling and purpose. As we teach our way through transitions, framed by our ongoing embrace of the Mennonite *Confession of Faith* as a guide for congregational belief and practice, we welcome a wide variety of people to join in the journey of being transformed into the image of Jesus.

"Now to him who by the power at work within us is able to accomplish abundantly far more than all we can ask or imagine, to him be glory in the church and in Christ Jesus to all generations, forever and ever. Amen" (Eph 3:20-21).

**31**

# The C3

## The Calvary Community Church Story

*Natalie A. Francisco*

### The birth of the church

Calvary Mennonite Church began in 1952 with a group of workers led by Nelson Burkholder. These workers were commissioned from Warwick River Mennonite Church in Newport News, Virginia, to pioneer a new church with the launching of street meetings in the downtown urban area of Newport News, inhabited primarily by African Americans. After meeting for Sunday school in the community, Calvary Mennonite Church moved into a facility at 3115 Wickham Avenue and held its first Sunday service on April 15, 1957.

Shortly thereafter, Leslie Walker Francisco II and his wife, Naomi, became acquainted with the Mennonite community and began participating in the life of the church. Leslie became a deacon in 1960 and was ordained into the ministry there in 1966. In 1971, he became lead pastor with Nelson Burkholder assisting, and the following year he took on the role as sole pastor. Evangelistic street and tent meetings were a focus of the ministry of the church from its inception and they continued under Leslie's leadership as an integral method of growth. These were effective, not only in drawing prospective disciples for Christ who would become church members, but also in helping to lay the foundation for a vision given to Rev. Leslie by God to build a new church in the neighboring city of Hampton.

There street and tent meetings were held during the summers of 1977–79. I can personally attest to the effectiveness of this evangelistic method, because the Gatling family—my parents, four siblings, and I—attended these meetings. After hearing the lively preaching of Rev. Leslie we decided in 1977 to leave our Baptist denominational roots to become Anabaptist members of Calvary Mennonite Church. Rev. Francisco was not only my pastor, but he also became my father-in-law when in 1983 I married his eldest son, Leslie Walker Francisco III.

## The ministry expands from Newport News to Hampton

From 1980 to 1985, evangelistic meetings continued to be held in Newport News, as well as in the Hampton area near where the Francisco family lived. The goal was to utilize preaching, dramatized productions, and music from our praise team, choirs, and band, which I directed and accompanied on piano, to reach those who were unsaved and unchurched. Our hope was for them to attend the meetings, accept Christ, and eventually become members of Calvary Mennonite Church in Newport News.

Rev. Leslie II was installed as a bishop in the Warwick District by the Virginia Mennonite Conference in 1984. His desire was to increase the size of the small Newport News congregation so that a team could be sent from that church to pioneer a new work in Hampton. That happened when on April 27, 1985, Calvary Community Church in Hampton opened its doors for its first Sunday service, with Bishop Leslie II as senior pastor and his middle son, Steven Hiawatha Francisco, as assistant pastor.

The new church edifice in Hampton was located at 925 Old Buckroe Road. It was built with the voluntary efforts of many Mennonite contractors and workers as well as the carpentry skills of the Francisco sons, Leslie III, Steven, and Myron. Leslie Francisco III was appointed to serve as interim pastor of Calvary Mennonite Church in Newport News; he was then ordained into the ministry in 1986 and was installed as senior pastor of the congregation on June 1 of the same year.

In 1988, Leslie III felt strongly impressed by God to speak with his father about merging the Newport News and Hampton congregations. By this time, the ministry had evolved and was reaching a more diverse demographic of African Americans. Leslie's rationale was to strengthen the bond between the two churches in an effort to build and sustain growth for one viable congregation. After speaking with his father and the church council, an agreement was reached and the plan went forward.

## The torch is passed to new, younger leadership

Unfortunately, Bishop Leslie II's health began to decline rapidly, and as a result, he asked his eldest son, Leslie III, to assume the role of senior pastor of the combined Calvary Community Church congregation in Hampton. Mentored by his father, Leslie III revamped the structure and governance of the church's ministry and the congregation doubled in membership.

Bishop Leslie II saw firsthand the supernatural growth of the ministry, which expanded to include a preschool and before- and after-school program launched in April 1991. These initiatives came as a result of a God-given vision to Leslie III, who asked me to research the feasibility of the projects and eventually to launch and oversee them. Calvary Christian Academy was born, and it soon had a bustling enrollment with a waiting list of students.

After placing the mantle of leadership upon his son, Bishop Leslie Francisco II continued to battle with health issues and passed away at the age of sixty-two on December 13, 1992. The following year, on August 15, 1993, Leslie W. Francisco III was installed by Virginia Mennonite Conference as a bishop in the Warwick District.

## Growth on all fronts—at home and in international contexts

In that same year, a three-thousand-square-foot addition was constructed to enlarge the sanctuary and provide new offices, classrooms, and restrooms to accommodate the growth of Calvary Community Church and

Calvary Christian Academy. Also in 1993, Calvary Community Church extended its spiritual guidance and financial resources to plant Calvary Community Church in Accra, Ghana. This included providing support for sending missionary teams and financial assistance to Nsiah and Janet Agyarko, who would become pastors of the church planted in Accra, as well as offering financial support to other churches in partnership with Virginia Mennonite Missions.

Calvary Community Church continued to grow locally as well:

- It became necessary to purchase another facility in Hampton at 2311 Tower Place to accommodate the expanding multifaceted ministries and as an extension of outreach in the community.
- Calvary Bible College was established in 1997, operating under the same roof as Calvary Christian Academy while retaining ownership of the 925 Old Buckroe Road location.
- We assumed that we could stop having two weekly Sunday morning services once the church moved to the twenty-five-thousand-square-foot Tower Place location. And for a time, one worship service each Sunday sufficed—until we began to grow quickly once again.
- In 1998, Calvary Community Church acquired another facility, Fellowship of Christ Church in Rocky Mount, North Carolina. Ronnie and Louvenia Pride, ordained ministers at Calvary, were sent there to become senior pastors.
- In the year 2000, a twenty-five-thousand-square-foot addition was completed to enlarge Calvary to a fifty-thousand-square-foot facility, including a gymnasium, restrooms, locker rooms with showers, a commercial kitchen, bookstore, parents' room, and an upstairs office complex and conference room, which accommodated Calvary's local growth.

Many new leaders were added to the ministry, some becoming licensed while others were ordained into the ministry to accommodate the spiritual and numerical growth of the congregation. Several new church plants were soon to follow:

- In 2002, Flinn and Karen Ranchod of Pietermaritzburg, South Africa, were ordained and financially supported by Calvary to serve as senior pastors at Calvary Community Church Chesapeake, located in Chesapeake, Virginia.
- In the same year, Cornelious and Yolanda Carroll were sent and supported to serve as senior pastors of Abundant Love Christian Center in Houston, Texas.
- In 2003, Bishop Francisco III's younger brother, Steven Francisco, and his wife, Karla, were commissioned and supported to serve as senior pastors at Calvary Community Church West in Carrollton, Virginia. The following year, Steven unexpectedly died, and the ministry, which continued independently for a while with Karla, later disbanded.
- On February 15, 2004, Calvary District was established and recognized by Virginia Mennonite Conference, to relate to churches and pastors sent from and supported by Calvary. Bishop L. W. Francisco III was appointed as overseer for the district.

## Building on our legacy to refocus and rebrand the ministry

As the ministry continued to evolve, Calvary Community Church in Hampton underwent an extensive rebranding process in 2010 and emerged as "C3 Hampton" with a three-fold mission:

- Building community
- Restoring hope
- Transforming lives

As of 2015, C3 Hampton has a membership of about twelve hundred under the leadership of senior pastor Bishop L. W. Francisco III. The growth of the ministry continues to abound as the next generation prepares to take the ministry to another dimension of growth. The legacy continues through the shared vision of our daughters: Lesley Francisco McClendon, who serves as youth pastor, and Nicole Francisco Bailey, who serves as chief financial officer. Three new church plants further extend the legacy:

- C3 South Africa in Pietermaritzburg, led by pastors Flinn and Karen Ranchod (2011)
- C3 Atlanta in Georgia, where I serve as campus pastor (2013)
- Zion Church, led by Pastor Sylvester and his wife, Minister Carlie Taylor (2014)

## Lessons learned

The thrust of evangelism that launched Calvary Mennonite Church in Newport News, Virginia, and C3 in Hampton, Virginia, continues to attract and engage communities at home and abroad. Most of C3's church plants in Virginia, North Carolina, Texas, Georgia, and South Africa started with home Bible study groups that eventually moved into facilities to accommodate growth.

Principle-driven, practical teaching and preaching for productive living is made available from the pulpit to the pew, to the virtual members and visitors who join us via Livestream each week for Sunday morning services, Tuesday women's noonday Bible studies, Wednesday evening life courses, E.P.I.C. youth ministry activities (E.P.I.C. stands for "Experiencing Power In Christ"), and many other specialized leadership and ministry events.

While our vision has always been to empower generations to have a mind to work at enlarging our coast for Christ, our mission of building community, restoring hope, and transforming lives guides us as God's Spirit empowers us. Together, we are creating a legacy and impacting generations for years to come.

32

# The Lancaster Mennonite Conference Missional Journey

*Conrad Kanagy and Brinton Rutherford*

## Historical development of missional initiatives

The Lancaster Mennonite Conference board of bishops elected Keith Weaver as conference moderator in 2000. As orientation to the new position, he met with leaders in each district of the conference. He asked them what they needed to better engage God's mission. Overwhelmingly, he heard pastors ask for help in enabling the people of God to more effectively engage the people in the communities where conference congregations were located. Those district meetings with conference leaders birthed "Vision 2010."

Vision 2010 began a ten-year intensive effort to embed missional thinking into Lancaster Conference congregations. Some of the important initiatives and outcomes of Vision 2010 were STEP (Study and Training for Effective Pastoral Ministry), a set of core values and training curriculum; a credentialing commission; website revision; work on the conference's corporate image; the *Shalom News* publication; an annual vital statistic data collection program; and Partnership for Missional Church and Natural Church Development.

As Vision 2010 neared its conclusion, conference leadership gave thought to considering the next decade. A process labeled *generational planning* was used to review the first ten years (2000–2010), to consider goals expected by 2030, and then to plan for the next decade (2010–20).

While Vision 2010 had been marked by many new programs, what became "2020 Vision: We See New Life" took a very different approach. 2020 Vision set aside programs in favor of initiative within the local congregation to engage missional experiments and congregational multiplication. 2020 Vision offered a common vocabulary to talk about missional church. It was not designed to give congregations more work, nor was it a plan that congregations were asked to adopt. The core focus for 2020 Vision was and is, in simplest terms:

> Consistently following Jesus,
>> the baptizer in the Spirit,
>>> and joining in God's mission in the world.

Resource persons like Stuart Murray, Alan Hirsch, Lois Barrett, Craig Van Gelder, and Alan Absalom challenged us at conference gatherings and helped churches missionally engage their neighbors, friends, and strangers. Congregations began moving outside their church buildings into their parking lots, neighborhood parks, and fairgrounds to engage people with the good news of Jesus. "2020 Vision: We See New Life" saw the emergence of the Church on the Other Side—a coaching network to support and foster congregational multiplication. Congregations began experimenting with different multiplication models, like Mid-Size Missional Communities, Simple Church, Launch Large, and other more traditional church planting initiatives. The following missional snapshots explore a few of the missional experiments underway in Lancaster Mennonite Conference.

## A few missional snapshot stories
### The Church for the Needy
The Vietnamese Mennonite Church in Philadelphia, Pennsylvania, established the Church for the Needy in 2013. God gave the church

a vision to assist people in finding jobs, to help children through an after-school program, and to provide a shower ministry for people living on the streets. The shower ministry offered an opportunity for these neighborhood folk to take a shower, put on clean clothes, and experience the love of the Father. God also provided a facility—the House of Hope—to further carry out the congregation's vision for the community around them. In this way, the ministry of the Church for the Needy fully focuses on preaching the good news of Christ and making disciples, while the House of Hope—which the Vietnamese Mennonite Church renovated—helps congregational members who are in need and reaches out to others in practical ways.[1]

## Habecker Mennonite Church

Some years ago, with only one day's notice, an older couple in the Habecker congregation opened their doors to a bewildered Karen refugee family. Since that day, nothing has been the same for this congregation. Struggling with declining attendance over several years, Habecker's open door to one family has led to the arrival of one hundred more refugees from Burma/Myanmar, who had been living for decades in refugee camps in Thailand. Says pastor Karen Sensenig, "Though not at all like we imagined, God is forming us into people of radical, relational hospitality. We are learning how to let others host us, as exemplified by the seventy Jesus sent out in Luke 10. God is transforming us, like all disciples who encounter Jesus in the 'other.' We are alert to the move of God's Spirit as on the day of Pentecost." Conversations at Habecker are energetic and full of new life and wonder. Worship services have become more participatory as stories of God's work flow in several languages. Sewing groups have become circles of care across language barriers. Karen leaders are finding their voices by preaching, leading worship, and seeking next steps in education and leadership training.[2]

## Elizabethtown Mennonite Church

In 2010, youth pastor Fred Zeiset proposed that the congregation offer a free lunch in the park nearby. The congregation agreed and the

---

1. Adapted from an article by David Choi, "House of Hope," in *Shalom News* (July–September, 2014): 14–15.
2. Adapted from an essay by pastor Karen Sensenig, "Who We Are," available at the Habecker Mennonite Church website: http://habeckerchurch.com/who-we-are.

borough gave permission. Each summer since then, volunteers serve up a delicious meal on Tuesdays and Thursdays for nine weeks in summer. Folks from both the congregation and the community serve, eat, visit, and play together. This past summer, leaders of "Lunch in the Park" reported that fourteen different persons gave leadership to serving the meals during the nine weeks and that more than two thousand meals had been served. They also noted that two girls who attended on the last day offered their allowances in hopes that Lunch in the Park would continue. One leader told the following story, "A woman began attending Lunch in the Park from the beginning. A summer ago, her girls came to Kids Week—it was their first time inside of a church. Since then, both girls and their mom have become involved in the church. In the meantime, this woman has invited her friends and neighbors to come to Lunch in the Park. And they come!"

## Vision Columbia

When the small, struggling Mennonite church in Columbia, Pennsylvania, decided to close its doors in 2010, the bishop for the district immediately began a discernment process to work at a restart. Clair and Beth Good responded and moved to Columbia to launch Vision Columbia. Both were experienced missionaries in East Africa under Eastern Mennonite Missions. They set about the task of asking God to bring the dry bones of Ezekiel back to life. Using lessons learned from their years of partnering with the Spirit to give birth to a church among the Maasai people of southern Kenya, Clair purchased a dog and began walking the streets of Columbia looking for the needy, the lost, the forgotten, and the outcasts. He concluded that God could build a church with these people. Meals, food distribution, service projects, Bible studies, a health clinic, and eventually a Sunday gathering tell the story of new life in Columbia. New leadership is emerging from among those now connected to Vision Columbia.

## Mosaic International Fellowship

When the management of Dial Apartments contacted Loice Byler about the possibility of visiting with the aged renters in the building, she embraced the opportunity with vigor. Visiting soon moved to praying with the renters, and then to a Bible study with them. Loice was soon joined by her husband, Jon Byler, and a missional experiment began in the basement community room on Sunday mornings. Using a "simple church" model of engagement with the Bible in a group setting, Mosaic International Fellowship was born. The Bylers attend West End Mennonite Fellowship and they represent one of over a dozen missional experiments that have emerged from within that congregation.

## Parkview Mennonite Church

When Martindale Mennonite Church outgrew their facility in 2009, they began conversations about starting a new congregation. Through a process of district discernment a leadership team was selected, a building was purchased, and planning went into fast forward. A "Launch Large" was planned. With Martindale District collaboration, involvement, and commitment, the first Sunday offered a full complement of traditional church opportunities for the more than 120 who gathered. This Launch Large provided a range of age-graded Sunday school classes, ushers, a kitchen committee, building trustees, and deacons—all in place and ready to go from the very first Sunday. Three years after that first service, Parkview Mennonite Church in Adamstown exceeds two hundred adults and children on an average Sunday morning.

## Multiplying missional Anabaptist communities

"2020 Vision: We See New Life" encouraged congregations to ask what the Spirit was saying to them. As an outgrowth of that sentiment, Lancaster Conference staff asked interested churches to join together in undertaking a missional journey of multiplication. The effort sought to mobilize small groups of congregations to engage multiplication in four steps:

- *Covenant.* First, the pastors prepared a covenant for multiplication to which each member was committed.
- *Cohort.* The model included working as a cohort for mutual encouragement and accountability.
- *Identity.* Included here was a commitment to missional Anabaptist identity formation.

- *Cycle.* Each member of the cohort further committed to prayer-fully discern a cycle in which multiplication would occur, per-haps within three to five years.

The first cohort—made up of congregations at Kinzer, Hershey, and Meadville—began in 2014. The group meets regularly to share ideas, plans, action items, and prayer. All of the leaders have "first steps" action plans in place to begin the process of missional multiplication. One of the realities that each leader has embraced is that the missional experiments that emerge may not increase the size of the traditional congregations they currently lead. They recognize that the multiplication may occur outside of the traditional church setting.

## Spanish Council, Coatesville

In 2014, the small and struggling Mennonite congregation in Coatesville, Pennsylvania, suffered some serious leadership difficulties. As a result, and with careful deliberation with the bishop of the district, the congregation decided to end its ministry and turn the building and assets over to the Spanish Mennonite Council of Lancaster Mennonite Conference. The Spanish Council located a young Hispanic couple from Harrisburg, Pennsylvania, who were willing to move to Coatesville and begin a formal restart. Coatesville is a very distressed city and has experienced major economic and demographic changes over the last several decades. In keeping with the intent of 2020 Vision: We See New Life, one of the newest missional experiments in Lancaster Conference is now underway in Coatesville.

# 33

# Atlantic Northeast Conferences

## The Joys and Struggles of Partnership in Mission

*Gay Brunt Miller*

A coming together. A rethinking of "territories." There was hope, vision, and a sense that God wanted to do something beyond what eight area conferences could do individually.

## The origins of a ministry partnership

The close of the twentieth century found increasing conversation between two long-standing denominations, the Mennonite Church (MC) and the General Conference Mennonite Church (GCMC). The two groups were "dating" and wondering what the future would look like if they were to get "married." A joint general assembly was held in St. Louis in 1999 and, though contentious at several points, support for the bidenominational *Confession of Faith in a Mennonite Perspective* and *A Mennonite Polity for Ministerial Leadership* gathered momentum toward a shared future.

Conversations were afloat in various areas concerning the possibility of regional conferences (Mennonite Church language) and districts (the term used in General Conference Mennonite Church circles) coming together across former denominational lines. What would happen in the northeast, some people wondered, where congregations from both denominations and various conferences already geographically overlaid one another?

The seed of what would eventually be known as the Atlantic Northeast Conferences of Mennonite Church USA—or ANEC MC USA—was originally planted in June of 1996, when leaders from Atlantic Coast, Franconia, and Lancaster Conferences (Mennonite Church) and Eastern District (General Conference) gathered at Groffdale Mennonite Church in Leola, Pennsylvania, for conversation.

It would be four years later—in June 2000—that leaders from these conferences again gathered at Conestoga Mennonite Church in Morgantown, Pennsylvania, and began developing more regular and intentional regional relationships. First referred to as "The Morgantown Four," the group soon became "The Morgantown Five" with the addition of Franklin Conference leaders. Eventually Virginia Conference (2003), then New York and Allegheny Conferences (2004) also joined the table. Later, representative leaders from Mennonite Church USA, Mennonite Mission Network, and occasionally Mennonite Church of Eastern Canada also participated.

The first of these meetings occurred during the initial formation of the Constituency Leaders Council, or "elders," of what would become Mennonite Church USA. National relationships were being built as well. Would each of these regional bodies choose to cast their lot with the new denomination? The answer to this question could not be taken for granted.

Early conversations focused primarily on issues of identity—who are we and who do we want to be?—and supporting one another through the challenges of committing to the newly forming denomination. There was much suspicion and distrust within the given constituencies, even as trust levels grew among leaders of these conferences.

Slowly, energy emerged beyond the transformation process of Mennonite Church USA and offered the northeast conference leaders new space for vision and dreaming together.

## A vision for church planting

Time was spent in the early meetings discussing the desired aim of these gatherings. Was the goal conversation? Cooperation? Collaboration? Alliance? Amalgamation? Merger? In May 2002, conference leaders agreed upon the following vision:

> We, the leaders of five conferences in Eastern Pennsylvania, agree that God is calling us all to greater engagement in the mission of planting and growing healthy congregations on the eastern seaboard of our nation. And that further:
>
> • We affirm our unity in Christ and around the great commission as the basis for our collaboration together;
> • We believe our ministries will be enhanced and the gospel given new credibility as we work collaboratively in this mission;
> • We value the counsel and support of other conferences in any new mission endeavors that one of our conferences and its congregations consider in this region;
> • We share information, learnings, practical resources, and personnel with one another in these missional endeavors;
> • We cultivate relationships of openness and trust, respecting the uniqueness of each conference, while we remain open to God's leading in further aspects of working together.
>
> This vision for collaborative mission grows out of the trust and joy we have found in fellowship and worship together over the past several years, and in our desire to support and uphold one another as we continue the mission of Christ in our region.

The vision crystalized further and more succinctly when Keith Weaver, Lancaster Conference moderator, articulated the idea of collaborating together to "plant Anabaptist churches and be an Anabaptist witness to the northeastern U.S. megalopolis—from Boston to Richmond."

## Struggles and successes in church planting efforts

Defining a vision is part of the challenge; living into it is another matter. How do eight conferences, with their own leadership structures, varying sizes and resources, unique histories, agendas, and guiding beliefs and practices begin to live into a shared vision?

Meeting two or three times a year, rotating leadership, and having no dedicated staff working on behalf of the whole meant slow progress. Those at the table represented moderators, executives, and administrators from conferences. Was this the right mix of people and gifts to actualize a vision of church planting?

Timing was frequently an issue. When some conferences were ready to move in an area, others were distracted with internal agenda. At subsequent meetings it would be a different mix of conferences who were ready and those who were not.

In May 2007, leaders of new missional experiments and faith initiatives were invited to meet with conference leaders. The expressions ranged from the Table and the Early Church (Harrisonburg, Virginia) to the Union Project/PULSE (Pittsburgh, Pennsylvania) and BikeMovement—a group of young adults who rode together across the United States and initiated conversations with young adults about the church and ways that a then-new social media initiative called Facebook was being used to network and build a virtual church among young adults.

Preparing for their November 2007 meeting, conference leaders realized that while they were *talking*, God was busy *doing*. The leaders plotted on a map "where either a church plant is taking place presently or where conversation is happening regarding possibility of a church plant." In awe, they placed forty-seven dots on a map of the U.S. East Coast. And in so doing, they were reminded that God was already at work!

Recognizing that much of the new growth across the church was happening among immigrant congregations, ANEC leaders met in May 2008 with church planters of African, Latin American, Indonesian, and Vietnamese congregations. In order to learn from them and further empower them, the church planters were invited to share their stories and responses to various questions, such as:

- How did your relationship with your conference develop and what are the benefits of that relationship?
- How has the dominant Anglo culture impacted your work?

- What do conference leaders need to learn about that struggle?
- What are your pressing, immediate needs?

Out of these meetings it was decided to interview as many church planters in the eight conferences as possible. Interviews explored:

- ways that conferences could continue to facilitate the vision and work of church planters;
- what was provided that church planters had found most helpful;
- whether there had been attempts to offer support that was not helpful; and
- any other significant points that emerged in the course of conversation.

Subsequent ANEC meetings resulted in a church planting vision and a proposal to carry out the vision. Meetings increasingly began to include conference and denominational staff whose roles related to church planters within their systems.

In November 2009, ANEC members took formal action to employ a person to implement the vision to support church planters and encourage church planting with "support in kind" from Mennonite Church USA. No hire was made. Instead, a church planting advisory team and a church planting coaching team were developed, with representatives from each of the conferences.

These groups planned three training events for church planters, held in Baltimore, Maryland (2010), Allentown, Pennsylvania (2011), and Arlington, Virginia (2012). The events were well-attended and appreciated by church planters. Rather than committing to making this an annual event, it was decided to simply make plans from one year to the next.

In May 2012, ANEC leaders again mapped current church planting initiatives. Nearly seventy church plants were identified within the eight conferences and Mennonite Church of Eastern Canada. These included many different kinds of initiatives and expressions of church plants, some of which, it was acknowledged, would likely not mature into actual congregations. It was also noted that:

- there was no uniform definition used across conferences to identify these groups;
- very few of these congregations were conference-initiated;
- the vast majority were the result of non-Anglo—immigrant or
  racial/ethnic—church initiatives.

Nonetheless, the minutes of this meeting captured a sense
of celebration:

> The church will look quite different as this continues. Since 2007, a number
> of church plants have "graduated" into full congregations. God's Spirit is
> moving and inviting us to join in the work of what God is doing. There is
> much to celebrate.

In May 2013, ANEC leaders invited church planters to meet together
for an engaging day of conversation and resourcing with Alan Hirsch,
a South African–born missiologist, author, and leader in the missional
church movement.

Revisiting the purpose and vision of ANEC in May 2014, it was
noted that the conversation about identifying staff for equipping church
planting work got lost in the reality of financial pressures conferences
were facing. A systemic approach to working together had not developed, but the question was raised whether they could work with what
was already happening and "goad each other on in our work rather
than trying to centralize." It was proposed to revise the vision statement
to read,

> Because we are called to participate in God's activities in our region, we
> gather to cultivate relationships of openness and trust and remain open to
> ways we can collaborate together in missional engagement.

## Leadership training, congregational revitalization, and other joint projects

While the most significant energy was invested in church planting,
the ANEC group also planned various other initiatives over the years.
In November 2005, conference leaders identified their top three areas
where collaboration might be useful as:

- Calling, developing, and equipping leaders
- Planting churches and making disciples
- Congregational transformation, revitalization, and health

Earlier initiatives around leadership cultivation included a multiconference publication called *Growing Leaders,* which was published over a four- to five-year period. During this same time, an Inter-Conference Pastoral Training Board evolved into the development of "Gateway Courses"—four core Anabaptist courses deemed important for pastors who did not attend Anabaptist seminaries. Eventually Eastern Mennonite University assumed management of these offerings, making them available to people living in eastern Pennsylvania.

Between 2001 and 2004, a subcommittee of ANEC conference representatives was appointed on behalf of Mennonite Church USA to develop a proposal for Mennonite World Conference to hold the 2009 World Assembly in eastern Pennsylvania. A representative from Mennonite Central Committee East Coast was also part of the planning group. Leaders from the Brethren in Christ, Conservative Mennonite Conference, and the Mennonite Brethren were also consulted in the process and issued invitations to Mennonite World Conference. Paraguay's invitation was eventually chosen for 2009, but this process laid the groundwork for the following world assembly, scheduled for Harrisburg, Pennsylvania, in July 2015.

On November 16, 2004, conference leaders agreed to plan a resourcing event to develop a common framework for church development in the megalopolis area. In January 2005 conference leaders met for a two-day retreat with author Mike Regele, who provided resourcing based on concepts from his book *Robust Church Development.* The November 2004 minutes concluded by saying, "It was noted that the trust level of the . . . group has increased over the years and this is to be celebrated!"

## Future unknown

Today, the future of ANEC—and of Mennonite Church USA more generally—is unknown. The 2014 year-end issue of *Mennonite World*

*Review* headline stated, "Sexuality issues test unity." Have the many years of meetings, trust building, praying together, and starts and stops of collaboration been in vain? Hopefully, not. However, this is *God's* church—and God will triumph in the end, likely more in spite of, rather than because of, human efforts.

# PART 6

# Missional Journeys: Multicultural Initiatives

34

# Redefining the Faith Family at North Goshen Mennonite Church

*Rebecca Helmuth and Jerry Wittrig*

## The early vision for a Mennonite neighborhood presence

The roots of North Goshen Mennonite Church (Goshen, Ind.) began in the early 1930s when a group of Goshen College students saw a need for ministry in the North Goshen neighborhood. Populated with Appalachian transplants who were largely poor and had little education, the area stood out to these concerned students. With no existing church in the immediate neighborhood, the students dreamed of starting a worshiping community and introduced the initiative to area Mennonite churches, selling twenty-five-dollar shares in the project. Worship services were initially held in a private home in the North Goshen community.

When the Beulah Baptist Church building in Wayland, Iowa, came up for sale, the students organized a project to buy the building for $300. They then took it apart—board by board—loaded it on two trucks, brought it back to Goshen, and reconstructed it at its current location.

In the early days the North Goshen church was a community church with local residents from the neighborhood making up the majority of its membership. In the 1940s, the congregation became a stopping place for many former Amish and Conservative Mennonites. The church grew rapidly, but the Appalachian community no longer felt comfortable at North Goshen and gradually left the church. Although church leadership was very missional and interested in the people living around the church, most of its members now had European Mennonite roots, largely from Alsace and Switzerland, and the congregation became a "drive-in" church, operating within but apart from the local community.

## Recalibrating the vision to changing circumstances

In the mid-1980s, the church started a gradual return to the vision of its founders when church leadership and other members began building new relationships with their neighbors. The demographics of these neighbors had changed; they were now about 30 percent Hispanic. The congregation started a monthly community carry-in supper, an annual block party with free food and entertainment, and a Christmas store where free gifts were gift wrapped for local parents and children. Using these events to build relationships, people from North Goshen were able to identify those families and individuals in need and provide them with assistance. Within a few years the Hispanic attendance at North Goshen Mennonite Church grew to about 30 percent.

*Clase de los Amigos*, a Sunday school class for North Goshen's Spanish-speakers, was formed and quickly grew in numbers. The congregation was challenged to meet the language and spiritual needs of its members and soon added Scripture reading and music to the worship services in both Spanish and English. Live Spanish translation of the worship services was also provided.

Congregational surnames have morphed from the overwhelmingly Swiss-German of Stoltzfus, Miller, Yoder, Nussbaum, Kaufman, and Troyer to a wonderful mix including Berdejo, Blacut, Elizalde, Hernandez, Morillo, Ortiz, Prieto, Quan, Ramirez, Rodriguez, and Tellez. In addition to our members who have European roots, we now have members from Mexico, Guatemala, Puerto Rico, Dominican Republic, Colombia, Brazil, and Bolivia. We are blessed to have a member of the pastoral team from Brazil and Hispanics serving as elders, commission chairs, Sunday school teachers, and music team members.

The North Goshen congregation continues to offer support to church families who face ongoing immigration issues, but with rapidly changing laws and the availability of legal counsel unpredictable, sometimes all the church can do is to walk with each family, love them, and help address their needs. Our hearts are heavy when we see families torn apart by legal decisions. Many times, as we have met the needs of people in the community, they have responded by wanting to be part of this community of faith.

## New and unexpected opportunities

God continues to work in ways we had never imagined. A couple of years ago, one of our members returned to his hometown in San Lucas, Mexico. When he came back, he said, "The people need Bibles!" On his next visit he took thirty Bibles with him. When he returned he said, "The people are getting together and reading their Bibles and they need someone to teach them." North Goshen Mennonite Church worked with Mennonite church leaders in Mexico City, and soon a pastor was going to San Lucas every two weeks. There is now a full-time pastor at the San Lucas church and the congregation is growing. Two North Goshen Mennonite representatives recently attended a baptism service at the Gulf of Mexico for fourteen new members.

35

# First Mennonite Church of Reedley

## Our Particular Missional Story

*Juan V. Montes and Stephen Penner*

### Celebrating with pipe organ and Latino flair

When First Mennonite Church (FMC) of Reedley, California, celebrated its one-hundredth birthday in 2006, those present were particularly cognizant of the multicultural, multiethnic nature of our church. Among the members of FMC, both English and Spanish were spoken. Tortillas were made in the church kitchen and zwiebach still showed up from time to time at the dinner table. During one worship service hymnals were held in hand while the sonorous pipe organ guided our singing. In another service, hands were raised in praise as contemporary Christian songs were sung and traditional Mexican melodies played.

The historians in our midst reminded us that while current dynamics may be different, they are nonetheless akin to what was happening in the early twentieth century when people of varied backgrounds united to form and establish our church in the first place. Some of those first members had Swiss ancestry. For others, the Russian Mennonite experience was formative. And for still others, later on, it was escaping the

Dust Bowl in Oklahoma that clearly emerged as the most critical event in their life story.

But for the last two decades the dominant multicultural experience has been the intentional blending of first- and second-generation immigrants from various Latin American countries with Anglo folk with roots in the former General Conference Mennonite experience. How did this come about and what have been the challenges?

## Becoming a multicultural, multiethnic church

First Mennonite Church has long been a faithful and steady supporter of the mission and service agencies of Mennonite Church USA. Many of our members have served over the years with Mennonite Voluntary Service and Mennonite Central Committee. But late in the 1980s, as the Latino population of Reedley began steadily increasing, the church decided to launch a modest outreach effort to these new arrivals. A small Bible study grew and graduated into a worshiping body known as Iglesia Vida Nueva (New Life Church). The clear intention of all persons involved was to eventually spin off Vida Nueva as an independent Mennonite congregation.

In 1995 a fifteen-member committee composed of eleven representatives from First Mennonite and four members of Vida Nueva began meeting to determine next steps in this process. One of the questions under discussion was whether we were ready at that time to release Vida Nueva as a new independent Hispanic congregation.

As the committee met to deliberate, a new idea began to emerge. Perhaps, instead of separating into two congregations, we should work intentionally at becoming one church together. After considerable discussion, *this* was the approach that came as the word of the Lord to us, and the congregation overwhelmingly agreed to combine our efforts and become one. The name Vida Nueva was dropped, as the two groups adopted the name First Mennonite Church (FMC), or alternatively, Primera Iglesia Menonita (PIM). Since that decision in 1996, we have had one budget, one membership roll, one governing structure, and two worshiping bodies.

## Questions and challenges still remain

The question is always with us, what can we do next to build our unity? How can this being one become more than just nice words on a piece of paper?

The dynamics that informed our missional impulse towards unity were diverse. Christian education was one important piece of the puzzle. As more children began attending the PIM service, the need for Sunday school teachers became more apparent. More teachers could be found in the FMC service. To fill this need, there was a clear, practical advantage to becoming one.

Our congregational discussions and decision-making process were clearly informed by the reading of biblical texts, particularly Jesus' prayer in John 17 "that they may be one" and stories in the Acts of the Apostles about the early church. If Jesus prayed for us to be one and if the early church dared to overcome cultural boundary lines to achieve unity, what might God be saying to us? As we looked around at each other it seemed more and more obvious that we should be directly engaged in these same questions.

The 1990s were also a time when serious work was beginning in some quarters of the North American Mennonite world to address racism in our congregations, church institutions, and individual lives. The familiar refrain was often heard, "The Sunday morning eleven o'clock hour is the most segregated hour in American life." These themes prompted us to examine ourselves, and not simply to point out the obvious sins of people in other faraway places.

A large number of people in our congregation had had previous experiences in cross-cultural settings, usually through Mennonite mission and service organizations. The skills we had learned, it seemed, could be applied in our church setting. Clearly, the church's many years of hearing and participating in missional stories from around the world helped to inspire our commitment and engagement in mission "across the street" as well.

It is our opinion that most people across the length and breadth of our congregation entered into the experience of "being one" with committed minds, if not with fully convinced hearts. There were, and remain, questions on all sides, and these questions are often framed with "we/they" language:

- How Anabaptist *are* they?
- What will happen if my true immigration status is known?
- Will they properly clean up the church kitchen?
- Why are they so unexpressive when they worship? Don't they care?
- Why is the music so loud? Don't they know it will damage their eardrums?
- Why do they read the Bible so literally?
- Why do they not bring a Bible to church?

As we embrace our missional calling to think and move beyond ourselves, simple but nevertheless haunting questions like these linger.

## Slowly, brick by brick, we are building unity

In the early church of the New Testament the observation that the Spirit of God was evident in the lives of the wholly different "other" was important in convincing Jewish Christians that the gospel could indeed travel across ethnic and cultural barriers. In a parallel way this has been our experience at First Mennonite Church.

When it became known that a Hispanic family in our church needed financial backing in their efforts to gain legal status, another family from the church put up their financial assets as a guarantee of financial stability. On several occasions in the recent past our congregation has held intentional "table talks" where we deliberately structure conversations around important, even controversial topics. Some stories have a dramatic quality, but it is the day-to-day crossing paths, working together in the church kitchen, and sitting together around a meal or meeting table that have over time made a difference. Slowly, brick by brick, we are building our unity.

The missional task of a congregation is not just for a select few members, but something that needs to be embodied by everyone. One way we think about this is in asking the question, "Can we detect something of Jesus in this sister, this brother?" Here we quickly run into the wide theological gulfs that have the potential to separate us.

For some of us, particularly those who attend our Spanish-language PIM service, the experience of Jesus has been life-changing and vital. Gone are unhealthy habits of the past. The heart and mind given completely to Jesus has led to transformed living. The theological focus is on encouraging ourselves and others to, in a similar way, encounter and experience the transforming power of Jesus. Jesus really *can* save a sinner from the miry depths.

For others of us, especially those who attend our English-language-only service, the decision to follow Jesus must lead to an exploration of the outer edges—the social and political implications—of Christian faith. How does our faith in Jesus influence our economic and political lives? How does Jesus speak to our views on Israel/Palestine? How does Jesus influence our use of the world's physical resources? Jesus really must speak into all aspects of our lives and how we understand and interact with the world around us.

Though our experience of Jesus may be different, it is important that within our congregation we trust and believe in the experience of Jesus in other persons. This translates into a strong and vibrant view of God's work among us, a belief that God can do far more than we can ask or imagine.

Local congregations go into mission "across the street and around the world," where they encounter an array of new and different ways of thinking and being. It has been our congregation's unique calling to experience the cultural, economic, and theological diversities of the world right here at the center of mission, our local congregation.

Our church is not a tidy place. Our organizational structures creak under the weight of our changing congregational dynamics. Our attempts to carefully strategize and envision what the future may hold have yielded only modest results. Rather, we have often relied on informal, ad hoc gatherings designed to confront specific issues. Overall, we have cultivated a relaxed spirit that allows us to flex as necessary while requesting patience of all. For the most part we have remained non-anxious about becoming a perfectly integrated, deeply and profoundly multicultural church. But we are at least on our particular missional journey—somewhere on the way.

# 36

# Living Water's Multicultural Journey

*Sally Schreiner Youngquist with Kristin Loeks Jackson, Sophorn Loeung, Amos Shakya, and other leaders*

In Living Water Community Church's Sunday worship, we pass the peace to one another in eight different languages: English, Spanish, French, Kirundi, Swahili, Khmer, Nepali, and Hindi. These language groups and more live in the surrounding neighborhood of Rogers Park in Chicago, Illinois. What enables this Mennonite congregation to hold together such a level of diversity? Besides giving a lot of credit to the Holy Spirit, we can name several ingredients contributing to this rich mix of cultural groups gathering around the Lord's table at LWCC.

## Diverse neighborhood context and diverse core group

The original church planters from nearby Reba Place Church studied neighborhoods and chose Rogers Park for its diversity in housing stock and people groups and its lack of any evangelical, Anabaptist, family-oriented church. We were counseled not to begin until we had diversity in our ranks. When we finally started public worship in 1995, we included African American, Anglo, Argentinian, Cambodian, Indian, and Laotian people. We came from diverse Christian and non-Christian backgrounds. We aspired to learn and model peacemaking and race reconciliation. Through various attempts, failures, and painful conversations, that journey continues with the present combination of racial and cultural groups. Lay Cambodian pastor Stephen Mum observes, "I see the people of LWCC really love people—no matter the color of their skin."

## Warm welcome and a culture of hospitality

Members who work with refugee resettlement agencies have given some newcomers their first invite to LWCC. Unity Choir leader Zawadi Silas recalls, "We had gone to some other churches first, but didn't like them. I remember Julie told us Living Water was her church. We didn't know where it was, but she arranged for someone to pick us up. We liked it the first day. Our kids said it would be our church. I liked it because they had a time for greeting everyone like our church back in Africa. They give anyone time to share a testimony or prayer request. They want everyone here to be free to share the gift God has given." Nepali pastor Amos Shakya agrees, "LWCC creates an environment that's fit for anybody to offer their gifts and talents. Everyone can work and learn together, doing ministry. LWCC is located in a center of refugee/immigrant people. When they come, they feel they are home because they are surrounded with love and care."

LWCC hosts a potluck lunch on the first Sunday of the month. Sarom Sieng, a longtime Cambodian member, sees cooking as her special gift. She puts long hours into preparing huge quantities of food to share at potluck. Breaking bread together and sharing our different foods builds relationships. Free food is distributed weekly from the LWCC building, sharing surplus with those who need it.

## Geographic proximity

Church members have intentionally chosen to buy and rent housing in close proximity to the LWCC meetinghouse and one another. This makes "life together" a 24/7 reality near the intersection of Pratt and Ashland. The big city has a village feel when you can bump into people you know on the way to the train or the grocery store. It is easy to give rides or advocacy, share job referrals, cars, childcare, prayer concerns, or gardening space when church members live side by side. Reba Place Fellowship's management of two multiunit apartment buildings with affordable rents close to the church offers additional opportunities for proximity.

## Cross-cultural friendships

LWCC pastor Kristin Jackson says it takes considerable time to build genuine friendships across language and cultural barriers. But she sees the fruit that has emerged because of such long-term investment. Reba Place Church members' experience with Cambodian refugee resettlement back in the 1980s was good preparation for entering relationships with more recent immigrants from Nepal, Congo, Rwanda, and Burundi. LWCC deacon Saysamone Putnam, resettled here from Laos as a teenager, understands what newcomers go through. She and her husband, George, mentor Nepali pastors Amos and Roma Shakya as they have developed the Nepali-speaking Saturday morning worship service. They have walked with the Shakyas through medical crises of a child with multiple heart surgeries. As we share each other's joys and sorrows, we are woven more closely together.

LWCC elder Sophorn Loeung came to the Reba mother church at age sixteen. Although he commutes a long distance to LWCC from the suburbs, he says, "I have a strong affinity and love for our church. It gave me life, hope, and a moral compass. I grew up here. I cannot leave these people I feel strong connections with as father and mother figures. I want my wife and kids to be formed by people who are not greedy and selfish. I want to live out my years and die with this church."

## Worship style incorporating different languages and cultures

LWCC's contemporary worship music selections vary from week to week as songs are introduced in English, Swahili, Khmer, Nepali, or multiple translations. The Swahili Unity Choir brings us lively singing and dancing two or three times a month. After a one-hour service using

English as the primary language, Khmer and Swahili-speaking groups disperse to other rooms to study the sermon text in their own languages. On our monthly communion Sunday we stay together. Sometimes the message is delivered by two pastors speaking in their own languages. We continue to experiment with how to weave the gifts and contributions of our different language groups together. Learning one another's music, dance, and history builds bridges of understanding and reciprocity. We all stretch and grow when we make room for the contributions of the other.

## Indigenous leaders and intentional leadership development

Our pastors have largely arisen from within our ranks among the different people groups. When necessary, we have recruited from outside to hire a needed staff member, such as a youth pastor. None of our immigrant groups came with any prior exposure to Mennonites or Anabaptist theology. We have shared the primacy of Jesus, community, and peacemaking. We study the *Confession of Faith in a Mennonite Perspective* as a membership preparation text.

Most LWCC folk from outside the United States have known the realities of war and loss of home. They see the value of nonviolence and forgiveness towards enemies. After many years of mentoring, Cambodian pastor Samrach Nuth was licensed and then ordained by Illinois Mennonite Conference. He says, "I choose to be at Living Water because the Mennonites support peace. I lived in Cambodia where war separated families. The Mennonites have a good idea about how to deal with that." Samrach has taken several mission trips back to Cambodia, preaching and baptizing new believers there.

Nepali pastor Amos Shakya came to us from Youth With A Mission training in Nepal and Wisconsin. He has been licensed for ministry and is working towards ordination. He and lay leaders from the Nepali and Cambodian groups are participating in the "Journey" program, a conference-based lay leadership development resource offered by Anabaptist Mennonite Biblical Seminary. This provides a great exposure to the wider denomination.

Young people from LWCC have developed their leadership gifts through teaching vacation Bible school to younger neighborhood kids. Graduating seniors are annually tapped to give a sermon on youth Sunday. Younger musicians are being mentored by experienced musicians in the LWCC music group. Experienced Sunday school teachers are teaming with newer recruits from the various language groups. Periodic election of elders gives opportunity to recognize and empower emerging leaders to team with LWCC pastors in discerning direction for the church.

## Tapping denominational and other resources

Churchwide support from other churches, our local conference, Camp Menno Haven, Mennonite Mission Network, Everence, and Mennonite Central Committee has encouraged the development of our young church. We purchased and renovated a storefront meetinghouse in 2005, thanks to gifts from many beyond us and a thirty-year mortgage from Everence. We have been able to provide monetary support to our Summer Service workers of color and Nepali pastor through community worker grants from MCC. Our kids have bonded across cultures at Menno Haven retreats, assisted by scholarship aid. We have offered an after-school program to local youth through grants from a number of not-for-profit organizations and partnership with students in a work-study program from nearby Loyola University. This kind of networking helps LWCC run a multifaceted program with a team of paid, part-time pastoral staff from a very limited budget.

## Stability amidst urban transiency

Last, but not least, many members have chosen to stick with LWCC over the long haul, despite internal conflicts and disappointments, external crime and violence, high turnover and burnout. LWCC has seen immense change of composition over the years, common to churches in urban areas. Young adults are particularly transient as they come for graduate studies or first jobs, but move on. The new immigrant groups are highly fluid also as they look for jobs and reasonable cost of living. So we expect to experience change in the coming years from who is here with us now. We feel pain from investing in others, forming deep bonds, then releasing members called elsewhere. Yet we also experience the joy of welcoming them back for visits, as they report from service abroad or elsewhere in the church. We have come to see ourselves as a sending congregation, embracing this role as part of our mission. We release to God the control of who stays or goes, trusting it is God's project. Those of us along for the ride get to cooperate with the twists and turns LWCC takes in its multicultural journey.

37

# Kingdom Builders Anabaptist Network of Greater Philadelphia

*Leonard Dow, J. Fred Kauffman, and Freeman Miller*

The late Mennonite bishop Luke G. Stoltzfus used to say that when he and his family moved to Philadelphia in 1951, there were four Mennonite churches in the city, but that these churches hardly communicated with each other or even recognized each other's existence. By the time Luke and Miriam retired and moved out of the city at the end of the twentieth century, there were more than twenty Anabaptist congregations with multiple connecting networks or organizations in one of the oldest and largest cities of America—the city where the first North American Mennonites had arrived in 1683. One of those networks with a long and consistent record of facilitating relationships across the city's Anabaptist community is the Kingdom Builders Anabaptist Network of Greater Philadelphia (KBN).

## Origins of the Kingdom Builders Anabaptist Network

In 1953 Mennonite Board of Missions opened a center for Mennonites living in Philadelphia called the Mennonite Student Center. Later named Student and Young Adult Services (SYAS), that ministry provided early impetus for getting the various churches and ministries together. One result of this initiative was the formation of the Philadelphia Mennonite Council (PMC), which, among other things, published a regular newsletter with news items from various congregations.

The PMC started in 1974 as a loosely organized group for the purpose of guiding the Interfaith Realty Corporation, the Christian School Committee, and the Meetinghouse—an initiative launched in 1976 as a Mennonite peace witness in Philadelphia's bicentennial celebrations. Occasional joint projects of the PMC included a summertime picnic in the park, a combined Christmas worship celebration moving from church to church, and several Easter sunrise services.

In 1993 the biennial Mennonite Church General Assembly met in Philadelphia at the brand-new Pennsylvania Convention Center. What a surprising turn of events for the mostly rural denomination to hold its convention in a large urban setting! The announcement surprised not only the "quiet in the land" Mennonites scattered across the country, but the city of Philadelphia itself. The newly formed convention center operations team appropriately wondered what six thousand Mennonite youth and adults would be like as they filled numerous center city hotels.

This historic moment provided impetus for the fifteen or so mostly young and newer Mennonite congregations across the city to begin meeting regularly to prepare for their new role in hosting the denomination. As they gathered, prayed, and planned, a new sense of "coming of age" emerged. Perhaps the Mennonite Church was going to take cities and urban churches seriously! More importantly, these pastors and church leaders gained a new appreciation for each other and decided to keep meeting after the General Assembly gathering. Most of them were, after all, pioneers in establishing an Anabaptist presence in Philadelphia—a challenging urban location. They needed each other. Building vibrant communities of faith needed to go beyond small individual hubs to embracing the city as a whole.

In 1999–2000, new and young Mennonite leaders chose the name Kingdom Builders Anabaptist Network, generally referred to simply as Kingdom Builders. The monthly pastors' prayer breakfast—which has remained the constant heartbeat of the group—eventually spawned various new events, ministries, organizations, and the launching of Philadelphia Mennonite High School in 1998. In addition to the new name the group adopted, the monthly gatherings of Anabaptist leaders became more focused on mutual support, worship, and prayer, with different congregations leading worship each month.

## A few highlights of KBN initiatives over the past fifteen years

Here are a few of the many activities in which Kingdom Builders have been in engaged since the founding of the network fifteen years ago:

### 2001

The ASSETS Micro-Enterprise training program partnered with KBN to launch a pilot project in Philadelphia. A series of classes were held, with participants coming largely from Anabaptist congregations. A handful of businesses started from this initiative and many more were strengthened.

### 2002

KBN organized its first joint Pentecost worship service. It was an organizational disaster! But it encouraged local churches nonetheless to continue joining together for Pentecost worship. For many Philly congregations, this service has been the highlight over the years of KBN's various activities.

### 2003

This was an active year for KBN, as the Mennonite Church USA Historical Committee partnered with the network for a three-day conference—"Philadelphia Stories: Kingdom Building in the City"—bringing together local leaders and national historians. In addition, KBN organized a three-day conference with Dr. John Perkins, culminating in Pentecost worship.

## 2004

Regional Mennonite conference leaders met with KBN for conversations about ways to be in ministry together. The Philadelphia Urban Ministry Partnership (PUMP) was born out of these conversations. PUMP was designed to be an active, entrepreneurial ministry and much of KBN's work was subsumed by PUMP at that time, though it has since closed. That year, KBN also invited Eastern Mennonite Seminary professor Anil Solanki to lead an MDiv-level course on the Psalms, and ten students completed the course.

## 2005

Mennonite Central Committee East Coast launched a major review of its urban programs with KBN as its prime partner in the process. Later in the year, MCC hired J. Fred Kauffman as the MCC program coordinator for Philadelphia. Kauffman, who had been serving as KBN chair, resigned his position and was replaced by Leonard Dow, pastor of Oxford Circle Mennonite Church. Dow agreed to take on this role with one condition, "That we stop doing everything that we have been doing to see if anyone misses it." With KBN monthly attendance already dwindling, the group agreed not to hold regular monthly meetings in 2006.

## 2006

KBN youth leaders and MCC Philadelphia organized a two-day peacebuilding event called "Packing the Peace of Christ." Over 120 youth attended the Friday evening launch or the Saturday workshops. One of the workshops dealt with gun violence. KBN and MCC together crafted a letter to Mennonite and Brethren in Christ churches in the surrounding counties asking for their support for legislation that would slow the flow of guns in the illegal gun trafficking market.

## 2007

Early in the year, KBN surveyed local Anabaptist pastors to ask them what kind of monthly meeting they would come to—and what they would avoid. Virtually all of the leaders expressed interest in a monthly meeting for mutual support, Scripture study, and prayer. "We don't want more work to do," they said. "But we do want to have fellowship and mutual support from other pastors." With this valuable feedback, KBN late in the year relaunched monthly meetings utilizing primarily the discipline of Scripture-based "dwelling in the Word" and prayer, reserving urban ministry business, planning, and visioning for pre-planned lunchtime conversations, when needed. Also that year, KBN began sponsoring a "Martin Luther King Day of Service" at MCC's Ephrata (Pennsylvania) Material Resource Center. This provided a wonderful opportunity for urban church members—not just pastors—to serve and fellowship together.

## 2008

Dan Umstead, with experience in residential construction, contacted MCC Philadelphia about ministry opportunities. This coincided with the needs of KBN congregations, but due to the poor economy, MCC had no funds for a new program. Oxford Circle Mennonite Church had, however, just purchased a large office building and needed to rehab it into worship, classroom, and office space. The congregation committed $15,000 to MCC to support the position of a Kingdom Builders Construction (KBC) coordinator. The Vietnamese Mennonite Church soon committed another $10,000. With that—and the hope of additional contributions from other Philadelphia congregations—MCC and KBN were convinced that the initiative could be sustained.

## 2009

Kingdom Builders Construction was thus launched early in the year and has continued functioning since then, doing larger institutional rehab projects in the summer with volunteer help and residential repair and rehab during the rest of the year to generate revenue.

## 2010–11

Since the launch of KBC, there has been increasing desire and conversation within KBN about ways to share resources beyond just the city itself. Two unique opportunities came about in partnership with MCC East Coast and KBN. The first was to help sponsor and plan the "Philly Festival"—similar to MCC's auctions elsewhere—where the proceeds go to MCC, with a percentage remaining with Philadelphia's KBN. The diverse KBN congregations have provided food for sale and logistics for the event, and many congregants have volunteered as workers throughout the day. Another way KBN has reached beyond the city is through the annual Advent hygiene kit drive and assembly. Contributing to the materials and assembly of these kits has proven to be another way for fellowship and work to occur within the network.

## 2013

Pentecost worship this year was a real highlight. James Krabill of Mennonite Mission Network led a KBN workshop regarding music and mission in multicultural settings. The twenty workshop participants broke into diverse small groups to compose songs. Two weeks later, at the citywide Pentecost worship event, we were treated to five new multilingual worship songs.[1] In addition, KBN legally formalized itself this year as a nonprofit organization with a functioning board. It began a time of recasting and visioning together, believing that this formal status will allow the group to achieve a level of both greater solidarity and intentionality as it relates to setting vision, priorities, and utilization of resources well into the future.

## 2014

From these conversations and planning in the summer of 2014, Chantelle Todman-Moore from MCC East Coast and MCC Global Family Program teamed with KBN to form the Out of School Time Collaborative. This brings together four KBN congregations who were already doing ministry, but who are now working together on planning, strategy, support, and visioning. In addition, in the fall of this year, KBN partnered with MCC East Coast and Mennonite Church USA to host the first Urban Anabaptist Ministry Symposium. More than one hundred participants attended over the two-day event. The gathering grew out of conversations happening between the three partners on how to continue to be a resource to each other and invite other urban Anabaptists into the network.

---

1. See clip at: www.mennonitemission.net/Stories/Multimedia/Pages/Combining worshipstylesinPhiladelphia.aspx.

## Assessing what God has done

For most of the years since Kingdom Builders' beginnings, Anabaptist pastors and leaders have met monthly to share stories, prayer, Bible study, and mutual encouragement. The group has continued to attract new pastors, church planters, and other ministry leaders. Initially, the monthly gathering was hosted by Messiah College Philadelphia Campus on North Broad Street. Later, it met at the Philadelphia Mennonite High School,[2] joining students for chapel and lunch. Eventually the gatherings moved to Second Mennonite Church in North Philadelphia and more recently to Oxford Circle Mennonite Church in the near northeast sector of the city.

At the outset of 2015, Kingdom Builders counts almost fifty churches and nonprofit organizations in its network.[3] Many of these represent African American and Hispanic indigenous Mennonites who have grown up in Philadelphia and who have been faithfully serving from day one! Pastor Juan Marrero, as an example, often notes correctly, "I am a fourth-generation Mennonite—an 'indigenary'!" Many of the KBN churches have become multicultural in composition, but others retain specific language and national identities—Vietnamese, Chinese (Mandarin and Cantonese), Ethiopian, Cambodian, Indonesian (various ethnicities), Filipino, Haitian, Ghanaian, Nigerian (various ethnicities), Lao, Palestinian, various Hispanic/Latino groups, along with a variety of Caucasians sprinkled in.

KBN has continued to have an ebb and flow of steady growth, diversity, and influence in Philadelphia and the larger church. The group now draws from outside the traditional male-dominated Mennonite and Brethren in Christ pastors and includes women NGO (nongovernmental organization) professionals and leaders, as well as neo-Anabaptists from a variety of urban nonprofits and other denominations. Occasionally even a brother or sister from "up country" in the traditional Mennonite heartlands will join us. We are busy planning and looking forward to hosting guests from around the world in July 2015 in conjunction with the upcoming Mennonite World Conference Assembly being held in Harrisburg, Pennsylvania.

---

2. Philadelphia Mennonite High School has recently merged into the City School.
3. See the current list at the end of this chapter.

In the midst, however, of all the things we are doing together, the focus of the KBN monthly gathering has remained constant around Scripture, prayer, and the unifying question of "What can we as urban Anabaptists do together in the name of Christ that we cannot do alone?" Philadelphia, like many urban communities in the United States, provides us with a lengthy list of areas where there is agreement for God's "justice to roll down like a mighty river": immigration reform, gun violence reduction, education reform, job creation, gentrification, incarceration/restorative justice, racism, militarism, and poverty, to name only a few.

Yet the fact is that in an ever-more-polarized world—and more specifically in our increasingly polarized Anabaptist/Mennonite church— the resolve of KBN is and will be increasingly tested with the question, How will we work together in the midst of our clear theological, social, and cultural differences? We continue to hope, to believe—and to pray!—that the day of Pentecost was not simply a one-time random gathering, but rather a model to remind us that there is strength in diversity. Such strength is required in seeking to partner with God in the building of God's kingdom here in Philadelphia.

## List of Anabaptist churches and ministries in the Kingdom Builders Network

### KBN churches in greater Philadelphia

- Abundant Life Chinese Mennonite Church—*Cantonese* and *Mandarin* (LMC)*
- Arca de Salvación Movimiento Menonita—*Spanish* (LMC)
- Centro de Alabanza—*Spanish* (FMC)
- Christ Centered Church (Koinonia)
- Circle of Hope, Broad and Washington (BiC)
- Circle of Hope, Frankford and Norris (BiC)
- Circle of Hope, Haddon and Fern, Camden, N.J. (BiC)
- Circle of Hope, North Broad Street (BiC)
- Church of the Needy (LMC)
- Church of the Overcomer, Trainer, Pa. (FMC)
- Germantown Mennonite Church (unaffiliated)

- Eglise Evangélique Harmonie et Solidarité—*Haitian Creole/French* (EDC)
- Ethiopian Evangelical Church of Philadelphia—*Amharic* (LMC)
- Iglesia Evangélica Menonita, Jesús es el Señor—*Spanish* (EDC)
- Iglesia Monte Carmelo—*Spanish* (BiC)
- Indonesian Light Church—*Indonesian* (FMC)
- Indonesian Mennonite Church—*Indonesian* (Harvest)
- In the Light Ministries (unaffiliated)
- Jesus Power and Love Ministry (LMC)
- Love Truth Chinese Mennonite Church—*Cantonese* (LMC)
- Manantial de Vida—*Spanish* (LMC)
- Nations Worship Center—*Indonesian* (FMC)
- New Beginnings Community Church (FMC)
- Nueva Vida Norristown New Life—*Spanish/English* (FMC)
- Oxford Circle Mennonite Church (LMC)
- Philadelphia Praise Center—*Indonesian* (FMC)
- Second Mennonite Church (AMEC)
- The Family Church (Koinonia)
- The Lord's House (Koinonia)
- Upper Darby Vietnamese Mennonite Fellowship—*Vietnamese* (LMC)
- Vietnamese Mennonite Church—*Vietnamese* (LMC)
- Way Thru Christ Ministries (LMC)
- West Philadelphia Mennonite Fellowship (FMC)

## Ministries participating in KBN

- Circle Thrift
- Circle Counseling
- City School (formerly Philadelphia Mennonite High School)
- CityTeam
- Crossroads Community Center
- Germantown Mennonite Historic Trust
- Heeding God's Call
- Kingdom Builders Construction
- Mennonite Central Committee
- NewCORE

- Oxford Circle Christian Community Development Association
- Timoteo Flag Football League

## *Abbreviation code for conference or denominational affiliations

- AMEC—Alliance of Mennonite Evangelical Congregations
- BiC—Brethren in Christ
- EDC—Eastern District Conference
- FMC—Franconia Mennonite Conference
- Harvest—Harvest Fellowship of Churches
- Koinonia—Koinonia Fellowship of Churches
- LMC—Lancaster Mennonite Conference

## 38

# Latino Mennonite Megachurches

## Lessons to Be Learned

*Martin Navarro*

### Latino faith communities—a challenge to traditional Mennonite patterns

Illinois Mennonite Conference currently has two growing Latino congregations. One of them embraces a charismatic style of worship.[1] The other one has developed a hybrid identity of charismatic beliefs and a seeker-friendly approach to worship. Both churches have a rich history of suffering *and* success. At this moment these churches are developing into a kind of Mennonite evangelicalism, with new perspectives on what it means to be the church. A Latino Mennonite megachurch challenges Mennonite tradition. Instead of hymns sung on Sunday in four-part

---

1. Some of the content in this essay is from memories of my upbringing in *Comunidad Cristiana Vida Abundante*. There has been very little historical research done on these congregations. The only study—barely scratching the surface—is that of Rafael Falcon, *La Iglesia Menonita Hispana En Norte America, 1932–1982* [Eng. trans. by Ronald Church, as *The Hispanic Mennonite Church in North America, 1932–1982*] (Scottdale, PA: Herald Press, 1985).

harmony, one is more likely to hear Caribbean-style worship with salsa beats, mariachi, and jazz filling the sanctuary.

Affluent Mennonites may observe these churches as outsiders and be quick to judge them as little more than "moneymakers." It is true that both congregations have theological tendencies toward a kind of the "prosperity gospel." Yet the history of these churches reveals their deep commitment to preach and live out the gospel. Both churches could and should nevertheless be enriched by various traditional Mennonite beliefs, like the role of the pastor, Christian discipleship, and a deeper understanding of community.

## The immigrant church reality

Soong-Chan Rah argues in his book *The Next Evangelicalism* that "the immigrant church carries a social status. Immigrants experience displacement by their experience in being a minority. They come from a country where they are the majority, to a country where they are a minority."[2] Comunidad Cristiana Vida Abundante and Sonido de Alabanza are no different than other such immigrant churches.

Both congregations moved from the city of Chicago to the town of Cicero in an era when the Latino community was experiencing pressure to relocate due to gentrification.[3] Pastor Andrés Gallardo and Apostle Juan Ferrera found the opportunity to minister to this growing and newly settled Latino community in Cicero.

## A few important themes for the two congregations

### History and growth

The example of Comunidad Cristiana Vida Abundante under Pastor Gallardo's leadership is a good one. The church had its origin at St. Augustine College in Chicago. It moved from having worship in the basement of a Reformed church to purchasing a new building of its own.[4] Every time the group has changed location it was due to outgrowing its current space. The church—first known as Fe Viviente—began

---

2. Soong-Chan Rah, *The Next Evangelicalism: Freeing the Church from Western Cultural Captivity* (Downers Grove, IL: InterVarsity Press, 2001), 176.

3. Falcon, *La Iglesia Menonita Hispana*, 108, 110.

4. See Allan Howe, "Centro Cristiano Grows to Two Services, 600 Worshipers," in *Missionary Guide* (December 17, 1996): 2.

with fifteen people. Today, Sunday meetings are held with one thousand or more in attendance.

## Diversity

The congregation's diversity is unique, with people coming from all walks of life. Some members are politicians and others are ex-gang members. The membership does not reflect a stable social class. A large percentage of the members are undocumented immigrants while others are economically well-established. Some members are construction workers and still others live in the shadows. This is where the prosperity gospel plays such a significant role. For the majority of the attendees, escaping poverty and moving to the middle class is an important thing to do.[5]

## Prosperity through generous giving and self-help

The prosperity gospel is an important theme for both Sonido de Alabanza and Communidad Cristiana Vida Abundante. Both congregations are located in impoverished communities. In regular services the pastor challenges members to give of their money with faith. Specific details of what the giver will receive in return is somewhat ambiguous. But clearly, people give of their tithes and offerings in hopes that their poverty will end.

The other part of the church's message, however, is the practice of self-help. People are encouraged to chase their dreams, to not be limited by their suffering, and to have faith in God. Chasing those dreams includes financial prosperity through giving to receive God's blessing. On some occasions the pastor has offered a prayer during collection time, stating that we give to God what is God's—money that represents faith—and to Caesar what is Caesar's—doubt. The leadership encourages members to open businesses, go to college, purchase homes instead of renting, learn English, and apply for citizenship. All these factors help people increase both emotional stability and wealth.

---

5. This happens frequently as church members find themselves saving money to open a business and then try to move into the middle class; see Donald E. Miller and Tetsunao Yamamori, *Global Pentecostalism: The New Face of Christian Social Engagement* (Los Angeles, CA: University of California Press, 2007), 172.

## Leadership development through small groups

Both congregations are committed to leadership development. The heart of leadership is in cell groups, now called small groups. This model places an emphasis on church growth, but also on the leadership development of the cell director. Opportunities to be cell leaders are crucial for both church communities.

## Focus on youth ministry in a context of gang violence

Both churches are located in communities where education is of poor quality and youth are at high risk to join gangs. The church offers a hope to succeed, while the schools become battlegrounds for gang violence.

Youth leadership is the heart of Vida Abundante. Each youth pastor in the past has had some sort of involvement with gangs or drugs. The testimony of the youth pastor must speak to the youth and be relevant to their context. The fact that several youth pastors at Vida Abundante are ex-gang members has helped to build bridges between the church youth group and Cicero gangs.

At one point, when Mario Tamayo was youth pastor, the youth group included members of two rival gangs—on one side the Latin Kings, with the rival gang, the Saint Disciples, on the other. Church vans sometimes picked up gang members from rival neighborhoods and youth pastors risked being caught in the crossfire. But Vida Abundante became known by gangs and they respected it as the sacred space—a place to listen to the Word of God. Some gang leaders have walked to the altar at Vida Abundante and changed their lives around.

## Community ministries

The youth of the church are well embedded in the community and in the city of Chicago. On one occasion, the youth and adults from Vida Abundante visited Farragut Career Academy, a high school struggling with gang wars, drugs and alcohol, teen pregnancy, and high dropout rates. Youth from the church walked around the school with a guitar singing *coritos*—Spanish choruses—and praying out loud. When the youth director and his group arrived in the back parking lot, they found a group of gang members holding a meeting. Out of boldness and faith, Mario Tamayo asked the gang members if he could pray for them.

Vida Abundante was addressing issues that other churches were ignoring. Youth director Tamayo with the church's youth built on relationships at Farragut Career Academy and created a mentoring program and a network of cell groups in the Little Village neighborhood where the high school was located. The strategy there was to reach the lost in the barrio—the neighborhood context where they lived.

Some members of the congregation were critical of getting involved in Little Village Chicago, when Cicero was "the location where God has placed us." As a matter of fact, however, Little Village was the neighborhood where the church had once been located and the youth leadership was well acquainted with it. And so, during a Sunday morning worship service, Pastor Andrés declared to the congregation, "God is taking us back to Egypt, but we are doing something different than the Israelites. We are transforming Egypt!"

## Struggles and challenges remain for both congregations

While there is much to celebrate in the lives and histories of these two Latino churches, there remain several key issues that they need to address:

### Retaining young adults

One thing that Vida Abundante has struggled with is keeping young adults. Youth during their college years begin to ask questions concerning their faith. Both churches tend to avoid the questions rather than answering them. They believe that if one is struggling financially it is due to unfaithfulness to God.

### Preoccupation with micro social issues

Both churches are often more concerned with micro social issues than with the macro social issues that cause poverty or violence.

### Tending to the spiritual growth of leaders

Discipleship is at the very core of Comunidad Cristiana Vida Abundante, though it is more focused on leadership development than on spiritual growth. The perspective of both congregations is making leaders who can "take over the city for Christ"—a *conquest* perspective.

## Keeping faith and discipleship connected

Faith can sometimes become separated from discipleship. One thing that these churches could learn from more traditional Mennonite churches is their emphasis on discipleship as faith. This is particularly urgent right now as many church members are searching for a discipleship that is more committed to following Christ than adhering to pastor's ideology.

## Pastoral accountability

Both churches need to better understand the pastor's role in serving the community. The churches are pastor-centered and lack accountability. On April 9, 2014, the youth pastor of Sonido de Alabanza was arrested on child abuse charges.[6] The church gave a simple apology but the hierarchy continued. The pastors did not use this opportunity to make a radical change and submit to the congregation. Both churches are increasing in membership and attendance, but the people do not have a voice holding the leadership accountable.

As the Mennonite church goes forward both of these Latino congregations are continuing to grow. These fellowships have much to offer the rest of the Mennonite church. And the Mennonite church has much to offer them as well. Our brothers and sisters at Sonido de Alabanza and Communidad Cristiana Vida Abundante are indeed the future of the church, giving a new face to the Mennonite Church USA denomination.

---

6. "Cicero Youth Minister Charged With Sexually Assaulting 6 Boys," CBS Chicago, http://chicago.cbslocal.com/2014/04/09/cicero-youth-minister-charged-with-child-sex-assaults/ (accessed September 12, 2014).

# Epilogue

*Stuart Murray*

No theological concept, however potent, is immune from the danger of becoming a catchphrase. Some of those who have been passionate advocates of "missional church" in recent years are becoming increasingly concerned that the reality often fails to match the rhetoric. Revamped denominational mission statements, program changes in congregations, and new training courses in theological institutions may all make helpful contributions, but activism and noble statements do not suffice to achieve the paradigm shift required.

It is encouraging, therefore, that the final sections of this book are entitled "Missional Journeys" and that earlier chapters explore many different dimensions and applications of what it means to be missional. The journey towards missional church is a multifaceted adventure. It will not be completed easily or quickly. It will encounter resistance and be prone to detours. What seems to be the destination may turn out to be only a staging post on the journey.

This is not surprising after centuries of church life in which missiology and ecclesiology were frequently detached; the pioneering ministries—apostles, prophets, and evangelists—gifted to the church by the ascended Christ were marginalized; and mission was perceived, if at all, as something that happened elsewhere. The Christendom legacy is powerful and pervasive, even in Anabaptist communities that should be more attuned to these issues.

The church has been operating in maintenance or pastoral mode for so long that progress will be halting and will require watchfulness and persistence if gains are not to be reversed. This journey has been likened to attempting to walk up a down escalator—stop for a moment and you are back where you started. Adopting a different metaphor, Anglican missiologist George Lings warns, "Pastoral mode is like a dominant gene. It is reproduced in the next generation with little effort. However, being missional is like a recessive gene and the perennial danger is that it will be bred out in the next generation . . . to eclipse mission, all that is needed is to do nothing."[1]

This impressive collection of reflections on the journey of MC USA towards missional church is best seen, then, as a progress report and encouragement to continue the journey. Hopefully, it will also be a resource from which other Christian communities can learn. For the journey towards missional church is one that numerous denominations, institutions, and congregations have embarked on. We have many fellow travelers. We have different histories, we prefer different terminology—missionary congregations, mission-shaped church, missional church, etc.—we face different sticking points, we make progress in different areas at different rates. But we are all on this journey and we have much to learn from each other.

Having worked on missional church issues with over thirty denominations in the past decade, I am saddened that many seem unaware of their fellow travelers and unwilling to learn together, but I am convinced that there is an opportunity to discover a new form of missional ecumenism that can take us so much further than the institutional ecumenism of the past. I believe the Anabaptist voice needs to be heard in these conversations alongside many other voices, not least because of its insistence that peace witness is a nonnegotiable dimension of being a missional church.

---

1. George Lings, *Encounters on the Edge* 41 (Sheffield, UK: The Sheffield Centre, 2009), 10–11.

What might I, a British neo-Anabaptist who has interacted with North American Mennonite churches over the past twenty years, highlight as ongoing challenges on your journey towards missional church?

## Verbal witness

I am aware of historical and cultural reasons why Mennonites have been reluctant, and of contemporary concerns about proselytizing and imposition, but this is an essential feature of a missional church—and deeply congruent with the early Anabaptist communities in a much less congenial environment. Lifestyle witness will not suffice in post-Christendom Western societies.

## Urban mission

More than 50 percent of the global population is now urban, and this percentage is growing rapidly. This is the primary frontier for mission today, hugely demanding but full of opportunities. MC USA will prioritize urban mission if you are serious about becoming a missional church, encouraging persons and congregations to move into poor urban communities.

## Church buildings

I have been deeply disappointed when visiting Mennonite churches in North America. Your church buildings do not reflect your Anabaptist heritage, nor are most of them missional in ethos or usage. They conform to standard institutional Protestant architecture, seating arrangements, décor, and ambience. Why not sell them and meet in places where you are hosted by others, or transform them into missional community centers?

## Money

When a congregation tells me it is now missional, I ask how they spend their money. Usually, most is still spent on pastoral staff, buildings, and church programs. I suspect this is true of many Mennonite churches, despite the radical engagement with financial issues in Anabaptist communities through the centuries. Jesus said that our hearts are where our treasure is. How we use our finances is a measurable indicator of progress on the missional journey.

## Missional ethics

I know that the issue of homosexuality is hugely contentious and has been deeply divisive in MC USA and that passionate convictions are involved on all sides of this debate. But what would it mean to engage in this debate from a missional perspective, exploring the implications of whatever stance is adopted for the church's witness in society and its impact on those it hopes to reach with the gospel? How does the way in which you have this conversation—whatever conclusions you reach—mar or enhance your witness?

## Apostles and prophets

If a denomination is to move from maintenance to missional mode, the dominance of pastors, teachers, and administrators at all levels will need to be challenged. The contemporary recovery of the pioneering ministries of apostles and prophets has been fraught with difficulty, with inappropriate hierarchical notions and unaccountable self-appointed ministries distorting the picture and discouraging others. Might your Anabaptist values enable MC USA to resist these temptations and recover ministries that were exercised in the early years of the movement and are vital for missional churches?

## Church planting

Realistically, many of your congregations will not become missional churches. They will not be able to make this paradigm shift. Some of them will persist for many years in pastoral mode; others are in terminal decline. Church planting does not guarantee that new churches will be truly missional, but it provides an opportunity to develop more thoroughgoing missional communities. And, as others have found, it functions as a "change lever" in denominations, stimulating others to push forward on the journey towards missional church.

Finally, a concern about the language of "missional church": Can this result in an unhealthy focus on the church at the expense of our participation in God's mission? A frequently quoted text today—offered as an analogy for post-Christendom Christians—is the letter to the exiles in Jeremiah 29, in which the prophet urged them to transcend their hopes and longings for their own community and instead "seek the shalom" of the society in which they found themselves. The earliest Anabaptists evidently had a vision of societal transformation, which is why they were perceived as so dangerous, but this became reduced to a concern for pure churches. It would be tragic if the missional church journey was limited to church renewal and failed to embrace the passion of God for social transformation and a renewed cosmos.

# A Missional Church Bibliography

## Foundational books on missional church

Bosch, David Jacobus. *Believing in the Future: Toward a Missiology of Western Culture.* Valley Forge, PA: Trinity Press International, 1995.

Gibbs, Eddie. *Church Next: Quantum Changes in How We Do Ministry.* Downers Grove, IL: InterVarsity Press, 2000.

Guder, Darrell L. *The Continuing Conversion of the Church.* Grand Rapids, MI: W. B. Eerdmans, 2000.

Guder, Darrell L., and Lois Barrett, eds. *Missional Church: A Vision for the Sending of the Church in North America.* Grand Rapids, MI: W. B. Eerdmans, 1998.

Hunsberger, George R., and Craig Van Gelder, eds. *The Church between Gospel and Culture: The Emerging Mission in North America.* Grand Rapids, MI: W.B. Eerdmans, 1996.

Newbigin, Lesslie. *The Gospel in a Pluralist Society.* Grand Rapids, MI: W. B. Eerdmans, 1989.

Shenk, Wilbert R., ed. *The Transfiguration of Mission: Biblical, Theological and Historical Foundations.* Scottdale, PA: Herald Press, 1993.

Shenk, Wilbert R. *Write the Vision: The Church Renewed.* Eugene, OR: Wipf and Stock Publishers, 2001.

Wright, Christopher J. H. *The Mission of God: Unlocking the Bible's Grand Narrative.* Downers Grove, IL: IVP Academic, 2006.

## Cultural contexts and the church's witness

Boshart, David W. *Becoming Missional: Denominations and New Church Development in Complex Social Contexts.* Eugene, OR: Wipf and Stock, 2011.

Branson, Mark Lau, and Juan Francisco Martínez. *Churches, Cultures and Leadership: A Practical Theology of Congregations and Ethnicities.* Downers Grove, IL: IVP Academic, 2011.

Chung, Paul S. *Reclaiming Mission as Constructive Theology: Missional Church and World Christianity.* Eugene, OR: Cascade Books, 2012.

Kirk, J. Andrew, John Corrie, and Cathy Ross. *Mission in Context: Explorations Inspired by J. Andrew Kirk.* Farnham, Surrey, UK: Ashgate, 2012.

## Missional leadership

Frost, Michael, and Alan Hirsch. *The Shaping of Things to Come: Innovation and Mission for the 21st-Century Church.* Peabody, MA: Hendrickson Publishers, 2003.

Robinson, Anthony B. *Changing the Conversation: A Third Way for Congregations.* Grand Rapids, MI: W. B. Eerdmans, 2008.

Roxburgh, Alan J. *Missional Map-Making: Skills for Leading in Times of Transition.* San Francisco, CA: Jossey-Bass, 2010.

Roxburgh, Alan J., and Fred Romanuk. *The Missional Leader: Equipping Your Church to Reach a Changing World.* San Francisco, CA: Jossey-Bass, 2006.

## Congregational transformation for missional vision and practice

Barrett, Lois. *Mission-Focused Congregations: A Bible Study.* Scottdale, PA: Faith and Life Resources, 2002.

Hirsch, Alan, and Darryn Altclass. *The Forgotten Ways Handbook: A Practical Guide for Developing Missional Churches.* Grand Rapids, MI: Brazos Press, 2009.

Krabill, James R. *Does Your Church "Smell" Like Mission?: Reflections on Becoming a Missional Church.* Elkhart, IN: Mennonite Mission Network, 2003.

Missional Church Consultation and Dwight J. Zscheile. *Cultivating Sent Communities: Missional Spiritual Formation.* Grand Rapids, MI: W. B. Eerdmans, 2012.

Murray Williams, Sian, and Stuart Murray Wiliams. *The Power of All: Building a Multivoiced Church.* Harrisonburg, VA: Herald Press, 2012.

Robinson, Anthony B. *Transforming Congregational Culture.* Grand Rapids, MI: W. B. Eerdmans, 2003.

Rouse, Richard W., and Craig Van Gelder. *A Field Guide for the Missional Congregation: Embarking on a Journey of Transformation.* Minneapolis, MN: Augsburg Fortress, 2008.

Roxburgh, Alan J., M. Scott Boren, and Mark Priddy. *Introducing the Missional Church: What It Is, Why It Matters, How to Become One.* Grand Rapids, MI: Baker Books, 2009.

Stetzer, Ed, and David Putman. *Breaking the Missional Code: Your Church Can Become a Missionary in Your Community.* Nashville, TN: Broadman and Holman, 2006.

Van Gelder, Craig. *The Missional Church and Denominations: Helping Congregations Develop a Missional Identity.* Grand Rapids, MI: W. B. Eerdmans, 2008.

Woodward, J. R. *Creating a Missional Culture: Equipping the Church for the Sake of the World.* Downers Grove, IL: InterVarsity Press, 2012.

## Studies and stories of missional congregations

Barrett, Lois, ed. *Treasure in Clay Jars: Patterns in Missional Faithfulness.* Grand Rapids, MI: W. B. Eerdmans, 2004.

Brownson, James V. *StormFront: The Good News of God.* Grand Rapids, MI: W. B. Eerdmans, 2003.

Stiller, Karen, and Willard M. Metzger. *Going Missional: Conversations with 13 Canadian Churches Who Have Embraced Missional Life.* Winnipeg, MB: Word Alive Press, 2010.

## Worship practices in the missional church

Gray-Reeves, Mary, and Michael Perham. *The Hospitality of God: Emerging Worship for a Missional Church.* New York: Seabury Books, 2011.

Schmit, Clayton J. *Sent and Gathered: A Worship Manual for the Missional Church.* Grand Rapids, MI: Baker Academic, 2009.

Steelberg, Donald R. *The True Meaning of the Last Supper, Welcoming Others: A Missional Approach to Holy Communion.* Bloomington, IN: West Bow Press, 2011.

## Understanding Christendom/post-Christendom

Hall, Douglas John. *The End of Christendom and the Future of Christianity.* Valley Forge, PA: Trinity Press International, 1996.

Kreider, Alan, and Eleanor Kreider. *Worship and Mission after Christendom.* Scottdale, PA: Herald Press, 2011.Bottom of Form

Murray, Stuart. *Church after Christendom.* Waynesboro, GA: Authentic Media/Paternoster Press, 2004.

# Authors

**Jim S. Amstutz** is lead pastor of Akron (Pa.) Mennonite Church. He also serves as cochair of the Lancaster County Coalition to End Homelessness.

**Lois Y. Barrett**, Wichita, Kansas, is professor of theology and Anabaptist studies at Anabaptist Mennonite Biblical Seminary. She is author or coauthor of seven books, including *Missional Church*; *A Vision for the Sending of the Church in North America*; and *Treasure in Clay Jars: Patterns in Missional Faithfulness*.

**Palmer Becker** has spent a lifetime serving the church as a pastor, church planter, missionary, conference executive, author, and educator. More recently he has traveled extensively on teaching assignments to various international locations. He is a member of Waterloo (Ont.) North Mennonite Church.

**David W. Boshart** serves as the executive conference minister for Central Plains Mennonite Conference. He holds a PhD in leadership studies, with an emphasis in missional ecclesiology, from Andrews University.

**Mauricio Chenlo** is the denominational minister for church planting with Mennonite Mission Network. He is a member of Raleigh (N.C.) Mennonite Church.

356 Fully Engaged

**Nehemiah Chigoji** is pastor of Upland (Calif.) Peace Church, a member church of Pacific Southwest Mennonite Conference of Mennonite Church USA. The congregation is a newly formed merger of First Mennonite Upland and Indonesian fellowship Gereja Kristus Injili Upland. Chigoji and his wife, Agnes, are parents of three children.

**Leonard Dow** has served for fifteen years as senior pastor of Oxford Circle Mennonite Church in Philadelphia, Pennsylvania. Prior to the pastorate, he had twelve years of banking experience and has served on a variety of boards and committees on which both his ministry and business background were utilized.

**Natalie A. Francisco** is the copastor of Calvary Community Church and cofounder of Calvary Christian Academy in Hampton, Virginia, alongside her husband, Bishop L. W. Francisco III. For twenty-six years she has served as a motivational speaker, teacher, worship leader, and author, but her greatest joys are found in serving God, spending time with her family and friends, and practicing self-care.

**Glen Guyton** is the chief operating officer for Mennonite Church USA. He is passionate about youth, families, and ministry that transforms lives.

**Rebecca Helmuth** is the advertising and subscriptions coordinator for the *Mennonite*, the monthly magazine of Mennonite Church USA.

**Michele Hershberger** teaches Bible and youth ministry at Hesston (Kan.) College and is active across Mennonite Church USA as a preacher, writer, and dramatist. She is a member of Hesston Mennonite Church.

**Kristin Loeks Jackson** is pastor of Living Water Community Church in Chicago and was part of the core group that started the church. Kristin received her MDiv from North Park Seminary. She is married to Julian Jackson and is mother to two sons, Liam and Elijah.

**Conrad Kanagy** is pastor of Elizabethtown (Pa.) Mennonite Church, consultant at Lancaster Mennonite Conference, and professor of sociology at Elizabethtown College. He lives in Elizabethtown.

**J. Fred Kauffman** completed studies at both Hesston and Goshen Colleges and served with Mennonite Voluntary Service in Puerto Rico. He married Minh Thi Nguyen and they served for nine years with Mennonite Central Committee in Guatemala, India, and Cambodia. Fred was pastor of West Philadelphia Mennonite Fellowship for eleven years and MCC East Coast program coordinator for seven. He is currently interim pastor at Methacton Mennonite Church.

**Tilahun Beyene Kidane** is the coordinator of the International Missions Association. He also serves as pastor at Living Word Bible Fellowship, Boyds, Maryland—a congregation of the Lancaster Mennonite Conference within the Washington-Baltimore District.

**Matthew Krabill** is a current PhD student in the School of Intercultural Studies at Fuller Theological Seminary in Pasadena, California. His research focuses on migration and ecclesiology within the African Mennonite experience in America. He is on the pastoral staff at Wholicare Community Missionary Church, a member congregation of Pacific Southwest Mennonite Conference.

**Alan Kreider** is professor emeritus of church history and mission at Anabaptist Mennonite Biblical Seminary, Elkhart, Indiana. For many years he and his wife, Eleanor, were mission workers with Mennonite Board of Missions in England.

**Eleanor Kreider** is a retired adjunct faculty member at Anabaptist Mennonite Biblical Seminary, Elkhart, Indiana. A former Mennonite Board of Missions worker in England, she is coauthor with her husband, Alan Kreider, of *Worship and Mission after Christendom*.

**Sunoko Lin** is the bivocational pastor of Maranatha Christian Fellowship, Northridge, California. He also serves as board chair of West Coast Mennonite Central Committee and board member of Mennonite Mission Network.

**Sophorn Loeung** is a pediatric respiratory therapist and an elder of Living Water Community Church in Chicago. Born in Cambodia, he and his wife, Vanny, are parents of three boys, Joshua, John, and Justin.

**Marvin Lorenzana** is the coordinator for New Initiatives at Mennonite Mission Network and a coach for racial-ethnic congregations with Virginia Mennonite Missions. He has planted a church, El Camino Discipular, and received an MDiv degree from Eastern Mennonite Seminary, Harrisonburg, Virginia.

**Mattie Marie Mast** attends LifeBridge Community Church in Dover, Ohio, and is involved in a church plant at Strasburg. She enjoys her *jubilación* ("retirement," meaning "jubilation" in Spanish), which includes being present as a spiritual director and mentor.

**Freeman Miller** is a retired bishop, pastor, and college teacher and has lived and worked in Philadelphia since 1975. He loves writing, teaching, studying cities, spending time with his grandchildren, and watching the Phillies.

**Chet Miller-Eshleman** serves as pastor and founder of LifeBridge Community Church in Dover, Ohio. He is a passionate church planter, evangelist, and conflict transformation practitioner.

**David B. Miller** is associate professor of missional leadership development at Anabaptist Mennonite Biblical Seminary, Elkhart, Indiana. He served twenty years as a pastor. David joined the AMBS faculty in 2009. He and his wife, Mary Kathryn Schmid, are the parents of four adult children and are members of Prairie Street Mennonite Church in Elkhart.

**Gay Brunt Miller** served as director of administration of Franconia Mennonite Conference from 2000 to 2015 and is involved in various regional and churchwide leadership groups. She lives in Souderton, Pennsylvania, and is a member of Spring Mount Mennonite Church.

**Stuart Murray** spent twelve years as an urban church planter in London and has continued to be involved in church planting since then as a trainer, mentor, writer, strategist and consultant. He has written several books, including *The Naked Anabaptist: The Bare Essentials of a Radical Faith*. Stuart is married to Sian and has two grown sons and two grandchildren.

**Juan V. Montes** is pastor of First Mennonite Church of Reedley (Calif.).

**Martin Navarro** is a graduate of Anabaptist Mennonite Biblical Seminary and currently works as the event coordinator for the Mennonite Education Agency. He holds church membership at Comunidad Cristiana Vida Abundante in Chicago but currently attends Prairie Street Mennonite Church, Elkhart, Indiana.

**Nelson Okanya** serves as the president of Eastern Mennonite Missions. Born and raised in Kenya, he now lives in Lancaster, Pennsylvania, with his wife, Jessica, and two sons, Barak and Izak, and is a member of Sunnyside Mennonite Church.

**Stephen Penner** has been a member of First Mennonite Church in Reedley (Calif.) since 1985. He has been a pastor at the church since 1999.

**Jamie Ross** is coeditor of *Anabaptist Witness* and on staff with International Ministries at Mennonite Mission Network. She has lived and worked in both Kyrgyzstan and Israel, and currently lives in Elkhart, Indiana, where she attends Belmont Neighborhood Fellowship.

**Brinton Rutherford** serves as a resource staff person for Lancaster Mennonite Conference of Mennonite Church USA. He also teaches theology and church history as an adjunct instructor at the Lancaster campus of Eastern Mennonite Seminary and Eastern Mennonite University.

**Amos Shakya** and his wife, Roma, pastor the Nepali-speaking congregation of Living Water Community Church in Chicago and parent their daughter, Yarona. Amos received his leadership training from Youth With A Mission in Nepal and Wisconsin and is currently enrolled in the Journey program connected to Anabaptist Mennonite Biblical Seminary.

**David W. Shenk** grew up in Tanzania and with his wife, Grace, has served in missions in Somalia, Kenya, Lithuania, and the United States. He has authored or coauthored sixteen books related to missions. In his interest in Christian engagement with Muslims, he has visited more than one hundred countries. As global missions consultant with Eastern Mennonite Missions, he has taught in universities and seminaries around the world.

**Sara Wenger Shenk** is president of Anabaptist Mennonite Biblical Seminary in Elkhart, Indiana. She served on the faculty and administration of Eastern Mennonite Seminary, and she and her husband, Gerald, taught in the former Yugoslavia. She has written extensively in both academic and church publications.

**Wilbert R. Shenk** lives in Elkhart, Indiana, and is a member of Belmont Mennonite Church. He has served as a mission agency administrator and seminary professor.

**Ronald J. Sider** is an ordained Mennonite minister, a member of Oxford Circle Mennonite Church in Philadelphia, and senior distinguished professor of theology, holistic ministry, and public policy at Palmer Seminary at Eastern University. He is the founder and president emeritus of Evangelicals for Social Action and has published thirty-five books.

**André Gingerich Stoner** serves as director of holistic witness and inter-church relations for Mennonite Church USA. He was pastor of missions at Kern Road Mennonite Church in South Bend, Indiana, for sixteen years and previously served for nearly seven years with Mennonite Central Committee on two peace assignments in West Germany. André and his family share life as intentional neighbors with four other households in South Bend's Near Northwest neighborhood.

**Ervin R. Stutzman** served in the roles of pastor, church administration, and seminary educator before taking on his current role as executive director of Mennonite Church USA. He is a member of Park View Mennonite Church in Harrisonburg, Virginia.

**Linford Stutzman** is professor of culture and mission at Eastern Mennonite University and directs the Biblical Lands Educational Seminars and Service (BLESS) program of Eastern Mennonite Seminary. Each spring he leads EMU's Middle East cross-cultural study semester.

**Heidi Rolland Unruh** is a consultant equipping churches and non-profits to develop more effective holistic community outreach. Heidi is the author of several books, including *Churches That Make a Difference*. She and her family are affiliated with First Mennonite Church in Hutchinson, Kansas.

**Isaac S. Villegas** is the pastor of Chapel Hill Mennonite Fellowship in North Carolina. He serves on the executive board of Mennonite Church USA and on the governing board of the North Carolina Council of Churches.

**Howard Wagler** is lead pastor of Journey Mennonite Church located in central Kansas. Over the past twenty-two years, JMC has become a multisite, multi-staff church with locations in South Hutchinson, Yoder, and McPherson, Kansas. JMC is a member of South Central Conference Mennonite Conference.

**Jerry Wittrig** is pastor emeritus at North Goshen (Ind.) Mennonite Church.

**Sally Schreiner Youngquist** is community leader of Reba Place Fellowship and a former pastor at Living Water Community Church in Chicago. She got her MDiv from Anabaptist Mennonite Biblical Seminary and studied and worked at Seminary Consortium for Urban Pastoral Education. Sally is married to Orwin Youngquist.

# Editors

**Stanley W. Green** is executive director of Mennonite Mission Network, the mission agency of Mennonite Church USA. Born in South Africa, Green lived under the apartheid system and first came to faith while attending evangelistic meetings. He has a degree in intercultural studies from Fuller Theological Seminary and has served in a variety of church-wide capacities. He and his wife, Ursula, have two children and are members of Waterford Mennonite Church in Goshen, Indiana.

**James R. Krabill** served for fourteen years as a Bible and church history teacher in Ivory Coast and other West African locations. Upon returning to the United States, he directed the mission advocacy and communications function for Mennonite missions, and he currently serves as senior executive for global ministries at Mennonite Mission Network. Krabill has worked as a teacher and has authored and edited numerous volumes, including *Worship and Mission for the Global Church* (William Carey, 2013). He and his wife, Jeanette, have three adult children and attend Prairie Street Mennonite Church in Elkhart, Indiana.